Managing Risk:
The Human Resources Contribution

Managing Risk:
The Human Resources Contribution

Editor

John Stevens
Managing Director, RiskFrisk®

LexisNexis®
Butterworths

Members of the LexisNexis Group worldwide

United Kingdom	LexisNexis UK, a Division of Reed Elsevier (UK) Ltd, Halsbury House, 35 Chancery Lane, LONDON, WC2A 1EL, and 4 Hill Street, EDINBURGH EH2 3JZ
United Kingdom	LexisNexis UK, a Division of Reed Elsevier (UK) Ltd, 2 Addiscombe Road, CROYDON CR9 5AF
United Kingdom	LexisNexis IRS, member of the Eclipse Group Ltd, 18–20 Highbury Place, LONDON N5 1QP
United Kingdom	LexisNexis UK, a Division of Reed Elsevier (UK) Ltd, 4 Hill Street, EDINBURGH EH2 3JZ and Halsbury House, 35 Chancery Lane, LONDON WC2A 1EL
Argentina	LexisNexis Argentina, BUENOS AIRES
Australia	LexisNexis Butterworths, CHATSWOOD, New South Wales
Austria	LexisNexis Verlag ARD Orac GmbH & Co KG, VIENNA
Canada	LexisNexis Butterworths, MARKHAM, Ontario
Chile	LexisNexis Chile Ltda, SANTIAGO DE CHILE
Czech Republic	Nakladatelství Orac sro, PRAGUE
France	Editions du Juris-Classeur SA, PARIS
Germany	LexisNexis Deutschland GmbH, FRANKFURT and MUNSTER
Hong Kong	LexisNexis Butterworths, HONG KONG
Hungary	HVG-Orac, BUDAPEST
India	LexisNexis Butterworths, NEW DELHI
Ireland	LexisNexis, DUBLIN
Italy	Giuffrè Editore, MILAN
Malaysia	Malayan Law Journal Sdn Bhd, KUALA LUMPUR
New Zealand	LexisNexis Butterworths, WELLINGTON
Poland	Wydawnictwo Prawnicze LexisNexis, WARSAW
Singapore	LexisNexis Butterworths, SINGAPORE
South Africa	LexisNexis Butterworths, Durban
Switzerland	Stämpfli Verlag AG, BERNE
USA	LexisNexis, DAYTON, Ohio

First published in 2005
© LexisNexis UK 2005

A CIP Catalogue record for this book is available from the British Library.

ISBN 0 406 97145 5

Typeset by Columns Design Ltd, Reading, Berkshire
Printed and bound in Great Britain by MPG Books Ltd, Bodmin, Cornwall
Visit LexisNexis UK at www.lexisnexis.co.uk

Foreword

In a fast-moving marketplace, risk management can sometimes become a reactive exercise or one of compliance rather than an effective management tool. But the climate for risk management is changing. Around the world, organisations are taking a fresh, hard look at risk and redefining the role of risk management in achieving performance objectives, and ultimately in driving their future success.

Organisations are constantly changing: products and services, markets and technologies continually evolve; organisational change, such as downsizing, new acquisitions or mergers, create new risks. Continual change can make long-established business risk management strategies ineffective; downsizing, new acquisitions or merging create new risks.

Successful organisations, whether in the private or public sectors, should not seek to eliminate risk; rather, they should actively seek to harness and manage it to their own advantage. Risk is no longer just a threat; when managed effectively it is a powerful asset that delivers competitive advantage, adds value and enables an organisation to achieve its aims.

The effective management of human capital and resource risks and the key aspects of managing people are vital to the creation of a successful strategy that will enable Human Resources professionals to operate effectively within their own organisations. This publication provides guidance and practical advice to Human Resources professionals about the contribution they can make to their organisation's risk management strategy.

Terry M. Neville

Pro Vice-Chancellor and Director of Finance
University of Hertfordshire

Preface

We aim to provide inspiration, guidance and practical advice to Human Resources professionals about the contribution they can make to the management of risk within their organisations. We show how changing to a risk-based approach enables Human Resources professionals to enhance their contribution and add value to the organisation, increase their level of influence and provide a valuable input to organisational development. We also demonstrate how they can use a risk-based approach to develop themselves, both professionally and personally.

We describe how Human Resources professionals can contribute towards risk management, and introduce our approach for identifying and managing risks within an organisation that Human Resources professionals, either directly or indirectly, can influence.

Core concepts, including organisational factors, are described and referred to throughout the book, and we discuss how key aspects of managing people risk, or human-capital risks and Human Resources risks are vital to the creation of a strategy that will enable Human Resources professionals to increase their influence on an organisation.

Collectively, we have gained significant experience of working within Human Resources to implement approaches that are risk-based and not just based on legal compliance. By risk-based we mean balancing the maximisation of opportunities and the minimisation of risks, not the too-often risk-averse legally compliant approach. We have used our extensive experience of applying the approaches we describe. This book enables readers to take advantage of that experience and knowledge to benefit them both professionally and personally, and to increase the success of their organisations.

We also prompt Human Resources professionals to create initiatives to increase their influence at higher levels of management decision-making, and therefore their added value, all within a business and risk management focused approach. The Human Resources function too often (like many other functions) undertakes its activities in accordance with its own self-image and based on 'external' perceptions and expectations of its contribution. This can cause many Human Resources professionals to contribute in a limited way, ignoring the potential contribution they can make to their organisation and to their professional and personal development. By changing to a risk-based approach, the Human Resources function will be able to enhance its contribution, be increasingly seen as organisationally relevant and make a significant contribution to organisational development and the achievement of an organisation's strategy and objectives.

We believe that there are three groups that can benefit from the approaches outlined in this book:

1 Organisations that are looking for a new approach to managing their Human Resources risks.
2 In-house Human Resources professionals and organisational development specialists who wish to understand the concept of risk management and the contribution that can be made.
3 Specialist external advisors on Human Resources and organisational development who are looking for an enhanced approach to assist their clients to manage their Human Resources risks.

Where appropriate, we have used case studies and checklists to highlight the key learning points and support action plan development.

List of contributors

John Stevens – Managing Director – RiskFrisk®

John spent 20 years in the public sector, including a public sector trades union, working in human resources, employee relations and training and development, gaining extensive experience of all aspects of human resources.
In the early 1980s, John joined the global BOC Group Health Care Products Division and, in increasingly senior positions, introduced some innovative programmes for Human Resources and health and safety.

John received a BOC Group award for his programmes and, in the early 1990s, was appointed Safety Director, International. He gained extensive and varied experience of the design and implementation of strategy, management systems, new processes, training and communications to match business needs and enhance business success.

From 1998, John has been Managing Director of RiskFrisk® (previously People Process Specialists) who provide risk management, human resources, health and safety and training interventions in the public and private sectors.

Jim Wright – Principle HR Strategy and Change Consultant – RiskFrisk®

Jim has international experience as a line manager and as a human resources professional in a number of multinational blue chip companies, including as worldwide Head of Human Resources for SmithKline Beecham Research and Development. His expertise is in integrating Human Resources and business planning and in helping organisations to anticipate changes in business and technology in order to respond creatively and flexibly.

His areas of interest are: strategic thinking and implementation, developing strategic human resources capability, change implementation, leadership development and education and executive coaching. Jim helps managers to think differently and assists organisations in growing their distinctive culture in order to release the potential of all employees to contribute to success and find fulfilment.

Vicki Jeynes – Principle HR Operations Consultant – RiskFrisk®

Vicki is a human resources professional with over 25 years' experience of Human Resources management gained in the NHS, British Gas and GlaxoWellcome. Vicki's experience has involved all aspect of human resources support – advising and counselling managers on people management issues, employment legislation and employee relation issues.

Vicki specialises in operational Human Resources support, working in partnership with managers to help achieve business objectives through practical, workable solutions to day-to-day people issues.

Elvis Cotena – Principle Organisational Psychologist – RiskFrisk®

Elvis is an Occupational Psychologist, Lecturer in Psychology and management trainer. His main areas of interest and expertise are organisational development, risk management, particularly in how it relates to organisational development and cross-cultural business communications. Elvis lived in Japan for two years whilst helping to set up Unilever's first plant in Japan. His role was to mediate cultural differences in business practices, attitudes and communication styles.

Elvis has also lived and worked in Australia where he was senior lecturer in Business Communications at the University of Technology, Sydney, and designed/delivered a wide range of extra-mural management training programmes. He continues to enjoy teaching psychology whilst also working as an associate to a number of organisational development and training organisations, including RiskFrisk®.

Contents

Table of Statutes

Table of Statutory Instruments

CHAPTER 1

Human Resources risk management

INTRODUCTION

1.1 What is 'Human Resources risk management' and what risks does it encompass? Our description of Human Resources risk management involves the integrated risk management of the following risks:

- Human Resources – Human capital or people risks.
- Human Resources operational risks.
- Human Resources professional risks.
- Human Resources personal risks.

1.2 We use the term 'Human Resources risk management' because we believe that the risks to be managed or supported by the Human Resources function are much broader that the organisation's human capital or people risks. Human Resources functions can make an enhanced contribution to the organisation's overall management of risk if it looks both outward and inward from its current position and contribution.

1.3 We will briefly explain each aspect:

Human Resources – human capital or people risks – this is an approach to Human Resources management that treats the organisation's people as a high-level strategic factor that is a positive and active asset to be developed, not a passive cost.

Human Resources operational risks – these are risks created by the operational management of the Human Resources function and its direct support for the organisation.

Human Resources professional risks – these are risks created as a result of the perceptions (often historical, and often created in other organisations) formed by managers and employees of the role and contribution that is currently being made, or can be made, by the Human Resources function to the organisation, and to managers and employees on a personal level.

Human Resources personal risks – these are risks created by a lack of role and personal development that restricts the individual Human Resources professional from making an effective contribution to the organisation.

Primary role

1.4   We believe that the primary role of the Human Resources function is to focus on the above aspects to support organisational development and success. But what is an organisation and what support can the Human Resources function provide? Our definition is:

> 'An organisation is a network of relationships between people who come together for a common purpose.'

1.5   Using the key words from the above definition, we can see that Human Resources professionals can support an organisation in the following ways:

1   Help to identify and maintain its common purpose, strategy and objectives.
2   Help to manage the relationships.
3   Help to maximise opportunities and minimise risks to people in the network and the organisation as a whole.
4   Help to ensure that people in the organisation have the competencies, knowledge and skills required to achieve the purpose, including to build effective relationships and successful networks.

1.6   The management of 'financial capital' within an organisation, along with the associated opportunities and risks is not something that is left to chance; therefore, neither should the management of an organisation's human capital or people risks. Human capital or people risks describes the organisation's people resources as an investment that can be used by the organisation to benefit the achievement of its objectives, rather than viewing them as a 'cost' that should always be reduced or its consequences under-'valued'.

1.7   We believe that Human Resources professionals can make an enhanced contribution to the success of organisations, by ensuring that there is an effective and beneficial structured process in three areas:

1   **The organisation** – by advising senior management about the benefits of making risk management part of the normal management process and supporting the enhancement of general internal control systems.
2   **The Human Resources function** – by making the identification, assessment and management of opportunities and risks a cornerstone of its approach.
3   **The Human Resources professionals** – by creating a structured process for the professional development of the organisation's Human Resources team, so that their individual and collective contribution is enhanced.

1.8   In our experience, many organisations are too often restricted in their approach to innovation and creative approaches to management challenges. They often also regard the Human Resources function as an administrative support function rather than an added value business partnership opportunity that can provide a valuable focus to assist the organisation to balance the management of opportunities and the minimisation of risk.

1.9   Restricting the contribution that can be made by the Human Resources function has important legal, moral, financial and business implications. Human Resources risks within organisations that are not effectively controlled can have a significant impact because of the increasing dependency of related business and operational functions. Some organisations have realised the criticality of key elements of their operation, that are often not replicated elsewhere, either within the organisation or externally. As a consequence, some organisations have undertaken business continuity reviews – thinking through the 'physical' risks that face the business, but many have not considered the Human Resources risks that are often equally as crucial.

1.10   Every organisation's risk profile is different. The key issue for any organisation is to identify and measure its exposures and opportunities and manage them to the benefit of all stakeholders.

Core concepts

1.11   There are five core concepts that are used as recurring themes:

1   Organisations should not restrict the management of risk to traditional areas, e g insurance or financial operations. Human Resources risk management strategies, and organisational policies and procedures must be included in risk management systems. The organisation must ensure that those who are responsible for Human Resources risk management are actively involved in broader organisational risk management systems.

2   A prime responsibility of the Human Resources function should be to provide the effective management of risk for organisational activities that have a people dimension – what we call 'people risks'. Human Resources processes should support and be recognised and accepted as supporting the management of risk, and not dismissed as administrative 'red tape'.

3   Human Resources professionals should use risk management techniques to identify risk exposures and evaluate control options to demonstrate how Human Resources risks can be managed and how their effective management adds value to the business. They must also demonstrate the cost of initiatives to improve the management of people risks compared to the cost of inaction.

4   Human Resources professionals must increasingly adopt a proactive risk-based and business-focused approach rather than a reactive and

risk-averse legislative compliance approach. This will create an environment where they can develop their professional and personal competency and demonstrate added value.

5   Human Resources professionals must form business partnerships with other key influencers within the organisation, e g financial management to support the minimisation of risk and the maximisation of opportunities. The proactive involvement of Human Resources professionals during an organisation's business strategy and planning processes is far more beneficial for the organisation, compared to a reactive involvement after the key decisions have been made.

Importance of Human Resources risk management

1.12   The effective application of legislation and the need for robust business-relevant and integrated Human Resources risk management processes are crucial for all organisations, where success is often dependent on the people within the organisation, and the contribution they can make. Regardless of what organisations say, in practice, Human Resources management is often not seen as core to the effective performance of the business. This can arise for a three main reasons:

1   Human Resources is seen as merely an administrative function that deals with, for example, payroll and records.
2   Human Resources activities are often described, whether linked to legislation or not, as administrative 'red tape'. This comment is made even where the risk of not handling certain aspects, e g individual performance, special leave, grievances and discipline, in a proactive, sympathetic, balanced and supportive manner can lead to serious consequences. Such consequences can include:
   ● Reduction in employee productivity and contribution.
   ● Additional management time.
   ● Increased employee absence and turnover.
   ● Employment tribunal cases.
   ● Legal costs, fines etc.
3   The reluctance of Human Resources professionals to get themselves on the 'risk and business agenda'. This may be either because of a concern that they may not be able to take a detached, independent view if they become too identified as part of the 'commercial' aspects of the organisation, within which it is perceived people risks are disregarded, or because they do not have the necessary competencies.

1.13   If Human Resources professionals can 'get on the business and risk agenda' within their organisations, then the risks of not managing the organisation's Human Resources risks come into sharper focus and the added value of the Human Resources function is much easier to demonstrate, understood and welcomed.

1.14 The secret is for Human Resources professionals to think 'risk' when evaluating their contribution and to use a cost-benefit approach that compares the cost of an intervention with the cost of inaction, ie leaving the risk uncontrolled. Using such an approach enables them to demonstrate how they can add value, rather than be perceived as a risk-averse legislative-focused function that only adds cost to the business. Changing the focus and perception of the Human Resources function can lead to new management approaches that identify different priorities and solutions, and thereby enhance the management of business and commercial opportunities.

Role of Human Resources

1.15 Before we start to discuss risk management in general terms and how Human Resources professionals can become more involved, let us consider the role of the Human Resources function. Future chapters will deal with these matters in detail, but for the moment let us consider some key points.

- **Broader business agenda** – The management of risk is an essential part of corporate governance and corporate social responsibility, both concepts that are increasingly becoming the sign of a well-run and responsible organisation. The protection of all stakeholders' 'capital' is a vital aspect of good business management, and the key method is to use risk management techniques throughout the business process. Human Resources professionals should be ideally placed to influence appropriate management system developments, and create a proactive internal environment for risk identification and resolution. Human Resources professionals must seek to ensure that the organisation includes the concept of risk management within its normal management of the business. It is vital that the identification and management of risk is not a reactive process when something goes wrong, but something that is considered at all stages of a business. Human Resources professionals need to proactively lead the creation of an organisation that has the management of risk at the heart of its culture and business processes.

- **Balancing opportunities and risks** – The organisation must ensure that its development of business opportunities within its strategic objectives must not be constrained by risk-averse approaches, nor continued without due regard to the risks. The management of risk must be effectively balanced with the identification and management of opportunities. In addition, the culture of the organisation must not include human factors that cause people to adopt risk-creating behaviours rather than intelligent risk taking. Human Resources professionals must support the identification of negative hidden belief systems. For example, the organisation may say, 'Our people are our most important asset' – but in reality all the organisation's focus is on the achievement of financial targets. This leads to the hidden belief that the organisation's real value is 'Our people are an unimportant asset'. Human Resources professionals must assist the organisation to identify with the concept that risk exists in not recognising or not implementing an opportunity, rather than the traditional view that risk management is only about minimising losses before or after they occur. One example of where the Human Resources function can add value is in the discussion of outsourcing. Some activities are often outsourced, eg payroll, car fleet management, site cleaning, where the activity is regarded as not core to the main organisational function and where the expertise required is very specialist or where the economies of scale make it cost effective to outsource. Whilst there can be significant benefits in outsourcing, the main organisation must be challenged to think very carefully about the risk of outsourcing activities that are strategic or linked directly to the product/service that the main organisation is providing.

The assumed cost-benefit of outsourcing may well be outweighed by a loss of control and a reduction in internal support and external customer service, and an inability to effectively manage the people risk management aspects, that can be core to effective performance.

- **Using key Human Resources skills** – Human Resources professionals must use their key skills of facilitation and relationship building to ensure that the organisation maintains an open culture and a challenging corporate 'mind' that it is prepared to operate as a matrix of opportunity 'teams', rather than each function within the organisation protecting its own responsibility areas and not thinking about or contributing to the overall strategic objectives. Human Resources professionals should seek out and create business partnerships with those parts of the business that have influence through other mechanisms, eg financial control, legal and company secretariat. In that way they will increase their influence via direct and indirect routes.

- **Human Resources role development** – Human Resources professionals should seek to use risk management to demonstrate added value, by identifying and managing risks across the whole range of Human Resources activities. Human Resources professionals need to get the basic administrative tasks and core people processes optimised. Once the most cost-effective and efficient systems are in place, they can concentrate on increasing their contribution to the organisation, by adopting proactive approaches rather than reactive responses to organisational developments, individual employment cases or changes in regulations. Human Resources professionals can contribute to a much greater degree if they use tools and techniques that demonstrate their risk management credentials and their business and commercial awareness and sensitivity. An increased contribution will enhance the professional and personal development of the Human Resources professionals.

- **Human Resources risk management** – If the Human Resources function is to develop its role and increase its added value, then it must actively identify the risks that it is managing or can influence elsewhere within the organisation, create mechanisms for control and ensure that business managers have the skills/knowledge to manage them on an ongoing basis. The identification of risk must be linked to a 'lost opportunity' approach of identifying the direct and indirect cost of inactivity, compared to the cost of activity. Each Human Resources activity has a cost of action, but equally has cost of inaction. For example, there is a cost to developing managers in undertaking effective recruitment and selection decisions, and performance management activities, but equally there is a cost of not providing them with the skills, so that turnover, absence and reduced employee development are not managed effectively, creating significant costs for the organisation. Unfortunately, such intangible costs do not appear on the balance sheet and therefore are often ignored during decision-making.

Types of Human Resources activities

1.16 Human Resources role development can also be viewed under different types of Human Resources activities, namely Human Resources operations, business-focused Human Resources and business partnerships. These will be discussed more fully in later chapters.

Human Resources operations

1.17 Essentially this includes Human Resources administration, policies and procedures, and Human Resources internal systems, to ensure full understanding by the Human Resources team, consistency of application, etc. The Human Resources function will have a general identification of what can go wrong and how to minimise these risks. Human Resources professionals must ensure that they deliver these base activities optimally with a high level of customer satisfaction, otherwise their efforts to get involved in 'higher' level activities will have no creditability. They can increase their added value by managing these activities in a proactive manner – providing management with core information, such as absence statistics, that can be used to improve costs and reduce risk. Too often, Human Resources information that is potentially useful to managers is held on a computer or hard copy system, under the control of Human Resources, but not extracted, analysed and shared with business managers so that the Human Resources professionals can work with them to influence a change in practice.

Case study

1.18 One organisation did not realise the level of absence arising from work-induced stress and employee turnover. When the level of absence and turnover was identified and costed under the absence and recruitment processes, the true level of the risk was identified. Management were then much more easily able to see the benefits of implementing a change in policy and the introduction of new work arrangements and management approach.

Business-focused Human Resources

1.19 As Human Resources professionals improve and optimise their operational activities, the organisation can begin to appreciate that they can add value to the business, but often they are still not 'welcome' in the boardroom. Consequently, they are only asked for a reactive input to business decisions after they have been finalised. They are often fighting a rearguard action and can only add minimal value if they are reacting to decisions that may have been taken without regard to people risks. They often have to resort to using changes in legislation as a way to introduce necessary changes in Human Resources policies, rather than being able to put these on the business agenda in a proactive manner. The Human Resources professionals need to be proactive in influencing their client groups to put people risks on the business agenda. They can demonstrate how they can add value by keeping tuned in to business developments in their client groups and getting themselves invited to management meetings to present proposals on the Human Resources implications of these developments.

Case study

1.20 An organisation made a decision to relocate one of its functions to another geographical area, without considering the risks of losing key employees. After the decision to relocate was made public, the Human Resources Director was asked to implement 'incentives' to encourage key people to relocate, but did not have the full authority to create proactive incentives as the 'budget' for the relocation had already been decided as part of the business justification. Certain key employees decided not to relocate and the Human Resources Director was blamed for the lack of success in encouraging the relocations.

Business partnerships

1.21 By taking the initiatives described in the preceding section, Human Resources professionals can get themselves involved in the discussion and decisions on future business strategies during the active development stage – rather than picking up the pieces once the strategies or implementation plans have been decided. Their overall aim needs to be to get themselves established as valued members of their client group management team in recognition of their contribution to the organisation. One measure of success is whether managers seek them out for one-on-one discussions and advice at an early stage of their thinking about new activities.

MANAGEMENT OF RISK

Overview

1.22 The need for organisations to identify, assess and manage risk has never been greater. The fast changing nature of the business environment, the speed with which products and services can be brought to market, and the way that established organisations can soon lose what was hitherto a strong market position has meant that all organisations, large and small, along with public bodies, need to think about the way their organisations are run and the inherent risks, across their total operations.

1.23 Risk is not something that comes into play when something goes wrong. Risk exists throughout the business cycle, from identifying a new product/service idea right through research, development, 'production' into distribution and after-sales support.

1.24 Risk management is a process consisting of well-defined steps that, taken in sequence, support better business decision-making by contributing to a greater insight into risks and their potential consequences, both positive and negative.

1.25 The process is as much about identifying and maximising opportunities as it is about minimising unplanned losses. An essential element of the risk management process is to ensure that the identified risks and their control processes are closely monitored. By adopting effective risk management tools and techniques, organisations, and in particular Human Resources professionals, can help to improve the management of the business and business performance that are linked to the organisation's strategy, goals and objectives.

Benefits of risk management

1.26   The benefits of risk management are many, and a selection is listed below:

- More effective strategic planning.
- Increased knowledge and understanding of exposure to risk and the ability to recognise and evaluate new opportunities.
- Better utilisation of resources, including human capital resources.
- Strengthened culture for continued improvement and collective risk management.
- Creating a best practice, quality-focused and risk-aware organisation.
- A systematic, well informed and thorough method of decision-making.
- Improving cost control.
- Reducing unplanned losses.
- Willingness for external review.
- Enhancement of shareholder value by maximising opportunities and minimising losses.

Risk-management vocabulary

1.27   Human Resources professionals should seek to understand their organisation's risk management vocabulary or develop their own for use within the Human Resources function. If no organisational vocabulary currently exists, then by developing and using their own vocabulary, Human Resources professionals will be able to demonstrate credibility.

1.28   Before embarking on the creation of a new or separate vocabulary, Human Resources professionals should liaise with risk management specialists within their organisation to agree a common set of definitions that they could use without confusing traditional risk-focused functions, such as insurance, that may already have their own terminology.

1.29   To assist this process, we have included definitions from two leading risk management standards to aid your understanding of the terminology we use in the book. The first Standard (United Kingdom) views risk management as the management of potential negative consequences, whilst the latter Standard (Australian and New Zealand) – the world's first published risk management standard – views risk management as the maximisation of opportunities and the minimisation of risk. As described earlier, our view is that Human Resources should approach and contribute towards an organisation's risk management system, based on the balanced principle of the maximisation of opportunities and the minimisation of risks.

United Kingdom Standard

1.30   The Institute of Risk Management (IRM), The Association of Insurance and Risk Managers (AIRMIC) and National Forum for Risk Management in the Public Sector (ALARM) jointly published a UK Risk Management Standard in October 2002 to 'set the scene for coherent thinking and application in the ever-widening field of risk management'. The Standard is aligned to ISO/IEC Guide 73 – Risk Management Vocabulary, and as an Appendix contains the ISO vocabulary. We have extracted some of the key definitions:

- **Risk** = 'Combination of the probability of an event and its consequence.'
- **Risk management** = 'Co-ordinated activities to direct and control an organisation with regard to risk.'
- **Risk management system** = 'Set of elements of an organisation's management system concerned with managing risk.'
- **Risk treatment** = 'Process of selection and implementation of measures to modify risk.'
- **Risk control** = 'Actions implementing risk management decisions.'
- **Residual risk** = 'Risk remaining after risk treatment.'

1.31   The above Standard says that the term 'risk' is generally used only to refer to negative consequences. The focus of this book, however, is towards a broader, more balanced approach, that also includes the management of potential opportunities within the process of risk management, whilst minimising risk within those opportunities.

Australian and New Zealand Standard

1.32   A joint Australian and New Zealand Risk Management Standard (AS/NZS 4360: 2004) also includes the following definitions, that, in general, take a broader, more balanced view of risk management:

- **Risk** = 'The chance of something happening that will have an impact upon objectives. It is measured in terms of consequences and likelihood.'

- **Risk management** = 'The culture, processes and structures that are directed towards the effective management of potential opportunities and adverse effects.'
- **Risk management process** = 'The systematic application of management policies, procedures and practices to the tasks of establishing the context, identifying, analysing, evaluating, treating, monitoring and communicating risk.'
- **Risk treatment** = 'Selection and implementation of appropriate options for dealing with risk.'
- **Risk control** = 'That part of risk management that involves the implementation of policies, standards, procedures and physical changes to eliminate or minimise adverse risk.'
- **Residual risk** = 'The remaining level of risk after risk-treatment measures have been taken.'

Risk management, corporate governance and Human Resources risk management

1.33   Corporate governance and effective internal control are vital ingredients of business processes that ensure risks associated with business and operational activities are managed for the benefit of all stakeholders.

1.34   As a consequence of an increasing focus on risk, organisations are beginning to realise that virtually none of their activities is risk free. Whether considering their people, their customers, suppliers, operations or their finances, there will always be risks arising from possible developments that could prevent or impede an organisation from realising its strategic objectives.

1.35   In general, 'risk management' has been a process that large organisations, or those with a heavy insurance requirement, have concerned themselves with. In addition, the majority of references to risk management relate to either insurance-linked activity or financial risk management. However, due to some recent high- profile cases, it is likely that future legislation will increasingly require all organisations – large and small, private and public – to take on board risk management concepts and include it within their strategic, tactical and normal day-to-day operational activities, rather than be reactive when things go wrong. There is increasing pressure for risk management processes to be extended beyond insurance and financial-based risks.

1.36   There is also a much-increased global focus on corporate governance as a result of significant failures in high-profile companies in many parts of the world, e g Enron and WorldCom. Effective corporate governance should also include the organisation's management of its Human Resources risks.

1.37   The Organisation for Economic Co-operation and Development (OECD) has published the following definition, which is widely accepted:

'The corporate governance structure specifies the distribution of rights and responsibilities among different participants in an organisation, such as, the board, managers, shareholders and other stakeholders, and spells out the rules and procedures for making decisions on corporate affairs. By doing this, it also provides the structure through which the organisation's objectives are set and the means of attaining those objectives and monitoring performance.'

1.38 The work of the OECD, and other global and national bodies in the major economies clearly shows that corporate governance will become increasingly important in the national and the global economy and key to the operation of all organisations, private and public, large and small alike.

1.39 The UK focus on corporate governance took a major step forward in September 1999, when the Turnbull Report was published by The Institute of Chartered Accountants in England and Wales. The Chairman of the Working Party was Nigel Turnbull, who was supported by representatives from commercial organisations and professionals service organisations. The Report was entitled 'Internal Control – Guidance for Directors on the Combined Code'. The Combined Code is linked to the 'Listing Rules' of the UK London Stock Exchange that apply to companies listed on the Exchange.

1.40 The Combined Code of the Committee on Corporate Governance (Code), and the Turnbull Report (Turnbull) include several key statements, which are very relevant to the contribution that Human Resources professionals can make to risk management:

- Code – 'The board should maintain a sound system of internal control to safeguard shareholders' investment and the company's assets.'
- Turnbull – 'The guidance is based on the adoption by a company's board of a risk-based approach to establishing a sound system of internal control and reviewing its effectiveness. This should be incorporated by the company within its normal management and governance processes. It should not be treated as a separate exercise undertaken to meet regulatory requirements.'
- Turnbull – 'A company's objectives, its internal organisation and the environment in which it operates are continually evolving and, as a result, the risks it faces are continually changing. A sound system of internal control therefore depends on a thorough and regular evaluation of the nature and extent of the risks to which the company is exposed. Since profits are, in part, the reward for successful risk-taking in business, the purpose of internal control is to help manage and control risk appropriately rather than eliminate it.'
- Turnbull – 'All employees have some responsibility for internal control

as part of their accountability for achieving objectives. They, collectively, should have the necessary knowledge, skills, information and authority to establish, operate and monitor the system of internal control.'

- Turnbull – 'Do the company's culture, code of conduct, Human Resources policies and performance reward systems support the business objectives and risk management and internal control system?'
- Turnbull – 'Do people in the company have the knowledge, skills and tools to support the achievement of the company's objectives and to manage effectively risks to their achievement?'

1.41 Two recent reports in the UK have taken the debate even further. Reports by Derek Higgs, 'Review of the Role of Non-executive Directors', and by Sir Robert Smith, 'Audit Committees – Combined Code of Guidance', were published in January 2003, and led to a revised Combined Code being published in July 2003. The revised Code came into effect in November 2003 for listed companies reporting years beginning on or after 1 November 2003.

1.42 The implications for Human Resources professionals are significant, and are discussed in detail in later chapters. The 2003 'Accounting for People' Taskforce sponsored by the UK Department of Trade and Industry (DTI) recommended that companies should clearly communicate the links between their human capital management policies and practices and their business strategies and performance, and the information should be reported in operating and financial reviews.

1.43 In May 2004, the Government published a consultation document on 'Draft regulations on the Operating and Financial Review and Directors Report'. This was in response to the work of the above taskforce and other inputs, including the recommendations of the independent Company Law Review and the Accounts Modernisation Directive from the European Union (EU).

1.44 Paragraph 2.5 in part states:

'Directors deciding in good faith what would be most likely to promote the success of the company, taking account of a wide range of factors, within and outside the company, which are relevant to achieving its objectives and to an assessment of its business. These factors may well include the company's impact on the environment and on the wider community, and its relationships with employees, customers and suppliers.'

1.45 A clear implication is that the management of human capital risks is a key component of this review and report; that Human Resources professionals should seek that the management of human capital risks are actively considered; and that comment on these risks is included in the Operating and Financial Review and Report (OFR).

1.46   When finalised, the requirements will apply to financial years starting on or after 1 January 2005 for large- and medium-sized companies. Companies will be studying the consultation document to determine what actions they need to take. Subsequently the timescale has been moved to 1st April 2005.

1.47   We believe that Human Resources professionals can assist and contribute to the thinking and the preparation of the organisation's OFR by posing the following questions:

- Does your organisation currently undertake such a review and publish such a report?
- Does it include aspects related to the management of Human Resources risks?
- What Human Resources risks are significant for your organisation?
- Has your organisation started to review its current methods of capturing the necessary data, including data on human capital risks to ensure it is able to comply with the new reporting requirements?
- Have you considered the matters relating to the management of Human Resources risks that could be appropriate for inclusion in the review and report?
- Have you been actively involved in the review and the broader discussions about the content of the report?
- Have you sought out and created new internal 'partnerships' to ensure that your contribution is timely and effective?

Competitive world

1.48   Increasingly all organisations need to appreciate that, in this competitive world, they must make sure that their employees are managed effectively to maximise their contribution to the organisation. Just concentrating on business growth and profits ignores the moral, legal and significant financial losses that can be caused by poor management of risk, especially human capital risks.

1.49   Human Resources policies and practices that are not relevant to the organisation's strategy, restrict rather than encourage creativity, create other restrictions, or do not add value, can seriously undermine the chances of motivating employees and meeting business targets.

Human Resources risks

1.50   Human Resources risk management aspects of organisations must be recognised and included as a core element of the delivery of the strategic vision of the organisation. Effective 'full employment' in the UK, coupled with the increasing scarcity of qualified and competent people within the labour market, and the large number of unfilled vacancies, is placing huge burdens on organisations that have not considered these aspects, particularly at the operational 'deliver' point.

1.51   People, especially knowledge workers, who have skills and experience that are in demand, are learning to use this to their advantage when negotiating pay and conditions with employers. They are less loyal to the organisation, and have been heavily influenced by employers who took the view that 'jobs for life' were no longer good policy. The demise of final salary pension schemes, due to senior management regarding them as being too expensive, and the view that 'employees over 50 years of age' are no longer adding value, has also contributed to a reduction in loyalty. This has resulted in the risks in being an employer changing and becoming more complex.

1.52   Organisations in a 'knowledge-based' economy will have to be much more proactive and innovative in their management of people. The risk of relying on old-style practices is too serious to contemplate. This can be highlighted by an example of an all-too-frequent approach to learning and development expenditure that is exhibited by many organisations.

Case study

1.53   An exchange of views took place between a Managing Director and the organisation's Learning and Development Manager, in response to a request for resources for learning and development. Managing Director: 'What if we spend all this money/time and then people leave?' Learning and Development Manager: 'What if we don't spend the money/time and they don't leave?'

1.54   The risk is that the knowledge and experience held by employees will not be identified or effectively utilised. When these employees leave, organisational memory is lost. The 'knowledge' that will be considered and 'valued' (although not generally an overt process) is that related to an individual's current role. Human Resources professionals have a great opportunity to influence this internal debate, and in the broader public policy debate, to encourage necessary changes both inside organisations and externally.

1.55   As a consequence, in western economies the changing balance of power and changes in the relationships between the employer and the employed is much more fluid and dependent on economic conditions. This is often referred to as 'the changing psychological contract' between employers and the employed. The existence of this 'contract' is particularly relevant when considering Human Resources policies for compensation and benefits, eg flexible benefits, but is also affected by the organisation's approach to, for example, cost cutting by reductions in employee numbers and the ending of the expectation of a 'job for life', as well as a final salary pension scheme.

Psychological contract

1.56   Although this subject is listed below as an organisational factor, we have included details at this point to link to the matters discussed in the above section.

1.57   The psychological contract, which has been widely researched and written about, influences employees' beliefs and behaviour in the workplace. From the recruitment stage of an employee's work life to retirement or resignation, it can have a profound effect on the attitudes and well-being of an individual. It is commonly understood as an individual's belief about the terms and conditions of a reciprocal exchange agreement with an employer or manager; a belief that some form of promise has been made and that the terms are accepted by all involved.

1.58   The psychological contract is an unwritten set of expectations between everyone in an organisation and, unlike the written contract, is continually changing. By nature it is a flexible and undefined set of terms, which may be interpreted by the individual in different ways at different stages in their working life. Although it is unwritten, it can be a significant determinant of behaviour in organisations, and perceptions of violation can have lasting effects.

1.59   When employees believe that their psychological contract has been broken, they often feel a great sense of injustice. Consequently, they are likely to reduce their contribution to their organisation both in terms of their own work performance and other 'good citizen' behaviours.

1.60   Human Resources professionals need to take the psychological contract into account when they advise their organisations about changes in business and operational processes and changes in Human Resources policies and practices. These concepts are particularly relevant when the organisation wishes to obtain the commitment of their employees to a change, eg trying to improve quality, customer service or efficiency of employees' work.

Organisational factors

1.61   Later in the book we will discuss the significance of organisational factors and the way in which they can create risks. Additionally, we will discuss how a review of organisational factors can be used for the identification and management of risk.

1.62 Organisational factors are organisational characteristics that can differentiate one organisation from another, and have a major impact on the behaviour and attitudes of employees. The creation of positive and proactive organisational factors is key to the success of an organisation, and must be managed as an active management process. Key factors are:

- **Vision statement** – a statement of the organisation's vision for its future (sometimes called a 'mission statement') that underpins everything it says and does.

- **Senior management commitment** – the extent to which management are committed to the management of risk and the management of an organisation's Human Resources risks.

- **Core values** – what particular aspects does the organisation focus on, what core values does it set for the organisation and its employees, and what hidden belief systems are actually in place, influencing attitudes and behaviour?

- **Leadership style** – the energy and inspirational qualities of an organisation's leaders are a major factor in making an organisation one of the best to work for.

- **Organisational culture** – what value does the organisation place on the effective management of risk and, in particular, people risks?

- **Hidden belief systems** – what hidden belief systems are actually in place, and what influences attitudes and behaviour when no formal 'rules' are available?

- **Psychological contract** – to what extent is the 'unwritten' balance of the relationship between the organisation and the employee changing?

- **Responsibility framework** – to what extent are responsibility, authority and the allocation of resources delegated to the correct level at which action is most effective?

- **Occupational stress** – occupational stress has many negative consequences for organisations, and therefore it is a strategic risk that needs to be identified, quantified and managed.

- **Job/role design** – the ability of an organisation to create a structure, management style and work environment that encourages the best aspects of team working is a vital component in successfully managing any activity within the business, especially risk management.

- **Business strategy and goal setting process** – to what extent are these elements integrated and goals and objectives formally set, cascaded, monitored and amended to take account of changing circumstances?

- **Performance management system** – to what extent is performance set, measured and managed to ensure active action-oriented activity?

- **Compensation and rewards policies** – to what extent are compensation and reward policies, aligned to the business, linked to business goals and objectives, including risk management, and reward those behaviours that are consistent with the organisation's core values, cultural framework and hidden belief systems?

- **Communication** – ensuring that communication systems are effective is a challenge in most organisations, but the issue becomes ever more relevant when related to the management of risk. Effective communication is the foundation on which risk management systems are based.

- **Learning and development** – the extent to which the organisational and individual needs for learning and development are considered as part of the means by which the organisation will achieve its objectives, and a key method used to enhance the contribution and productivity of the individual employee and teams.

DEVELOPING A RISK MANAGEMENT STRATEGY

Overview

1.63   As boards, directors and managers increasingly become accountable for losses and ineffective management of risks, they need a strategy that assures they understand the implications and risks associated with every decision they make. Without a risk management system in place, their accountability and the consequences can be a lottery!

1.64   Any organisation, private or public, large or small, can benefit from using risk management tools and techniques. Many large organisations have some form of risk management in place. However, very few involve Human Resources risks.

1.65   Every organisation's risk profile is different, even within the same sector. The crucial issue is to identify and measure the organisation's exposures and opportunities and manage them to the benefit of all stakeholders. In our experience, the tools and techniques included within this book can be used by any organisation to this end.

1.66   *The development of a process to identify Human Resources risks, and the creation of a strategy for their effective management, is covered in Chapter 8.*

Risk-management processes and Human Resources

1.67   Organisations simply cannot allocate responsibility for risk management to 'risk managers' and expect that the processes they are able to put in place will be welcomed, accepted and maintained by managers and employees who are already overburdened by their workload. Managers and employees are generally focused on day-to-day operations (driven by the organisation's focus on short-term 'production') and do not take a longer-term view or focus on identifying and managing intangible risks. Therefore, 'risk managers' cannot expect to get their concepts on the broader business agenda and incorporated into the way that the organisation runs, if they take a risk-averse approach. There is nothing more frustrating to managers who are heavily focused on business and commerce, than to have within their risk management functions or external advisers, people who do not understand the realities of business, and therefore advise on strategies and approaches that restrict effective, risk-balanced decision-making.

1.68   As risk is inherent in any business decision/process, those within 'risk management functions' must advise on the potential risks, but must also seek to add value by offering alternatives that are consistent with the general strategic direction that the organisation has chosen to take. 'Risk' must be on the board agenda, but it must not become a 'bored' issue that serious business managers seek to avoid because unrealistic 'risk-averse' approaches are all that is on offer. All managers within an organisation must accept the responsibility for managing risk within their area of responsibility but, equally, must be given the skills and tools to do so. Additionally the organisation must ensure that the full business process for each area of operations is considered when risk exposures are being identified.

1.69   Organisational factors identified in the previous section generally have organisation-wide implications and therefore must be taken into account during the creation of risk management processes. The activities of the Human Resources function normally requires consideration of organisationally wide processes, but often the Human Resources function is not viewed as part of the general risk management system, and very often is not involved in risk management. In general, organisations do not see the Human Resources function as part of 'risk management', and Human Resources professionals would not typically see themselves as operating a 'risk management' activity or contributing towards managing risk.

1.70   If the Human Resources function is to be included within risk management, then those whose primary function is to advise on risk management must be helped to understand and accept that the Human Resources function is part of risk management. The benefits of including the Human Resources function in risk management can include:

- An organisation's human capital is likely to be a major cost to the business. Minimising human capital risks will contribute towards the success of the organisation, both in tangible ways, e g 'productivity', but also in intangible ways, e g morale and compliance with internal controls. Research has shown – see **Chapter 2** – that the majority of risks that concern managers have a human capital element. Indeed, of the top three risks, two were entirely related to human capital.

● Human Resources professionals are the specialists in the management of human capital risks, and therefore can support the implementation of, and compliance to, internal controls, especially risk management. The success of internal controls, including risk management, is ultimately dependent on people, not technology.

● Human Resources professionals are ideally placed to assist with the implementation of internal controls, as they can take an organisation-wide perspective, and they typically operate at all levels within an organisation – strategic, tactical and operational.

● Human Resources professionals can bring to bear their expertise in these areas, such as organisational development, training and development, performance management systems and compensation and benefits, to ensure that the risk management system goals and objectives are integrated with these organisation-wide systems.

● Human Resources professionals can use their key skills of influencing, facilitation, strategic thinking, non-silo-constrained thinking to assist in identifying innovative ways to ensure risk management systems are maintained.

1.71   The issue is that Human Resources functions do not typically see themselves as risk management functions, but in reality that is one of their fundamental roles, and needs to be one of the core competences of Human Resources professionals.

1.72   As organisations grow and develop into complex organisations, they do not always develop and create the necessary in-house risk management expertise, and often need to call in external experts. Unfortunately this is often only done on a reactive basis. In particular, for input on Human Resources risks, many organisations often rely on in-house risk management resources that lack the required level of Human Resources competency to identify Human Resources risks, implement and maintain the required systems, and provide proactive advice before things go wrong. Many organisations often see the Human Resources function as a necessary evil (and label it as administrative 'red tape') and something that can be allocated to a general administrative function, along with payroll, pension or other 'payment'-linked requirements. Such organisations do not see the need or value in creating the appropriate in-house expertise. This prevents the organisation from taking advantage of a structured process to manage Human Resources risks using internal expertise.

1.73   Consequently, the challenges facing Human Resources professionals are:

1   To influence the inclusion of 'risk management' on the broader business

agenda, particularly at board level, and influence the corporate governance/internal control processes.

2   To assist management in developing the organisation to ensure that it effectively balances the management of its opportunities, whilst minimising its risks, thereby supporting the achievement of its strategic objectives.

3   To use its generic influencing, facilitation, blue sky thinking, non-silo-constrained skills.

4   To develop its role, and acceptance of the role change, to one of managing risk within the total range of its Human Resources activities, and to increase the added value of the Human Resources function across its range of activities.

5   To increase the influence on the business by changing the Human Resources role from 'admin' to 'business partnership'.

Trust and risk management

1.74   Building successful working relationships and partnerships is of fundamental importance in managing risk in organisations. Trust is fundamental to creating these relationships. In the current climate of pressure for growth and profits, corporate greed, cost cutting and changes in the psychological contract, which all have the potential to destroy trust, Human Resources professionals have a key role to play in acting as the agents of co-ordination of the tensions and conflicting interests in organisations. They are uniquely placed to encourage leaders and employees to invest sustained, focused attention on building and maintaining trust within the organisation.

1.75   Failure to build the levels of trust in organisations carries the risk that it could result in:

* Turf issues and less-than-effective working across organisational interfaces.
* Employee commitment and discretionary effort being suboptimal.
* Disconnection between the interests of the organisation and those of the employee.
* Loss of innovation, risk taking and creative energy.
* Reduced organisational performance and increased operating costs.

1.76   Although these are significant people risks that Human Resources professionals need to manage, there does not appear to be much evidence that Human Resources professionals recognise that building and maintaining trust needs to be a specific objective.

1.77 In **Chapter 7** we explore the meaning of trust in the context of the workplace, factors that build or destroy trust, the value of trust to the organisation, and the role of Human Resources professionals in developing trust in the organisation.

Structured and integrated approach

1.78 The effective management of Human Resources risks requires a structured approach to be adopted, and the resulting controls integrated with normal business and operational processes. Many organisations approach the management of risk either in a piecemeal manner, or reactively following a loss.

1.79 In our experience, the most effective and well-managed organisations will use a structured approach that takes account of the profile of the organisation, will identify where they are exposed to risk, will evaluate existing control mechanisms, and will evaluate what more needs to be done to ensure that the risks are tolerable and effectively managed to the level decided.

1.80 The most effective risk management tools and techniques are those that are designed to provide answers to key questions at each stage of a structured process, and to enable the organisation to select the factors they wish to concentrate on during the next step.

1.81 In our experience, using a step-by-step approach enables the organisation to adapt the area of review and adapt the depth of study to match the precise requirements of their organisation. In this way the necessary information is identified and decisions can be made about proportionate actions.

1.82 But often organisations do not have the resources to resolve all their risk exposures in one big exercise. Consequently, a step-by-step approach, that progressively concentrates the focus of the review and at the same time increases the level of investigation, is an effective management approach.

1.83 A description of a structured process for building a 'Human Resources risk register' and a strategy for increasing the influence of Human Resources professionals on risk management, is explained in **Chapter 8**.

SUMMARY OF REMAINING CHAPTERS

Chapter 2 – Changing mindsets and setting the scene

1.84   Chapter 2 addresses the process of stimulating Human Resources professionals to think about the change in mindsets required both in themselves and their organisation to manage people risks effectively. It describes some scenarios for how they can make an enhanced contribution and add value.

1.85   It discusses some of the main areas of human capital, or people, risk, their relative importance, how to identify them and how to treat them. It reviews the roles of the Human Resources function in risk management and discusses the importance, for the Human Resources professional, of developing strategic partnership with other functions. It describes a process for developing the capability of the Human Resources function and its members through administrative excellence, people process management and business partnership to strategic leadership.

Chapter 3 – Organisational and human factors

1.86   Chapter 3 examines how effective risk management requires organisational and human factors to be managed as part of an overall business and operational systems approach.

1.87   'Organisational' factors are the structures and processes that largely determine the culture of an organisation and include factors such as responsibility frameworks, learning and development programmes and job/role design. 'Human' factors are fundamental human characteristics that need to be understood and managed as part of the risk management process. They include the nature of human error, how risk is perceived regardless of actual risk and what motivates individuals in the workplace to take risks.

1.88   The cross-functional nature of Human Resources and its focus on people management in the form of its involvement in learning and development, performance management, reward, responsibility frameworks and the like, provide Human Resources professionals with the expertise to become an integral and vital part of the risk management process.

Chapter 4 – Human Resources policies and procedures

1.89   Chapter 4 focuses on the identification, design and implementation of effective business-focused 'risk-based' Human Resources policies and procedures to improve organisational effectiveness and maximisation of opportunities. It will also explain the need to reduce a typical focus of some Human Resources professionals on changes that are only 'justified' by changes in legislation.

1.90   Human Resources professionals must avoid the approach that views the introduction of new legislation:

- As an opportunity to be risk averse and regulation focused.
- As an opportunity to exert some influence 'through the back door'.
- As an opportunity to enhance controls for current poor management systems.
- As an opportunity to increase the concentration of 'power' over Human Resources matters within the Human Resources function.

1.91   The key steps in the process will be explained and checklists used to assist risk identification, the evaluation of existing controls, the detailing of residual risk and action plan creation.

Chapter 5 – Human Resources administration

1.92   Chapter 5 highlights the fact that, whilst Human Resources administration is typically seen as the routine end of the spectrum of Human Resources services by both organisations and some Human Resources professionals, it is still vital that there are effective and robust systems in place to ensure that the basics are performed with 100% accuracy.

1.93   Human Resources will never be able to climb out of its administrative support box and graduate to higher levels of involvement and influence if it cannot manage the basics.

1.94   This chapter identifies the risk exposures within Human Resources administration and will demonstrate the types of controls to reduce the risk to tolerable levels.

1.95   The key steps in the process will be explained and checklists used to assist risk identification, the evaluation of existing controls, the detailing of residual risk and action plan creation.

Chapter 6 – Business transformation

1.96   Chapter 6 focuses on the identification and assessment of risk exposures and the evaluation of control options that are appropriate and proportionate for use during the consideration of business and operational process changes.

1.97 Human Resources professionals have a major role to play in business transformation and business and operational process change. Often the senior management in the organisation addresses the financial and legal risks associated with major changes, such as mergers and acquisitions or major reorganisations, but fails to address, or addresses inadequately, the human capital risks.

1.98 **Chapter 6** discusses some of the main human capital risks associated with business change and transformation and then reviews one core issue – the effect of change on relationships within the organisation and the impact of these relationships on business effectiveness. It discusses an approach to evaluating the quality of relationships and variations in these as a consequence of business changes. It also describes an approach to understanding the potential impact of proposed changes on relationships.

Chapter 7 – Business partnership – the way forward

1.99 **Chapter 7** describes the model of Human Resources involvement as business partners with senior managers, other managers and with employees. It also discusses the importance of partnership between line managers in different functions, between managers and employees and between employees.

1.100 It reviews the importance, for risk management, of trust levels within organisations. It discusses factors that build or destroy trust and suggests how Human Resources professionals can influence these. It addresses the relevance of limiting beliefs for risk management and discusses how these limiting beliefs can be brought to the surface and changed. Finally, it reviews situations where trust is not appropriate.

Chapter 8 – Getting started – increasing your contribution

1.101 **Chapter 8** will show how Human Resources professionals can identify, assess and classify Human Resources risks. In addition, an explanation will be given of the creation of a strategy for the implementation of improvements in the management of Human Resources risks, thereby increasing the contribution of the Human Resources function and demonstrating its potential for enhanced added value.

1.102 A concept of a Risk Register will be included that can be used to list risks and potential risk treatments. Other key aspects covered include:

- Human Resources risk identification.
- Input, activity and output risk identification.

- Process approach to risk identification.
- Classification and risk assessment.
- Implementation challenges.
- Strategy for increasing contribution.

1.103   Particular reference will be made to the professional and personal development of Human Resources professionals.

Chapter 9 – Pulling it together

1.104   **Chapter 9** pulls pull together the key points from earlier chapters and summarises the way forward for Human Resources professionals to identify and assess Human Resources risks and enhance their contribution to risk management.

WHAT NEXT?

1.105   **Chapter 2** starts the process of getting Human Resources professionals to think about the change in mindsets required both in themselves and their organisation, and how to start setting the scene for an enhanced contribution and added value.

REFERENCES

The 2003 'Accounting for People' Taskforce sponsored by the UK Department of Trade and Industry (DTI) (www.accountingforpeople.gov.uk)

The Accounts Modernisation Directive from the European Union (EU), Directive 2003/51/EC of the European Parliament and of the Council – 18 June 2003 amending Directives 78/660/EEC, 83/349/EEC, 86/635/EEC and 91/674/EEC on the annual and consolidated accounts of certain types of companies, banks and other financial institutions and insurance undertakings (www.europa.eu. int / eur-lex / pri / en / oj / dat / 2003 / 1178 / 1178200307 17en00160022.pdf)

Combined Code on Corporate Governance, UK Financial Services Authority, 2003. The Financial Reporting Councils' Combined Code – Listing Rules for UK Stock Exchange Listed Companies (www.frc.org.uk)

Draft regulations on the Operating and Financial Review and Directors' Report – A consultation document – UK Department of Trade and Industry, www.dti.gov.uk/cld/condocs.htm, May 2004

The Higgs Review, www.dti.gov.uk/cld/non_exec_review, 2003

The Organisation for Economic Co-operation and Development (OECD), OECD Principles of Corporate Governance, www.oecd.org/dataoeced, 2004

The Smith Report, www.frc.org.uk/publications/content/ACReport.pdf, 2003

Turnbull Report, Internal Control: Guidance for Directors on The Combined Code, The Institute of Chartered Accountants in England and Wales, www.icaew.co.uk/internalcontrol, September 1999

White Paper, Modernising Company Law, www.dti.gov.uk/cld/modern/index/ htm, published in July 2002 – Cm 5553 – I & II, July 2002.

CHAPTER 2

Changing mindsets and setting the scene

WHAT IS RISK MANAGEMENT FOR THE HUMAN RESOURCES PROFESSIONAL?

2.1 This chapter addresses the changes in mindset required both by Human Resources professionals and by their line management colleagues about the contribution of Human Resources professionals to risk management. It also addresses new and additional ways to enhance the contribution of the Human Resources function to add value to the organisation.

2.2 Risk management is often not seen by Human Resources professionals as a key element of their contribution to the organisations in which they work. If it is thought about at all, risk management is seen as something that is the responsibility of people in Health and Safety, Information Technology, Finance (Governance) or Insurance functions. It is seen as something that is best left to the risk management professionals. Alternatively, at best, it is seen as a part of the project planning process in Human Resources, where the risks of something going wrong are assessed in a potential problem analysis step as part of the contingency planning prior to implementation.

Risk management as a core competency for Human Resources

2.3 Our thesis is that risk management should be seen as a core competency and a key responsibility of any Human Resources professional. When we discuss this with colleagues, their first reaction is often 'Oh, but isn't that a very negative way of thinking?' Or, 'How boring. So you want to control everything to avoid risk?' Or, 'Our role is to be creative and opportunistic, rather than removing risk.' These comments betray a misunderstanding of the contribution that a risk-based approach brings to the work of the Human Resources professional. The commonly held view that risk is always a negative to be avoided is not sustainable. Risk is something that all people and organisations face and can, indeed, be an opportunity. This is exemplified by considering one of the main roles of the Human Resources function, which is to facilitate the development of a culture that encourages innovation. Implicit in this is the ability to take intelligent risks.

Risk management and innovation

2.4 People in organisations are often afraid to take risks, because, in spite of what is said in the organisation's values statement about encouraging innovation, they know that it is only acceptable to take risks as long as they 'get it right'. Most organisations do not reward the taking of risks that do not deliver the expected results. People often feel that they will be punished if they 'get it wrong'. In part, the anxiety may arise from their inability to assess risks effectively and to plan appropriately to minimise the risks or their effects. If they were more skilled in this aspect of risk assessment, they would be in a better position to take intelligent risks rather than hoping that everything will work out right. But this damage limitation aspect is the minimum that can be gained by Human Resources professionals from addressing risk management. Even more important is the benefit to be gained from reviewing the external and internal environment of the organisation to identify:

- Risks that could be potentially harmful to the organisation and adopting a risk management approach to increase productivity.
- Opportunities that may be missed and ensuring that the risk of missing the opportunity is minimised.

What is people risk?

2.5 In our experience, Human Resources professionals are faced with many problems and ambiguities. The example below illustrates some of the people risks, or human capital risks, that are inherent in many organisations.

2.6 Senior management wanted harmonisation across the organisation of the way that people were managed. Departments each managed employees in their own way and with very different styles. Performance and development reviews were carried out effectively in some areas, were done haphazardly in others and missing entirely in others. Departmental managers were supposed to be accountable for assigning merit increases and rewards to their people, yet senior executives on occasion intervened to award special bonuses for people that they identified. Although company policy required people to transfer between departments for their career development, mobility between departments was determined by the way that individual departments manipulated the salary progression and promotion policy for their own advantage. Recruitment practice varied widely between departments and costs of recruitment were much higher than the benchmarks. The way in which managers used the disciplinary policy and fired employees varied widely and the costs of industrial tribunals and litigation were spiralling out of control. Some parts of the company had comprehensive career development and training practices while others had none. Communication between departments was poor, decision-making was slow and erratic and departments each blamed the others for inefficiencies, taking no accountability for their actions.

2.7 Human capital risk can be considered to be made up of three domains:

1 **Compliance** – Financial or reputational damage to the organisation due to failures to meet legal or regulatory requirements.

2 **Productivity** – Loss of productivity or output due to under-skilled or under-motivated employees; or an organisational culture that does not encourage discretionary effort (the extra contribution over and above what is required to keep the boss off your back) from employees.

3 **Growth** – Failing to maximise organisational capability or to identify and achieve internal or external opportunities for innovation or major growth or development of the business.

FIGURE 1

ELEMENTS OF HUMAN CAPITAL RISK

2.8 Some examples of the risks in each of these domains are included in the following list, which is intended to be illustrative, rather than comprehensive:

- Compliance:
    - Employment law.
    - Sex or race discrimination.
    - Health and Safety.
    - Harassment, bullying or violence in the workplace.
    - Disciplinary and grievance procedures.
    - Stress.
    - Occupational health.
    - Safety/accidents and security.

- – Human Resources metrics.
- – Diversity.
- – Unfair or wrongful dismissal.
- – Corporate governance.
- Productivity:
  - – Performance assessment.
  - – Core skills training.
  - – Succession planning.
  - – Absence management.
  - – Minimising loss of organisational memory and core skills and talents through major reorganisations, mergers, takeovers or downsizing.
  - – Reward and recognition.
  - – Attracting and retaining talent.
  - – Health and safety.
  - – Employee surveys.
  - – Employee satisfaction/commitment.
  - – Organisation redesign.
  - – Organisational development.
  - – Diversity.
- Growth:
  - – Recruitment strategy – identifying potential skill shortages in the recruitment market and planning initiating action in advance.
  - – Strategic training – identifying skills and capability gaps in the workforce, and initiating an appropriate training strategy.
  - – Leadership development.
  - – Performance development and career planning.
  - – Succession planning.
  - – Strategic thinking capability.
  - – Reward and recognition processes. Recognising and reinforcing behaviours and attitudes required to develop the desired organisational culture.
  - – Corporate governance.
  - – Clarifying and embedding core values and vision to align people and activities.
  - – Developing a communications capability that ensures people understand and are committed to the vision, values and objectives.
  - – A systemic approach that ensures that Human Resources policies and practices work in an integrated manner to deliver what the organisation requires.
  - – Developing an organisational culture that encourages, recognises and rewards intelligent risk-taking; changing mindsets and limiting beliefs.
  - – Building trust, effective working relationships and team working.
  - – Employee opinion surveys.

–   Diversity.

2.9   Different organisations with different profiles are likely to have different lists, depending on their strategies and challenges. A number of human capital risk elements could be placed into several domains, as can be seen above. For example, corporate governance can be seen as a compliance risk, necessitating meeting the minimum requirements of the regulators or the shareholders. Or it can be seen as a growth risk, by failing to operate the business in a sustainable and sound manner if employees at all levels do not understand their roles, the organisation's objectives and the right way of conducting business and behaving in an ethical manner. Similarly, diversity can be seen as a compliance risk that the organisation needs to address by simply paying lip service to legal or regulatory requirements. Or it can be seen as a risk for growth and development of the business if individual differences are not valued, and people are not given the opportunity to grow and develop and contribute to their maximum capability – regardless of their gender, ethnic origin, sexual orientation or any other factor that, in the worst circumstances, can be used to differentiate and discriminate against individuals or groups. Managers often view absenteeism as a compliance risk that they need to manage by avoiding legal claims arising from this risk. It can also be seen as a productivity risk, that can be avoided by proactively managing individuals with higher-than-average absenteeism in order to identify causes and remove them (the causes, not the people). Alternatively, high levels of absenteeism in an organisation may be due to a variety of behavioural risks associated with employee health, well-being and morale that, when addressed at a strategic level, can lead to significant growth.

RELATIVE IMPORTANCE OF DIFFERENT RISKS

2.10   What are the most important risks faced by organisations? According to a survey conducted by Chicago-based Aon Corporation (Nickson, 2001), risk managers feel that they must expand their view of risk to include Human Resources. More than 300 risk managers were asked to rank seven major risk categories. Human capital risk was ranked first, with employee recruiting, retention and compensation being the main contributors.

2.11   Randy Nornes, a managing director in Aon's strategic accounting unit, is quoted as saying, 'It's a reflection of the labour market – the demands of all businesses trying to hold on to people'.

> 'It's a huge issue, and it's only going to get bigger. What it's also saying is the human resource interests, which were just operational issues in the Human Resources department, are now a key issue to other managers. These managers are saying that if they don't get this right, their business strategy is going to fail.'

2.12   Marsh, a leading risk and insurance services firm, surveyed 600 mid-sized European businesses on their attitude to risk in 2002 (Marsh, 2002). For the purposes of the study, the mid-sized sector was defined as having annual revenues between €50m–500m and staff numbers between 50–500. The top issues listed by UK companies are shown in Table 1. It is informative to note that the majority of these risks involve human capital. Two of the top-three risks, losing key staff and absenteeism, are completely human capital risks, whereas many others, such as not responding to technological advances, wrong strategy or IT security failure, have a strong people component.

TABLE I

MOST IMPORTANT RISKS IN UK MID-SIZED COMPANIES

Risk	Percentage rating
Losing key staff to competitors	81
Supply chain failure	80
Staff absenteeism	77
Not responding to technological advances	72
Increased competition	71
Legal and contractual non-compliance	70
Changes in customer demand	69
Workplace injuries	67
Wrong strategy – lack of market data	66
IT security failure	65
Employee misdeeds	65
Changes in demographics and customers	63
System failures	61
Fire and disaster	60
Business interruption	58
Misinterpreting market information	56
Employee injury	55
Physical security breach	51
Wrong investment strategy	50

People skills and risk management

2.13   People skills and organisational culture are at the heart of risk management:

- People are a source of risk. For example, they may leave the organisation, taking key skills and knowledge with them. They may be the cause of industrial accidents or business catastrophes through being careless or inadequately trained. They may, as in the case of Barings, Britain's oldest merchant bank, bring the company to collapse through failure to establish effective company procedures to prevent misdemeanours, or through management carelessness. In this latter case, the management of Barings effectively let the trader, Nick Leeson, settle his own trades by putting him in charge of both the dealing desk and the back office. This is tantamount to allowing the person who works a cash till to bank the day's takings without an independent third party checking whether the amount banked at the end of the day matches the till receipts.

- People are also important for managing risk. A well-trained and committed workforce in a company with a positive organisational culture and clearly stated values and corresponding behaviours can understand, anticipate and respond to risks.

- We get impatient with the tired old maxim 'our people are our most important resource', because it is patently true and yet few organisations behave as though they really believe it. Investment in capital equipment is managed very carefully with intensive checks and balances and monitoring processes. Yet people policies are implemented in a relatively haphazard way in many organisations with little attempt to apply systems thinking to ensure that the implications and outcomes of any changes in people policies or practices are examined holistically. How often have you seen a systematic analysis of the risks of introducing a change to the reward policy and practices in an organisation? As an example, we have seen organisations that state that teamwork is a core value and that effective team working is essential to the success of the organisation. Yet they implement merit pay practices that reward individual performance and make no attempt to recognise or reinforce effective team working behaviours. Most organisations claim that people development is one of their top priorities. Yet organisations that specifically recognise and reward managers who invest time and energy in people development are in the minority. Our experience has been that such managers complain that they probably suffer financially or from a career point of view from investing time in people development as it takes time out from delivering their business and operational objectives. If an organisation is committed to people development, this needs to be included in managers' performance objectives and the managers need to be rewarded for successfully achieving them.

2.14   As people really are an organisation's most important resource, particularly as intellectual capital becomes more explicitly valued and with the increasing numbers of knowledge workers, then should we not have in place systematic methods for assessing the risks associated with this resource? The challenge to leadership and to Human Resources professionals in managing people risk is to change thinking about the relevance and importance of these risks, and to find ways of changing the way people behave so that they actually manage these risks.

IDENTIFICATION OF RISKS

2.15   We address the identification of risk factors in detail in **Chapter 8**. In this section we summarise some of the principles involved in behavioural risk analysis. Reddy (2003) argues that a full behavioural risk analysis penetrates into every aspect of an organisation's operation. It includes, for example, a review of fraud and theft, computer sabotage, promulgation by employees of pornographic material through internal and inter-organisation email, substance abuse, diversity and disability issues as well as the more obviously people-related risks associated with all aspects of people policies, processes and practices – such as employee sourcing, interpersonal conflict, unwanted employee turnover, grievances, job performance short-falls and disciplinary offences.

Focus on human capital risks

2.16   The challenge for the Human Resources professional is not to identify numerous potential risk areas, but to decide which of the many potential human capital risk areas to address. Organisations have rarely tackled these in a systematic, comprehensive way. This is partly from a sense that it is difficult to identify the nature of these risks and to quantify their costs, and partly from a concern that the magnitude of the task of changing people's behaviour makes it too daunting or difficult a programme to take on. Our recommendation is that Human Resources professionals would be well advised, initially, to focus primarily on the risks associated with the people policies and practices for which they are responsible, rather than addressing risks in areas for which they are not directly responsible, such as financial risk, business continuity or IT risk. In particular, Human Resources professionals should assess the full breadth of Human Resources risks (discussed in detail in **Chapter 8**). We emphasise that it is essential to take a cross-functional, rather than a silo-thinking, approach to the risk analysis, as many of the areas of risk require interventions across departmental and functional interfaces. We will develop this theme in **Chapter 7**.

2.17   'Behavioural Risk Analysis,' says Reddy (2003) 'is in the first place about controlling the risks of employing people. In the second place it is about how organisational practices allow or even foster the behaviours that give rise to people risks.' A striking example of this is the way in which organisations embark on major change programmes, planning carefully for the financial and structural objectives and yet paying insufficient attention to the softer issues such as communicating to employees the need for the change and taking people's concerns and anxieties about change into account. This often has unanticipated negative consequences for the effective and smooth implementation of the changes, with consequent impact on organisational performance.

Human capital risks associated with senior management decision-making

2.18   In 2002, PricewaterhouseCoopers commissioned a global survey to gauge attitudes in the prevailing climate of uncertainty. The research was designed to establish what strategies companies were adopting to address market shocks and volatility and the key drivers behind the decisions they were taking (PricewaterhouseCoopers, 2002). Over 590 senior managers, mostly at Chief Financial Officer or equivalent, level were surveyed in medium and large companies in a range of industry sectors worldwide. Their key findings were shocking, but supported what many Human Resources professionals probably knew intuitively:

- **Senior managers were making short-term cuts to please shareholders, not longer-term strategies to build businesses** – Companies confuse short-term shareholder appeasement with effective cost control. Confronted by economic uncertainty, managers worldwide will all too readily resort to slash-and-burn cost cutting, instead of approaching cost control strategically for the longer term.
- **Companies were not practising what they preached** – 86% of respondents agreed that significant short-term cost reduction programmes can be strongly detrimental to employee morale and loyalty, and 55% agree that obvious cost cutting is more about impressing analysts and shareholders than improving the business. But knowing this does not stop most companies from making the same short-term cuts they know to be damaging to the longer-term prospects of the business.
- **Too much cost cutting could be fatal, leaving companies underresourced for the future** – The survey showed that companies have yet to understand this – quick-fix cost reduction dominated the global agenda, with 60% of companies putting recruitment and investment on hold. Most companies did not appear to have learned the lessons of the early 1990s, and seemed intent on making sure history repeated itself.
- **Weeding out costs would not stop them coming back** – 57% of respondents agreed that the costs they were currently cutting back

would be back in their organisations within two to three years – short-term solutions rarely attacked the root of the problem.

2.19   A century ago, labour was plentiful, cheap and many jobs were relatively unskilled, which meant that employers could, if they chose, treat their employees as dispensable and readily replaceable. As intellectual capital becomes more explicitly valued and knowledge management becomes integral to the management of the business, people (behavioural) risk management assumes a high level of importance. Yet the PricewaterhouseCoopers study shows that nineteenth-century attitudes still prevail in some quarters. There have been many examples of this type of thinking in recent years, perhaps exacerbated by the economic downturn and the consequent business volatility and unpredictability at the start of the twenty-first century.

Case study

2.20   An article in *People Management* (2004a) stated that an airline lost very skilled people as a result of job cuts in the wake of the terrorist attacks of 11 September 2001. Less than a week after the event, the airline decided to lose 25% of its employees, and just a month later, 1,200 employees had gone. Eventually 1,700 people lost their jobs, mostly through voluntary redundancy, although many of these were rehired later. The company announced expansion plans including the recruitment of up to 1,400 staff in early 2004. Could a longer-term approach have minimised some of the trauma and expense associated with the job losses and subsequent hiring of similar numbers of people? We are not suggesting that these issues are simple. But the example epitomises the challenge to Human Resources professionals to devise more innovative approaches to agile resourcing in times of rapid change.

RISK TREATMENT

Levels of intervention

2.21   Reddy (2003), describes three levels of intervention in risk treatment: remedial, preventive and systemic.

- **Remedial** – This is the level of damage limitation, of taking action to deal with problems after they have occurred, or of implementing short-term measures to address areas of people risk.
- **Preventive** – This is where people are enabled to make themselves and

the organisation more risk-aware. Provision of training and raising awareness of risks, providing skills of risk assessment and risk management, changes the way people do things to minimise people risks and develops an organisational culture that supports innovation and risk taking.

- **Systemic** – This is the level of organisation change. This is achieved by changing mindsets and limiting beliefs, reflecting the new mindset in new policies and procedures, and the collection, monitoring and reporting of management information relating to people (people measures).

Prioritisation or assessment of risks

2.22 It's one thing to undertake risk analysis to identify long lists of Human Resources risks. But where do busy Human Resource professionals begin to break into the list, particularly as they already have a longer list of pressing tasks than they can manage? How do they begin to change mindsets and, consequently, change behaviours and risk profiles in their organisations? In some respects it depends on whether you are at the corporate centre or in a unit of a large organisation. Hard-pressed Human Resources professionals in small- to medium-size organisations may become concerned about the additional workload that will be added to their long list of tasks and objectives. But there is a way through, as we will show.

Probability/impact matrix

2.23 Once you have identified the main risks using the processes outlined in **Chapter 8**, they need to be prioritised. One approach that we have found useful is to assess the risks across two dimensions:

1 The possible impact of the risk in terms of costs, or impact on business effectiveness.
2 The likelihood of the event occurring.

2.24 The risks can then be located on a four-quadrant matrix and efforts can be made to prevent the occurrence or to reduce the likelihood of it happening (see Figure 2).

2.25 Clearly, risks falling into Quadrant 2, which are high probability and high impact, are high priority. Action needs to be implemented to reduce either the probability of the risk occurring, or the impact that it causes, or both.

2.26 For example, if an organisation has experienced numerous tribunal cases for unfair dismissal complaints or discrimination and the majority have

FIGURE 2

CLASSIFYING RISKS ACROSS THE TWO DIMENSIONS

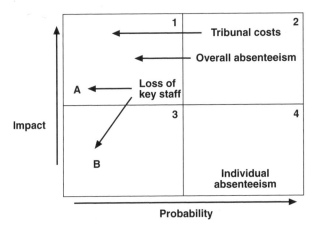

been found against it, this is a high-probability and high-impact risk. Providing appropriate training for managers could reduce both the impact and the probability of the risk. For a low-probability but high-impact risk such as losing key staff with scarce skills (Quadrant 1), the probability could be reduced by implementing effective career development processes and, possibly, appropriate recognition and reward practices (A). Alternatively, by introducing appropriate training, combined with encouraging people to make career transitions, to generate a larger pool of people with scarce skills, both probability and impact of the risk could be reduced, moving the risk to Quadrant 3 (B).

2.27 Absenteeism is a risk that has a low impact on the total organisation for an individual employee, even if that person has a poor attendance record (Quadrant 4). But if it occurs sufficiently frequently across large numbers of employees (high probability), it can have a major impact on company productivity (Quadrant 2). Since an individual manager may not have many employees with a high level of absenteeism, it falls to Human Resources professionals to keep records of absenteeism and to monitor them and report regularly to managers in order to reduce the probability of the risk and therefore the overall cost, shifting the risk to Quadrant 1.

2.28 Using this approach helps to decide whether the appropriate level to intervene is remedial (urgent, fire fighting), preventive (more time to address the issue at a deeper level) or systemic (a major risk that needs more diagnosis and a more strategic approach to ensure that the probability of the risk occurring is minimised and/or the potential impact on the organisation is minimised).

2.29 Often the approach adopted by busy Human Resources professionals is to tackle the major presenting problem immediately (the remedial level).

The pragmatic Human Resources professional may judge that it is wise to identify what the CEO's main concerns are and to go for number one on his list – the preventive level. That may or may not be a minimalist strategy for survival, but we believe there is a better way, namely, to take time to step back and think, prior to developing a strategy and implementation plan – the systemic level.

THE ROLE OF THE HUMAN RESOURCES FUNCTION

2.30   Some Human Resources functions have the capability to provide strategic leadership in their organisations and to influence major change in the way things are done. Unfortunately they are not the majority. A very good example of this is the current concern amongst institutional investors and other stakeholders about corporate governance, that has given a wake-up call to many organisations.

Corporate governance

2.31   There have been highly publicised failures in corporate governance recently in companies such as Enron, Shell, WorldCom and Parmalat. These, and the increased risks from terrorist activities following the 11 September 2001 disaster, have focused the attention of Boards and senior managers on risk management. Not surprisingly, their main focus of attention has been corporate governance. New standards and legislation, including the Sarbanes–Oxley act in the USA and the Financial Reporting Council's new Combined Code on Corporate Governance in the UK reflect widespread concerns about the way companies are run. Many of the FTSE 100 companies have established teams to review corporate governance, and have implemented new systems and procedures for corporate governance and introduced processes to monitor their effectiveness.

2.32   The Financial Reporting Council's new Combined Code on Corporate Governance brings together a number of reports, including the Higgs report into the role and effectiveness of non-executive directors. But Corporate Governance is not only about board structure, pay and processes – the main focus of Higg's recommendations. Neither is it just about introducing control mechanisms to ensure that companies comply with regulatory requirements.

2.33   Alan Judes of consultants Hewitt, Bacon and Woodrow made a key point when he said:

'Corporate governance is about operating the business in a sound and sustainable manner and that means employees have to understand their roles, company objectives and the right way of going about business and behaving in an ethical manner' (*People Management*, 2004b).

2.34   Good corporate governance means that the organisation (in other words, all the people that work in it) can be trusted and that it holds itself accountable to all its stakeholders by providing figures and measures to demonstrate this. In other words, it is about how people behave; it is about establishing integrity and trust both within, and, in organisations and encouraging people to hold each other accountable for what they say they will deliver.

2.35   This is something that the Human Resources function should be involved in, but a Hewitt, Bacon and Woodrow survey, published in November 2003, revealed that while the Human Resources function generally took some part in activities to improve corporate governance, most often in designing board-level remuneration, in some of the companies, Human Resources professionals had no role at all.

2.36   John Drummond, Chief Executive of the ethics and corporate governance consultancy, Integrity Works, said:

'HR isn't as involved as it ought to be. If there is a gap between board rhetoric, including adherence to corporate governance standards, and actual behaviour in the organisation, this produces unacceptable levels of corporate risk' (*People Management*, 2004b).

2.37   Often Human Resources professionals are invited in at a late stage in the process when the plans have been made, rather than being involved in the strategic thinking and planning stage. This is true, not only in the area of corporate governance, but in all areas of corporate strategy and organisational change, that can only be delivered through people. Failure to deliver this strategy fully and effectively is an unacceptable risk to the organisation. So why are Human Resources professionals not involved in the early stages more often? We address this question at **2.49–2.74**.

Mergers and acquisitions

2.38   Mergers and acquisitions (M&As) are fraught with difficulties, many of which relate to Human Resources issues. International mergers and acquisitions are even more problematic. When engaging in cross-border deals or acquiring an organisation with operations in many countries, legislative frameworks, ways of doing business and cultural differences will all provide hurdles not found to the same extent in single-country deals. In more cases than not, mergers result in a destruction of shareholder value, irreparable damage to organisations that were previously working satisfactorily and/or serious harm to the livelihood or careers of thousands of people. Despite this, chief executives and boards, not to say merchant bankers and venture capitalists, still generally view M&As as a legitimate business strategy. The questions for Human Resources professionals are: 'How thorough is the risk assessment that we did before embarking on the merger?' and 'Have I done everything possible to ensure that the senior management fully understand the people risks and opportunities of the merger or acquisition?'

2.39 A new Chartered Institute of Personnel and Development (CIPD) research report on mergers, 'Human Resources' Contribution to International Mergers and Acquisitions' (CIPD, 2004) considers why mergers and acquisitions fail, and what Human Resources professionals can contribute to reduce the associated risks and enable them to succeed. The report assesses the factors that determine the level of influence Human Resources is able to have in international M&As, and how, when Human Resources is more actively involved, mergers are more successful. The report concludes that, when going through mergers and acquisitions, organisations usually focus primarily on the financial, economic and commercial aspects of the deal, and often only consider the people dimensions as an afterthought, if at all. Taking full account of the people issues in a merger or acquisition and managing them effectively can reduce the risks associated with mergers. This approach will generate better short-term and long-term results for employees, customers and shareholders alike.

2.40 In an interview on BBC Radio 4 following the merger of Morrisons and Safeway, the Chairman, Sir Ken Morrison, said that the different cultures of the two companies was contributing to some of the problems in improving the performance of the merged company. A similar situation occurred with the merger of GlaxoWellcome and SmithKline Beecham, where the differences in the cultures of the two companies slowed down integration.

2.41 Another report by the CIPD, 'People and Performance in Knowledge-Intensive Firms' (CIPD, January 2003) highlights the importance of people processes such as coaching, communication and learning in high technology, knowledge-based organisations. This, by implication, highlights the potential organisational risks arising from paying insufficient attention to the people issues in a reorganisation or restructuring.

Developing strategic partnership

2.42 Although the role of the Human Resources function has been developing slowly over the last ten years to become more of a strategic partner with line managers, in many organisations Human Resources professionals are still expected to, and in many cases are apparently content to, operate at an administrative or policy policing level, providing pay and rations. The Human Resources input often starts at the stage of implementing business plans, change projects or reorganisations, whereas, if they are professionally competent and willing to take a lead, they should be involved from the beginning in the thinking and planning processes and raising awareness of the people issues. They should be able to bring about change through influencing employee behaviour and changing the way that people do things within organisations and interact with their customers and suppliers.

2.43 The CIPD has said much in recent years about the need for the Human Resources profession to become recognised as a strategic partner in the business. But the change has been slow in coming. Why is this? Partly it is the chicken and egg situation that, while Human Resources professionals are weighed down with the heavy workload of delivering the administrative and operational outputs that the organisation expects of them, they find it difficult to raise their heads above the water and find time and energy to identify some of the strategic people needs of that organisation. This makes it a challenge for them to begin to think about how they can influence the senior managers to do something about these needs.

2.44 This is reinforced by a Chartered Institute of Personnel and Development study of heads of Human Resources and development functions in 2003 (CIPD, October 2003). The study, that involved 1,200 organisations, found that many Human Resources professionals were having trouble freeing themselves from their day-to-day operational and administrative activities in order to carry out a more strategic, higher-value-adding role. Partly, it is also down to the lack of appropriate skills, such as strategic thinking, process improvement, project management, consulting influencing and change management among Human Resources professionals.

2.45 This is exacerbated by the discontinuity in the career ladder for Human Resources professionals. The skills required to be effective as a Human Resources professional in leading strategic thinking and change are very different from those required to be an effective operational Human Resources person. Operational Human Resources professionals risk hitting a career ceiling unless they can diversify their skills and experience to gain the required competencies to operate at a strategic level.

2.46 If the expectation of the organisation is that the role of the Human Resources function is just an implementer of decisions made elsewhere, it takes determination, vision, business acumen and high-level professional capability to change that mindset. These are not simple quick fixes where you can produce an equation that demonstrates that 'If you do this, the payoff will be £X million.' We are talking about organisations that are complex systems where the outcomes of some of the required interventions will be unexpected and surprising.

2.47   In Enron, there was a culture that regarded people as 'hunters and therefore they needed to be allowed to eat off their kills'. Although it is tempting to go off at a tangent to examine this language construct and the mindset that underlies it, we will resist the temptation. It would have taken a tough and courageous Human Resources professional to be able to argue the case for the downside of this approach, namely that if the reward philosophy is so strongly linked to making business 'kills', it carries the risk that people may be tempted to take risks that could be unacceptable to the company. How do you carry that argument when apparently the philosophy is driving the growth of the company to unprecedented levels that seemed almost too good to be true? The answer is that Human Resources professionals will not succeed only by tackling these sorts of situations when they have run into difficulties. They need also to be involved in the discussions that determine the values that the organisation wishes to espouse and to be able to influence the thinking about how this goal is achieved through its people. This is not a short-term fix, but involves a long-term strategy for developing the capability of the function. Like any good strategy, it will involve a number of steps.

2.48   It is essential for Human Resources functions that want to operate at a strategic level in the organisation to have a strategy for developing the capabilities and competencies of Human Resources professionals. They need to be able to operate at a strategic level to influence the thinking of the senior managers about the people issues and to contribute to the strategic thinking process. Unless this can be achieved, the Human Resources function will be ineffective in enabling the organisation to manage Human Resources risks and opportunities. The following section describes a process we have used to develop the strategic capabilities of the Human Resources function.

STRATEGY FOR DEVELOPING THE EFFECTIVENESS OF THE HUMAN RESOURCES FUNCTION

2.49   Each organisation is different and each Human Resources function is operating in its own individual context. So the following guidelines can only be general and cannot be applied without thinking. Nevertheless, the underlying principles are valid and have stood the test of building a strategic Human Resources function that has operated effectively over a sustained period in a number of organisations.

2.50   The following four capabilities that are required to operate as a strategic Human Resources function can also be regarded as developmental steps. The development of the capabilities is described in the following sections as sequential, although in practice the steps are, to some extent, developed concurrently. Often loop-backs are needed to revisit and further develop capabilities that have been achieved earlier.

Administrative excellence

2.51   In our experience, when Human Resources professionals first get enthusiastic about operating at a strategic level, they want to focus immediately on business partnership with their line clients. The new interest in strategic change and organisational development can result in administrative or operational tasks becoming regarded as of minor importance and relegated to low priority, or even ignored. The first step in establishing a high-performing Human Resources capability, however, is to build the capability to deliver operational excellence. If Human Resources professionals cannot deliver a new employee to the timescale agreed with line managers, they should not expect managers to respect them enough to want to engage with them on thinking about how they can help them to make their organisations more effective. If they cannot provide managers with reliable records and information about the people in their organisation, they need not expect them to seek their counsel on strategic thinking about their people. Human Resources needs to establish its credibility as a function that can manage its basic activities effectively. In addition, Human Resources professionals need to be able to understand what the issues are that bother their managers and deal with those first, before they can begin to tackle some of the more strategic issues.

2.52   This means surveying, and talking to, their internal clients to discover the things they value about the Human Resources function and the things they would like them to stop doing, start doing, do better, or do more of. Carrying out a client survey with clients who do not regard the Human Resources function as perfect (to say the least) can feel like committing professional hara-kiri. Leaders in Human Resources will need to carry their people with them and to allay some of their concerns about how the survey data will be managed. For example, will they be fired if there is negative feed back on their performance? Although there are sensitive issues to manage, the data gathering exercise will achieve a number of things:

- Being prepared to go out to clients and admit that the Human Resources function could do, and wants to do, things better will immediately send a signal that there is a strong desire to meet their needs more effectively. More importantly, it will demonstrate that Human Resources wants to get away from the old blame or punishment culture that pervades so many organisations (sometimes under the surface) to build a culture of openness, accountability and trust.
- It will provide a wealth of information about how the function is perceived by its clients and even though some of the feedback may seem off the mark, it lets Human Resources know what their clients think.
- The very act of engaging with them – through surveys, interviews and focus groups – will demonstrate a desire for partnership and a willingness to engage.

- The process will provide the Human Resources function with hard data that will help them to achieve a change in attitudes and behaviour among the Human Resources team. To change the role of the function can feel scary for many of the Human Resources professionals, most of whom will not have the skills needed, at this point in time, to operate at a more strategic business partnership level.
- Reporting back to clients with the outcomes from the data-gathering exercise demonstrates a willingness to receive feedback and to act on it, as well as showing that Human Resources have listened to what their clients regarded as important.

2.53 The wealth of information gained from the data gathering exercise can assist the identification of areas for performance improvement for the Human Resources professionals individually and for the function as a whole. As the outcomes from the survey are discussed with clients, Human Resources will begin jointly to identify and agree what they will do differently. Human Resources professionals will need to contract formally with each of their client groups on what will and will not be delivered to them over the coming year. The identification of Human Resources risks and the creation of a Risk Register is dealt with in **Chapter 8.**

2.54 We strongly support the benefits of drawing up a written contract that summarises clearly and simply what Human Resources will, and will not, deliver to a client over the next year and what is needed from the client to be able to deliver this. This introduces the need for contracting and negotiating skills, that may be new to Human Resources professionals, and for the capability of establishing service-level contracts, that demonstrate the need for mutual accountability between the Human Resources professional and the client.

2.55 At the same time, the outcomes from the data gathering exercise and the results of the contracting meetings with the clients will enable the Human Resources Director, with the team, to set performance targets to establish performance excellence, and to set up measures for monitoring and improving performance. Human Resources professionals will need to identify what skills gaps exist in the function and implement appropriate learning activities. It will be important to discuss these targets and measures with clients and to provide them with regular reports on how the function is performing against the targets.

2.56 The difficulty of establishing meaningful targets should not be under-estimated. We have seen evidence in the recent events with the UK National Health Service of the dangers of establishing targets that do not reflect the real underlying needs of the organisation. In recruitment, for example, the manager might want to agree a minimum time to deliver a new recruit from the date the vacancy was identified. But Human Resources professionals may not wish to act as a recruitment agency that exists merely to supply 'another of the same'. They may wish to negotiate over agreeing a review step to ensure that the skills and 'shape' of the new recruit are the most appropriate for the needs. Could an alternative approach be used, such as part-timers, job shares, outsourcing? This could lengthen the 'time to fill' measure. Agreeing and reporting targets again demonstrates openness and the willingness of Human Resources professionals to be held accountable for what they have committed to deliver.

2.57   Although the foregoing may seem somewhat mechanistic, it is a vital first step in establishing the effectiveness of the Human Resources function. As well as achieving clarity between the Human Resources person and the client on what will be delivered and how, it establishes a new way of working. It demonstrates openness and accountability and starts the process of building trust and better working relationships. It gets away from the old patterns of making excuses for failure to deliver, or blaming and shaming and punishment. It provides a mechanism for reviewing when something goes wrong, establishing the cause and implementing actions to do it better next time. Also, it clarifies the part the client plays in ensuring that the performance measures are met and builds mutual accountability.

2.58   Not only does this improve the effectiveness of the Human Resources function and the working relationships with its clients, it provides an opportunity for Human Resources professionals to open dialogue with their line managers on how they might consider working differently with their internal and external clients. It can start the process of giving Human Resources professionals openings to affect the overall culture of the organisation and to start conversations around risk and innovation.

Process mapping, standardisation and improvement

2.59   The second phase of developing a strategic Human Resources function is the development of process management capabilities. No matter how strategic, conceptual, theoretically based and academically sound Human Resources function and Human Resources professionals are, ultimately they need to deliver results to the organisation. There is a start point and an end point for the delivery. This means that there must be a best way of delivering the result – in other words, a process. Many progressive Human Resources functions have identified, mapped, standardised and improved their processes and have established performance measures to monitor effectiveness of the processes. Yet we still encounter Human Resources professionals who may talk about a Human Resources process, but who have never mapped the process, and who would run a mile rather than be held accountable for establishing measures of effectiveness by which the process's (and the Human Resources professional's) effectiveness could be monitored.

2.60 This is not a textbook on process improvement and therefore we will not go into great detail about how to implement process management in a Human Resources function. But it is necessary to give an overall summary in order to clarify some of the benefits that flow from Human Resources process management. The main steps in process improvement are as follows:

- Identify all the Human Resources processes.
- Prioritise them in order of effectiveness or need for improvement.
- Select one process for improvement and set up a process-improvement team.
- Map the process flow, identifying all the steps, timings and people who are involved and their roles and responsibilities.
- Identify inefficiencies in the process; steps in the critical path than can be improved; overlaps in responsibilities; delays; variations in the process among different people, etc.
- Standardise the process.
- Identify measures to monitor the effectiveness of the process.
- Train people in the new process.
- Implement the new process.
- Appoint a process owner who is accountable for maintaining, monitoring and improving the process.
- Monitor the process, gathering data on the measures.
- Improve the process.
- Identify the next process for development and continue the cycle.

2.61 Why would busy Human Resources professionals want to distract themselves from their workload to focus on process improvement? What are the benefits? In our experience the benefits are significant. They include the following:

- **Effectiveness and efficiency** – Human Resources practices for which there are not effective processes represent an unacceptable risk to the organisation. How do Human Resources professionals know whether the service they are providing is effective and efficient and value-for-investment unless they know what the process is for delivering the service and have established measures of effectiveness? When they have done this they can measure the process performance against the agreed targets and identify opportunities to improve it. Also, delegating process ownership to different people in the Human Resources function provides a focus on process improvement and quality of service to the clients, in a measurable manner.
- **Building better relationships with clients** – Once the process has been standardised, Human Resources professionals can contract with their customers on the service levels that they can realistically expect for the delivery of this particular service. Sharing the performance data with clients demonstrates openness and accountability and builds trust.

Sharing the process with clients ensures that they understand their roles in delivering optimum performance for the process and facilitates the building of mutual accountability and partnership.

- **Customer focus** – Spending time with internal clients will assist Human Resources professionals in understanding the business. It does not necessarily mean that they will know what their clients' needs really are, or that they will be able to meet them. Adopting a process management approach will ensure that delivery of measurable, top-quality customer service becomes a way of life for the Human Resources function.
- **The reputation of the Human Resources function** – Implementing process improvement enhances the reputation of the Human Resources function for efficiency and effectiveness. One of the problems of a support function is that, no matter how well they do, there is always something more that the client can look for in terms of performance and delivery. Ensuring clients understand the process, the part they play in it and the measures of effectiveness provides a basis for contracting on any changes in performance or delivery.
- **Demonstrating efficiency and providing supporting data in discussions about resourcing levels** – Human Resources functions are everlastingly under pressure to cut headcount and costs in organisations that view them as an overhead, rather than an investment. By implementing effective process management, the function demonstrates a commitment to efficiency, which facilitates difficult negotiations on resourcing levels and service delivery levels.

Business partnership

2.62   During the latter part of the last decade, the need for the Human Resources professional to become a member of the management team – to become a business partner – was a common theme in Human Resources literature. Much was said, and is still being said, about the need for Human Resources Directors to be invited on to the Board or the executive committee of the organisation. But the real challenge for the Human Resources professional is not to achieve an invitation to join the Board or the management team. It is to start to demonstrate the quality of contribution that they make to developing the business and supporting the achievement of the business objectives so that they are perceived as being essential members of the senior team. Mentioned earlier was the problem faced by Human Resources professionals when asked to implement people policies to support the business strategy, or a change plan that had already been decided, and that often ignored key people issues that put the strategy at risk. Since this is the reality for many Human Resources professionals, we will start here. The problem is often that the line managers do not understand what Human Resources professionals can contribute. The challenge is one of changing mindsets or mental models.

2.63 The starting point for the Human Resources professional who wants to develop effective business partnership is to work at understanding the business strategy and the external and internal influences facing the organisation. It is essential to network with peers in the supporting functions, such as Finance, Strategic Planning and IT to get a feel for potential business, operational and commercial developments. Human Resources professionals need to get themselves invited regularly to management meetings, to understand at first hand the issues they are addressing. This will also give them an opportunity to observe and critique their business processes, their interactions and relationships (for example, whether they listen well or talk over each other) and their decision-making processes. They will have the opportunity to give their clients feedback in a supportive way and facilitate some of their discussions. As they demonstrate added value over a period of time, it is likely that they will be invited to attend regularly. Even if their role is initially that of facilitator, rather than business partner, they will be starting to establish their credibility and become recognised as a full member of the business team. At the same time they will have the opportunity to begin to make contributions to their business thinking and to raise awareness of some of the people issues that need to be considered by the team in their business planning and execution.

2.64 There is a powerful case to be made for involving Human Resources expertise at the most senior levels, as well as at other levels, of strategic and organisational planning, from concept through analysis, to execution. Chris Bartlett and Sumantra Ghoshal (1994) have written about the need for organisations and executives to move beyond thinking about strategy, structures and systems to focus on 'purpose, processes and people'. Once the Human Resources professionals are considered part of the team, they can start to influence thinking in this direction and ensure that people risks and opportunities are appropriately considered in implementation of strategy and plans.

2.65 It can feel daunting to Human Resources professionals if their line clients regard them as operational implementers whose responsibility is to deliver new hires, pay salaries and arrange training courses. But if they can understand their clients' issues and then start to engage them by asking insightful questions, making proposals and getting involved in some of the issues that they are tackling, they can begin to change mindsets. In meetings with individual line managers, Human Resource professionals will have the opportunity to talk to them about their longer-term issues, as well as the fire-fighting issues that they want them to deal with. They can review some of the fire-fighting topics that are continually asked to deal with, analyse the root causes and make proposals to the manager about how these root causes can be tackled. They can take a longer-term view of some of the people issues that need to be addressed and make proposals to the manager about how to overcome them. For example, what are the turnover statistics in general? What is the turnover of the higher performers? What are the the causes? What are the absenteeism figures and what are some of the causes? They can review some of the employee relations issues, such as disciplinary actions or grievances and look for themes and trends to identify some of the underlying causes. They can make proposals on how to deal with these causes. They can examine the quality of the upward and downward communications in the department and see whether there are opportunities for improvement to address some of the people issues.

2.66   Employee-sensing surveys can be useful for finding out what employees' views are on a variety of topics, such as people policies and practices, management styles and behaviours, organisational change programmes, employee morale and topics that concern them. A sensing survey is a very important tool for identifying people risks. It can help to surface many of the issues that are impeding the discretionary effort (in other words, that extra effort over and above the minimum required for acceptable performance) in the organisation and can provide a rich source of information about how the Human Resources professional can support the business. The direct link to the business objectives is very clear. Unfortunately the employee survey is often misused, for example, when higher management institute the survey, analyse the results and undertake to act unilaterally to resolve the identified problems and issues. The reality is that senior management rarely have the capability to deliver, by themselves, all the expectations raised by the sensing survey. Even when they do have the capability to deliver change on a specific issue, the danger is that they may not follow through adequately. Rather than improving employee morale and engendering engagement and participation, a top-down approach can achieve the opposite unless higher management are super-humans. A more effective way is to ensure that the data are gathered in a way that enables reports to be produced providing information about the individual departmental levels. Feeding back the information at the work-group level, engaging the work groups to use the information to identify the key issues in their immediate area and to generate their own solutions, generates more participation and involvement and produces more effective and more sustainable changes. This also provides an opportunity for the Human Resources professional to partner with leadership in engaging the workforce and in facilitating the review of the survey data and planning appropriate action.

2.67   Some of the foregoing may seem like low-level operational activity. In fact, many of these types of activity will be happening when the Human Resources person is an administrative expert. The point we are addressing is that, by standing back and taking an overview, Human Resources professionals can raise the discussion to a higher level than fire fighting and begin to educate their clients to understand how taking a risk-based approach to people issues can have a significant impact on the organisation. Implementing some of these proposals will also enable them to interact at a more forward-looking level with their client group as a whole. Human Resources professionals need to push themselves forward to make the case for participating in their clients' regular business team meetings and must not allow themselves to be discouraged by possible initial rebuffs. They need to prepare their 'marketing' pitch. What is it that they can bring to the party? Where can they add value to their clients' business meetings and to the organisation as a whole? They need to orientate their pitch to the real issues and opportunities that their clients are addressing and to use specific examples to demonstrate what they have to offer.

2.68 They need to develop a Human Resources strategy that is totally focused on supporting the people issues that need to be addressed for the successful delivery of the business strategy. They need to be rigorous in striking off their action list all the Human Resources activities that are 'good to do' unless they can demonstrate a direct link to the business strategy. They need to develop the mindset in the Human Resources function that every activity gets questioned to ensure that it supports the business strategy. They need to educate their line clients to ensure that they understand the links between the people initiatives and the business strategy.

2.69 The competencies required to operate effectively as a business partner are different from those required to be a good operational Human Resources professional. We get concerned when we observe how often the Human Resources people are like 'cobblers' children', who run around in bare feet. They work hard with their clients to establish good people practices, but often do not put them into practice in their own function. A prime example is often people development. If the Human Resources function is serious about developing a business partnership, it will be essential to have a development strategy for the Human Resources team in order to equip them to be able to intervene effectively as business partners. Some of the competencies needed include consulting, facilitation, strategic thinking, influencing, marketing, contracting, change leadership and process management. These competencies and capabilities are not developed overnight. There will need to be a sustained effort over several years to build the required level of capability.

Strategic Human Resources

2.70 The fourth stage in the development of the Human Resources function is Strategic Human Resources. It may at first sight seem pedantic to distinguish between Human Resources Business Partnership and Strategic Human Resources, as the latter is a growth and development from the former and the two overlap significantly. However, in terms of Human Resources function development, the first challenge is to win a place at the management team table by merit and to begin to be accepted as a partner. Often, in the early stages of growing the business partner relationship, Human Resources professionals will encounter decisions and plans that have already been made by the management team and be faced with the task of 'adding on' the Human Resources strategy. Although this is not the ideal situation, it is acceptable as a starting point so long as Human Resources professionals recognise that their goal eventually is to be involved in the thinking and planning processes in order to contribute as an equal. This will enable them to bring their particular expertise to ensure that the people risks and opportunities are built into the team thinking at an early stage. In order to achieve this goal, they need to develop strategic thinking and planning skills and capabilities. This will enable them to get involved in the facilitation and planning of strategic thinking sessions with the client group management teams.

2.71   Another key element of this phase of development of the Human Resources function is to have an effective people-planning process that is integrated with the overall business-planning approach. It is beyond the scope of this book to go into detail on business planning and strategic thinking. But it will be helpful to outline the main steps and principles involved.

2.72   The overall purpose of the people-planning process is to achieve integration of business and Human Resources planning. It is *not* to produce a Human Resources strategy. There is the danger that the latter would be seen as something for the Human Resources professionals to deliver and may be seen as separate from delivering the business objectives. It *is* to ensure that mindsets are changed to understand that there is only one strategy for the business, that the people plans and organisational development opportunities are an integral part of that strategy and that line managers and Human Resources professionals work in partnership to deliver the strategy. Of course, the Human Resources function, like any other function, will still have its function strategy, which will be an expression of the people elements of the overall business strategy.

2.73   For the purposes of this description, we will assume that we are dealing with a small organisation or a major unit in a large organisation. Developing comprehensive, business-aligned plans requires co-ordination of three levels of activity:

- Organisation-wide planning and objective setting.
- Planning and objective setting for the Human Resources function as a whole.
- Planning and contracting within each functional area in the organisation (Manufacturing, Sales and Marketing, etc).

2.74   In the following, we will focus primarily on the development of the functional area plan. A four-stage annual people-planning process that we developed is outlined in Figure 3.

FIGURE 3

PEOPLE-PLANNING PROCESS

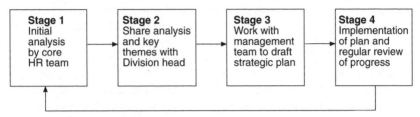

2.75   A preliminary stage involves planning by the Human Resources team. The composition of this team will vary, depending on the way the Human Resources function is organised – but it could, for example, comprise the Human Resources Business Partner for the division, and representatives from Organisational Development, Employee Sourcing, Compensation and Learning and Development. This is essentially a pre-planning stage in which the Human Resources team:

● Reviews the existing business plan to identify the people implications.
● Gathers data on external and internal influences that may have an impact on the next business plan and identifies the people implications.
● Reviews the current Human Resources initiatives and core processes and activities and assesses both their relevance to the business priorities and their effectiveness.
● Identifies key people themes that may be relevant to the next business plan.

Stage 1

2.76   Stage 1 requires a rigorous review of all the core Human Resources data, including: turnover levels and their causes; themes from exit interview data; skills gaps in the organisation; recruitment difficulties (eg shortages of certain types of skills); vacancy levels; compensation issues, such as groups where the salary levels may be less competitive than required; emerging people-development needs arising from development reviews. It also requires a thorough review of the business priorities and possible changes in the future. This stage requires creativity and pragmatism. The Human Resources Business Partner needs to use intuition and business awareness to guide the team to home in on the key issues.

Stage 2

2.77   The purpose of Stage 2 is to engage with the Head of the Division to test the conclusions from the initial analysis and to gain confirmation of the key themes and conclusions or to amend and improve them. This type of discussion engages the Human Resources professional and the Division Head at a strategic level and enables the Division Head to understand how a strategic approach to the business issues can help him to be more effective in meeting his objectives. It also involves the Division Head as the sponsor and the champion of the process so that the management team sees Stage 3 as 'their' activity, rather than something imposed by or limited to the Human Resources function. When all the Stage 2 discussions have been completed with each of the Division Heads, the senior Human Resources team, comprising the Head of Human Resources, the Human Resources Business Partners for each of the divisions in the unit and the Heads of the Human Resources Specialisms (Compensation, etc), meet together to identify the emerging issues, to look for common threads or potential conflicts between activities and begin their initial thinking about how to integrate some of the themes into the Human Resources function strategy and objectives for the coming year. This step ensures that the Human Resources Business Partners do not over-commit to any activities and that the Human Resources team takes a total systems approach to the planning process. It also ensures that the Human Resources Business Partners remain tuned-in to the overall business strategy as well as that of the business division that they support.

Stage 3

2.78   In Stage 3, the Human Resources Business Partner supports the division head in leading a business planning session with the divisional management team and acts as facilitator. If the business has a strategic planning process, this would take place within that cycle of activities. More often there is no planning process or, if there is, it is effectively a budgeting process. This meeting provides the Human Resources Business Partner with the opportunity to coach the line managers in strategic thinking, whilst at the same time achieving integration of the people requirements into the process. It also enables the Human Resources Business Partner to be seen as a strategic thinker and changes perceptions about the role. The themes agreed with the Division Head in Stage 2 form the basis for the planning process. It is important to ensure at this stage that there is a clear 'line of sight' between the people issues that are presented and the concerns or problems that are on the line managers' minds. Making this transparent immediately engages the attention and involvement of the line managers. It is important that the Human Resources Business Partner is also prepared to accept criticism of the contributions of the Human Resources function and to respond to any requests for improvement in service levels. It is to be hoped that if the Human Resources function has developed administrative excellence and process management capabilities, these types of inputs will be few. The conclusion of this stage is a draft plan for the division. Between Stages 3 and 4, the Human

Resources senior team integrate all the Divisional plans, identify priorities and resources and make a preliminary assessment of the core objectives for the Human Resources function for the coming year. If there is an overall business strategic thinking and planning process, the division plans will be incorporated into the overall business plan. It is important to set appropriate expectations for the divisional management team at this stage so that they realise that their plan may be subject to change.

Stage 4

2.79   Stage 4 is the finalisation of the divisional business plan, including the people-planning elements, and implementation. This enables the Human Resources Business Partner to contract specifically with the management team on what the Human Resources team will deliver in partnership with them over the next twelve months and what the responsibilities of the management team are to ensure a successful outcome. The contracting element of the overall process is one of the key outcomes and must not be ignored. We have found it helpful to draw up a 'formal' contract outlining the key deliverables and timescales. This demonstrates accountability from the Human Resources Business Partner and builds trust when the contract is delivered. Or if, at a later date, there is a danger that parts of the contract will not be delivered, the contract can be renegotiated, again building trust in the reliability of the Human Resources Partner and developing a stronger working relationship with the client group. The contract becomes the basis for monitoring progress during the year in the regular management team meetings and in meetings with individual members of the management team.

IMPLICATIONS FOR HUMAN RESOURCES

2.80   By developing their role as strategic business partners, Human Resources professionals will be able to assist their client groups to become more aware of the people risks and opportunities in running the business and to adopt a risk management approach. This is not to minimise risk. Businesses are about taking risks. It will enable people to be more aware of the risks and to evaluate the potential benefits from taking an intelligent risk. Equally importantly, the Human Resources professionals can play an important function by forming alliances with other functions such as Finance, Information Technology, Health and Safety, to begin to develop the culture of the organisation to be more risk aware and therefore to be more innovative and supportive of intelligent risk taking. We will develop this theme of partnership further in **Chapter 7**.

REFERENCES

Bartlett, C A, and Ghoshal S, Beyond Strategy, Structure, and Systems to Purpose, Process, and People: Reflections on a Voyage of Discovery, in Duffy, P B (ed), *The Relevance of a Decade: Essays to Mark the First Ten Years of the Harvard Business School Press*. Boston, MA: Harvard Business School Press, 1994

CIPD, Research Report, *People and Performance in Knowledge-Intensive Firms*, January 2003, CIPD, London. ISBN 1843980312

CIPD 2003 Research Report, *Human Resources' Contribution to International Mergers and Acquisitions*, CIPD, London, November 2003. ISBN 0852979765

CIPD Study, *Human Resources: Where We Are and Where We Are Heading*, October 2003

Marsh survey, *Managing Risk in UK*, www.marsh.co.uk/uk_localreport.pdf

Stephen Nickson, *Risk Management*, 48(2), 25, 2001, 'The Human Resources Balancing Act, Cooperation between risk management HR'

People Management, 10, 14, 2004(a)

People Management, 10, 29–31, 2004(b) 'Truth on Shares' R. Johnson

PricewaterhouseCoopers, *Strange Days*, 2002

Reddy, M, *ICAS Group Report*, February 2003

CHAPTER 3

Organisational and human factors

INTRODUCTION

3.1 This chapter discusses how organisational psychology can provide a valuable perspective in the management of organisational risks. This approach to risk management has been evolving into a unified field over the past 15 years and is now becoming a key perspective in understanding the causes and motivations associated with risk-related behaviour in the workplace. 'Organisational' and 'human' factors are discussed as part of an integrated approach to risk management. Organisational factors are the structures and processes that influence the culture of an organisation and include responsibility frameworks, communication frameworks and job/role design. Human factors describe fundamental human characteristics that need to be managed as part of the risk-management process. This section includes an analysis of the perception of risk, the nature of human error and the motivations that drive individuals to take risks in the workplace.

3.2 It is argued that Human Resources professionals operating at a strategic level are well placed to play an influential role in enabling organisations to manage the risks associated with organisational and human factors because, essentially, risk management is about implementing the procedures and practices that lead to changes in behaviour, attitudes and values. The Human Resource focus on people management in the form of its involvement in learning and development, performance management, establishing systems of rewards and sanctions and the like, provide Human Resources professionals with the necessary expertise. In addition, the cross-functional nature of Human Resources allows it to become an integral and vital part of an integrated risk-management process.

3.3 The management of risk-related behaviour via an examination of organisational and human factors provides an invaluable focus for organisational development because developing systems to avoid human error and manage risks necessarily results in the development of quality standards. A systematic focus on limiting human error and controlling risk acts as a mechanism for organisational development, as the potential for human error is largely synonymous with inefficient organisational systems.

3.4 The main purpose of this chapter is to explain:

- How organisational and human factors result in error and risk-related behaviour.

- How and why Human Resources should manage organisational and human factors as part of an integrated risk management system.
- How the management of risk leads to organisational development.

INTRODUCTION TO ORGANISATIONAL FACTORS

3.5   Organisational factors are the systems, procedures and practices that ultimately determine the culture of an organisation. They influence the values, beliefs and expectations that members of the organisation come to share. Implementing an effective risk-management system will require an understanding of how organisational factors affect risk related behaviour. Designing organisational factors that minimise the risks of loss and accidents, maximise intelligent risk-taking to develop opportunities and better control the uncertainties associated with being in business will, over time, result in the creation of a positive risk culture.

3.6   Where organisational factors are not aligned to minimise risk, latent failures may occur. Latent failures are an accumulation of uncontrolled risk such as a lack of clear responsibility for job/roles, poor communication processes and a lack of training that come together unexpectedly to create failure and loss. Catastrophic organisational failures are often the result of poorly managed organisational factors.

3.7   The organisational factors referred to in this book are listed in **Chapter 1**, and used for a risk-identification process in **Chapter 8**.

3.8   This chapter concentrates on organisational factors that are believed to be more significant in creating the structural framework of an organisation and therefore provide a focus for organisational development. Implementing an integrated risk-management system is essentially an organisational-development process. The organisational factors discussed are:

- Senior management commitment to the risk-management process.
- Organisational cultural and risk management.
- Responsibility frameworks.
- Occupational stress as a risk factor.
- Job/role design.
- Communications frameworks.
- Learning and development.

SENIOR MANAGEMENT COMMITMENT TO THE RISK-MANAGEMENT PROCESS

3.9   No organisation can eliminate all risks, nor is it sensible to do so. Almost all human activity involves risk; indeed, the advancement and the improvement of society necessarily involves the evolution of new approaches that may result in exposure to new risks. Surviving and thriving in a business environment is much the same. Organisations are required to make continual progress, for example, by finding new ways of using resources, becoming more efficient and more competitive, developing new product niches, utilising new technologies, etc. The very business of being in business involves risk. The key, is to ensure that the management of risk is a balance, between the maximisation of opportunities and the minimising of risk. What needs to be avoided is to engage in a risk-averse approach that stifles the creativity of the individual within the business and therefore the organisation itself. Intelligent risk taking is a prerequisite for the development of a successful organisation.

3.10 All organisational change involves risk, and failure to change in a rapidly changing business environment also entails risk. Risk management is essentially good management and therefore requires a commitment from senior management to identify and manage risk, be they current business process and operational risks, innovation risks, or risks associated with deep-seated organisational and human factors that could result in organisational failure and loss. If responsibility for risk management is taken at senior level, this will help to ensure that those responsible for implementing strategy will have the necessary support, authority and resources.

3.11 A commitment to establishing a risk management process requires, in the first instance, that the business and human case for implementation are clearly understood and communicated to all levels within the organisation and to all stakeholders including external agencies. The benefits derived from implementing a risk-management strategy include the traditional benefits of avoiding hazards, minimising the likelihood of failure and the general prevention of loss. However, as is discussed throughout this book, effective risk management also has other important positive outcomes. These include enhancing performance, improving communication systems, providing opportunities for organisational development and allowing the organisation to expose itself to greater business opportunities because existing organisational risks are better controlled and the uncertainties associated with new business development are better understood. Changing the culture of the organisation so that the management of risk becomes a core capability will, over time, lead to the following specific benefits:

- An enhanced organisational culture that develops the capability for balancing the maximisation of opportunities and the minimisation of risks.
- Increased likelihood that organisational objectives will be achieved as the discipline of risk management ensures that potential risks are identified, opportunities maximised and losses minimised.
- Enhanced shareholder value as the rewards derived from engaging in managed risks are realised.

- Better communication as risk management will require an organisation-wide framework for communication and a common language to discuss risk.
- The promotion of improvement via a risk-management cycle that continuously reviews the organisation's responses to system failures and human error.
- Fewer negative unforeseen circumstances as the organisation becomes better at forecasting risks and potential outcomes.

3.12   The foundation on which successful risk management is based therefore comprises of a senior-level responsibility for risk management because there is a clear understanding of its benefits. Once this is in place, risk management strategies can be aligned to organisational objectives and integrated with the strategic planning process.

3.13   Some commentators have argued that the lack of senior management commitment to (safety and) risk management is 'more perceived than real' as senior managers are intimately involved in business processes, operational processes and innovation risk management, albeit often in an unstructured manner. Senior managers are also acutely aware that poor risk management can potentially impact on corporate profits and reputation, particularly if the stakeholders' view of the organisation were to become tarnished by what would be ultimately perceived as poor management. These commentators suggests that barriers to risk management are largely created by the resistance of middle managers to focus on risk-management issues, perhaps with some justification as the role for which they are employed is primarily concerned with meeting 'production' targets. Although they may hear the rhetoric from senior management of the need to manage risks, they are confronted by other, often stronger and more urgent messages such as the need for cost-cutting, driving up 'productivity' and meeting business and commercial objectives. From the perspective of this book however, it is argued that effective senior management necessarily involves the management of middle managers to manage risk. The key to developing a positive risk-management culture is therefore to implement an effective risk-management strategy that has senior management support, and the active involvement and accountability of all managers.

ORGANISATIONAL CULTURAL AND RISK MANAGEMENT

Background to organisational culture

3.14   The concept of organisational culture is widely acknowledged to be very useful in helping to understand an organisations identity and performance aspirations. Schein (1990) defined organisational culture as 'the values, beliefs and expectations that members in an organisation come to share'.

3.15 Organisational culture is influenced by, and evolves as a result of, a number of interrelated variables such as the organisation's procedures, goals, management style, structure and human capital management. The term 'human capital management' is discussed in **Chapter 8**. Despite its negative connotations that individuals are resources that can be bought and sold, the term seeks to emphasise that an organisation's people are a 'capital' resource, equally as important as financial capital. They are vital to the success of an organisation and should attract investment rather than being seen as a potential cost. Organisational culture is also related to broader variables such as the organisation's function, size, history and, ultimately, national cultural variables. Organisational culture provides employees with information and direction as to how they are expected to respond to organisational initiatives such as organisational change, innovation or developing risk awareness.

3.16 Organisational culture may be very homogenous, fragmented or there may be very little consensus. Organisations without strong cultural norms may develop subgroup cultures built around successful 'local' leaders or as a result of geographical or functional separation. The aim of most organisations is to develop a unified culture that is consistent with the strategic goals of the organisation. Assisting organisations to develop a positive risk-aware culture is one of the aims of this book. The extent to which there is a consensus among employees in how an organisation is perceived, particularly with respect to subcultures, relates strongly to measures of organisational climate. Organisational climate, as distinct from organisational culture, attempts to identify and measure an employee's subjective perceptions such as morale, motivations and attitudes rather than the values, beliefs and expectations that organisations seek to inculcate.

3.17 The value of attempting to measure organisational culture and climate has been increasingly acknowledged over the past 15 years because of its usefulness in mobilising employee effort through the creation of 'appropriate systems of shared meaning' (Morgan, 1997). The successful development of organisational culture has wide implications for the effective implementation of planned interventions such as encouraging new entrepreneurial styles, coping with mergers and acquisitions or embedding a risk-management system. It attempts to create or impose a sense of corporate identity, by seeking to generate in employees a sense of commitment to goals that are larger than individual self-interests or the interests of functional groups.

3.18 Morgan (1997) highlights the fact that 'since organisations ultimately reside in the heads of the people involved, effective organisational change always implies cultural change'. An organisation is at least as complex as the employees that make it up, as people will have their own agendas and perceptions based on their own personal histories and motivations and these may be different to those promoted by the organisation. Therefore simply changing policies, procedures and technologies will not immediately result in a change in culture, because culture lies in the perceptions, attitudes and values of individuals.

3.19　Organisational culture evolves over time and is nurtured by appropriate learning and development programmes, the learning by good example and the use of rewards and sanctions that seek to modify attitudes and behaviour. It is sustained by a corporate vision that seeks to successfully manage and achieve organisational goals.

A positive risk culture

3.20　The term 'positive risk culture' has its roots in the concept of organisational culture. Essentially it describes an organisational culture that recognises consistent and effective risk-management practices throughout the organisation.

3.21　There are numerous definitions that focus to a greater or lesser extent on organisational or human factors, but for the purpose of this discussion a positive risk culture is considered to be the result of an interaction between these two variables. This is because organisational factors are determined by human factors, i.e. the perception, attitudes and capabilities of those who design and implement the risk management system, and by the behaviour and thinking of employees that are influenced by organisational policies, practices and procedures. Human factors such as the perception of risk and motivational aspects of risk-related behaviour are discussed in detail later in this chapter.

3.22　In order to be effective, a risk-aware culture requires 'buy-in' by all stakeholders. Effective risk management results when there is a 'collective acceptance' of risk-management practices and that this exists at all levels, individual, group, division and organisational levels (Schein, 1990).

3.23　Traditionally, attempts to improve risk management in the workplace have focused primarily on safety issues. They concentrated on the development of machinery to safeguard against injury and procedures to limit human error and accidents. However, a series of major accidents such as the meltdown of the nuclear reactor at Chernobyl, the fire at King's Cross and the explosion on Piper Alpha have highlighted the role that organisational culture contributed to each incident. Following the Piper Alpha inquiry, Lord Cullen stated that, 'it is essential to create a corporate atmosphere or culture in which safety is understood to be and is accepted as, the number one priority' (Cullen, 1990). More recently, Lord Cullen's inquiry into the Ladbroke Grove rail accident in 1999 (Cullen, 2001) pointed to evidence that suggests that a large proportion of accidents, incidents and near misses occur as a result of a culture that did not seek to manage risks effectively.

3.24   As knowledge of the factors that lead to organisational failure and loss has developed, so it has become increasingly clear that, from an organisational perspective, there is little value in blaming such failures on chance environmental factors, technological failures or the behaviour of individuals who are responsible for triggering an incident. In the final analysis, responsibility for such incidences rests with those who are charged with running the organisation and the culture they develop to manage its risks.

Embedding a positive risk-management culture

3.25   The first stage in creating a positive risk management culture is to identify appropriate strategies, policies, procedures and standards to manage risks. These are discussed throughout this book. Once these are in place, the embedding process results from allocating roles to these structures and assigning responsibilities. Roles and responsibilities can then be monitored, supported and enforced. In addition to the above, clear delegation of responsibility at all levels for key organisational objectives will create, over time, a culture where the management of risk is seen as an intrinsic part of how the organisation operates.

3.26   As people in the organisation change, it is necessary to ensure a continuous understanding of the roles and responsibilities related to the management of risk. The risk environment is also continuously changing. Therefore, as organisations adapt to a changing business environment or engage in new initiatives, priorities with regard to risk will also change. Assumptions about risk therefore require regular review and consideration. A common practice for organisations that manage risks effectively is to hold regular reviews of the risks associated with each of the key organisational functions. In this regard the Combined Code on Corporate Governance published in July 2003 provides a clear description of how organisations should monitor their internal control systems, including the management of risk.

3.27   The Human Resources function can play a pivotal role in monitoring risk-related behaviour, providing suitable learning and development, and ensuring that performance management, compensation and rewards are linked to risk accountability. The involvement by Human Resources becomes particularly valuable if they have been involved from the outset in designing risk-management policies, strategies, standards and practices. These aspects are discussed in greater detail in other chapters.

RESPONSIBILITY FRAMEWORKS

3.28   A risk-management process requires an iterative cycle of identifying risks, assessing their impact and prioritising actions to control and reduce risk. Implementing this cycle requires that responsibility for each phase of the cycle at different levels of decision-making is well defined. Because risk management is an integrated process across the whole organisation, it is important that accountability for specific areas of risk management is clear and that those responsible actually have the authority and capability to fulfil their responsibilities. It is also important that these roles and responsibilities are communicated and understood by others in the risk-management process, and the wider organisation.

3.29   Middle managers are a key group because, although they may have the authority to decide work practices, they may not have the responsibility for risk reduction or may not consider themselves accountable for negative outcomes. This can lead to a conflict of interest. As has been discussed above, productivity may be seen as incompatible with risk management, particularly when risks are perceived as insignificant. It is important, therefore, that the delegation of responsibility is linked to accountability. Shared or unclear lines of responsibility and accountability between individuals or functions will impact negatively on the risk-management process.

3.30   In order to increase responsibility for risk management, especially at the operational level, middle mangers and employees should be involved in the identification of risk and risk assessment processes. This will lead to greater ownership of risk and help inculcate a positive risk-aware culture.

3.31   The integrated nature of risk management will benefit from a group specifically established to facilitate and co-ordinate risk management across the organisation. This group can promote an understanding and assessment of risk, be responsible for reviewing systems and procedures and advise on the introduction of enhanced controls. Each organisation needs to decide on the most appropriate composition of such a group, taking account of their organisational structure, existing responsibilities, etc, but the following functions, as a minimum, should be considered for representation at the highest level: finance, risk/insurance, operations, Human Resources, a non-executive director and a number of operational-level managers.

3.32   Traditionally, the functions mainly involved in risk management are finance and insurance. They have tended to manage the risks associated with their function independently of the rest of the organisation. The implications of this type of 'silo management' are discussed in greater detail in **Chapters 7** and **8**. The argument presented in this book, however, is that Human Resources professionals operating at a strategic level are well placed to play an influential role in enabling organisations to manage organisation-wide risk because, essentially, risk management succeeds or fails depending on altering employees' perceptions, attitudes and behaviour with regards to risk. This involves learning and development programmes, performance management, reward and sanction systems and developing work practices and procedures that limit human error, increase job satisfaction and reduce stress. The above mechanisms are cross-functional and interrelated. They are essentially Human Resources functions in which Human Resources professionals take a lead in partnership with line managers. Human Resources cannot be marginalised without seriously undermining the risk management process. In the UK, the Turnbull Report (1999) (a significant contributor to the thinking on the Combined Code on Corporate Governance (2003) mentioned at **3.26** above) recommended that risk management should be imbedded in the operations of an organisation and form part of its culture.

OCCUPATIONAL STRESS AS A RISK FACTOR

3.33 Occupational stress has many negative consequences for organisations, and therefore it is a strategic risk that can be identified, quantified and managed. Numerous studies have shown that workplace stress adversely affects work performance, morale and commitment to the organisation. Workplace stress may cause absenteeism through physical or psychological ill-health, or an increase in turnover as employees leave the organisation for less-stressful working conditions. This has significant implications for managing and developing an organisation's human capital, especially with regards to resourcing plans. In addition, workplace stress is implicated in reduced productivity and an increase in the likelihood of risk-related behaviour that results in negative consequences. Negative consequences include increased costs resulting from poor quality work, increased errors and accidents and increased customer dissatisfaction. Where organisations have suffered catastrophic failures, failure to manage workplace stress is often implicated as a causal factor.

3.34 The existence of workplace stressors are costly to organisations and to society in general. Figures published by the UK Health and Safety Executive (HSE) (2003) estimated that work-related stress costs employers about £380 million *per annum* (in 1995/1996 prices) and, to society, about £3.8 billion. Since these calculations were done, the number of days lost due to stress has been estimated to have more than doubled (Jones et al., 2003). The 'hidden' costs of stress to an organisation can be substantial and insidious because excessive workplace stress can create a dysfunctional organisation where the culture is one of resisting change and being unwilling to co-operate. In extreme circumstances a subculture may develop that actively seeks to undermine the organisational goals and feels justified in doing so.

3.35 The work stress literature is replete with advice and guidance on how to identify and quantify work-related stress and how to manage stress on a personal level but, until recently, there has not been much guidance on how to actually tackle the organisational factors that cause stress. The HSE has published for consultation a draft 'management standards' document on occupational stress. When finalised, it will assist organisations to tackle the challenges of reducing stress in the workplace. The HSE has recognised that many health and safety professionals are acutely aware of stress as a heath and safety issue but are not in a position to do much about it because tackling the organisational factors associated with stress often involves major organisational reconstruction in work practices and would also involve challenging deep-seated attitudes and management styles. In most cases those involved in occupational heath and safety will not have the skill to undertake such large-scale changes or the authority to do so. The publication of the 'Management Standards' will highlight the role of 'general' management in tackling work-related stress. It is hoped that the standards will provide an opportunity for Human Resources professionals to raise the profile of workplace stress with senior managers and to initiate debate on what needs to be done to address it.

3.36   Stress is caused by the interrelation of a number of human and organisational factors. Human Resources professionals can therefore do much to advise on the modification of organisational factors to improve stress levels while also improving productivity and job satisfaction. Consequentially, this presents Human Resources professionals with a major opportunity to become actively involved in managing the risks in this area. As work demands and business competition increases, so organisations will need to seriously consider the moral, legal, financial and business benefits of managing stress as a risk issue. Human Resources professionals can take a lead in the identification, evaluation and resolution of work-related stressors as part of their involvement in risk management.

Stress and stressors

3.37   Stress can be defined as a physiological, psychological and emotional response to threatening situations or events. It results when there is a mismatch between the perceived demands of a situation and the perceived abilities of the individual to cope with these demands. The implications are that different people can interpret the same stressors in a different way, because they have different perceptions of the demands and their abilities. Stress is therefore a human factor but the causes of stress in the workplace, ie occupational stressors, are organisational factors. The focus of this section is on stress as a stressor and is, therefore, included as an organisational factor. Organisations can do much to redesign job/roles so that demands are achievable and employees feel they have the required abilities to meet the demands. Stress is caused by the interrelation of human and organisational factors. Human Resources professionals are therefore well placed to modify human factors such as the perception of risk via learning and development programmes and organisational factors such as job/role design.

3.38   Examples of improvement strategies that require Human Resources involvement include:

- Clarification of roles and responsibilities to remove stressors.
- Increasing individual job control and decision latitude.
- Building and supporting effective teams.
- Creating a supportive working environment.
- Ensuring focused learning and development to meet organisational needs and individual requirements.

Work overload

3.39   A common source of stress at work is being required to carry out more tasks than can reasonably be achieved in the time available or having to work at excessive speeds on a continuous basis. Work overload can also be qualitative; that is, work that requires excessive concentration or when employees do not have the necessary competencies to carry out the task without expending excessive effort. Stress arising from work overload is likely to be exacerbated by other stressors in the workplace.

3.40   A practice that is becoming increasingly common as a result of work overload is to take work home to complete. The long-term implications of this coping strategy are, of course, that occupational stress will leach into an individual's home life, thus allowing less time to recover from workplace stress with all the consequences that brings.

3.41   The drive to increase productivity, for example, by reducing head-count, has increasingly led organisations to make greater demands on their employees and this has resulted in workloads growing over time. However, increasing workload beyond a certain point does not automatically lead to an increase in productivity. An organisational culture that requires employees to exert excessive effort in carrying out their work is probably one that is poorly managed. Productivity is much more likely to be increased by well-designed job/roles and procedures, ensuring that employees have the appropriate competencies via effective learning and development programmes and ensuring that recruitment results in new employees with the required knowledge, skills, aptitudes and attitudes.

3.42   A risk-management approach to reducing stress caused by work overload would therefore actively seek to identify workload stress areas as part of the performance management process or via a stress rating question-naire. Managers and employees can work together to make use of this type of organisational feedback to improve work flows, learning and development programmes and recruitment functions.

Role ambiguity and role conflict

3.43   A major source of workplace stress for individuals results from a lack of clarity about their responsibilities. Ambiguity is experienced as a lack of control in being able to set work priorities or being controlled by the inconsistent expectations and demands of others.

3.44   A related source of workplace stress is role conflict. Role conflict occurs when employees are asked to carry out roles that they perceive to be incompatible or when their roles are in conflict with their personal values and beliefs. For example, a manager may be required to canvas employee opinion on a contentious work issue while knowing that the exercise is merely playing lip service and employee opinions will be ignored.

3.45   The negative health effects of stress caused by role ambiguity and role conflict have been demonstrated by numerous studies. For example, Shirom (1989) found a positive correlation between role conflict and coronary heart disease. Human Resources professionals, with Occupational Health professionals, need to play a role in reviewing and analysing statistics on stress-related illness in the organisation, such as coronary heart disease, irritable bowel syndrome, ulcers or depression and making senior management aware of the costs to the organisation.

3.46   Clarifying roles and responsibilities via job descriptions, especially when job/roles have altered, can result in a significant reduction in an employee's stress levels because work objectives and the expectations of co-workers are clearly defined. An effective performance-management process should enable employees to raise concerns about any uncertainties or conflicts they have in their role and responsibilities. Unfortunately the performance management process, as applied, does not always encourage open and honest dialogue between employees and managers. This is a major area for Human Resources professionals to address because it inhibits important feedback on the effectiveness of processes and procedures that would otherwise require modification. Organisations can also clarify roles and responsibilities by ensuring that employees understand how their job/role fits into the overall aims and objectives of the organisation or department.

Job control and decision latitude

3.47   How well an employee performs at their job or role is the result of a multitude of organisational and personal factors. However, a key factor appears to be the degree of control they have over workflows, deadlines and demands. Nearly four decades ago, Hertzberg (1966) argued that employees are intrinsically motivated to achieve high levels of performance if job/roles are designed to increase personal or team responsibility and encourage autonomy and problem solving. Research evidence with regards to stress now shows that, when employees have little decision-making latitude, and when work demands are high, imposed inflexibly and without consultation, this is likely to lead to major negative health effects. For example, Karasek and Theorell (1990), in a wide-ranging landmark study, concluded that such working conditions resulted in up to three times the risk of heart attack in professionals and executives who had equally stressful jobs but had some degree of control over their work. Having little control over one's work is also linked to poor work performance and an increase in the likelihood of accidents.

3.48 The increased involvement of employees in setting work targets via mechanisms such as goal setting within performance management and the delegation of responsibility for solving and completing work tasks, perhaps via the development of work teams, will almost inevitably encourage employees to take greater responsibility for their actions, improve job satisfaction and reduce the likelihood of errors due to misunderstanding.

3.49 Increasing autonomy in how job/roles are carried out can however, also lead to greater stress. Therefore it is important that adequate learning and development programmes and other support mechanisms accompany any increase in responsibility.

Workplace support and relationships

3.50 Humans are social beings; we are constantly socialising and interacting with others. However, relationships can be a major source of stress as well as support. It is not surprising therefore that the quality of relationships at work can have a significant impact on well-being, work performance and the likelihood of stress-related errors and accidents.

3.51 Poor work relationships are often the result of interactions with colleagues and line managers that are characterised by a lack of trust, little support, and low interest in listening and attempting to tackle workplace problems. More direct causes of stress include abrasive personalities, authoritarian leadership styles, group pressure and workplace bullying. Workplace bullying can be very subtle and implicit, yet it is commonly recognised as being extremely distressing to victims.

3.52 Line mangers can help to support employees by setting achievable goals in consultation with employees and providing regular and constructive feedback as to how work tasks are being undertaken. Managers can also provide support by giving encouragement and praise for good work and by ensuring that employees have the necessary resources and competencies to carry out their job/role. At an organisational level, there should be systems in place to respond to individual concerns such as bullying, the use of authority without justification and unhelpful criticism.

Employee assistance programmes

3.53   The occupational stressors discussed above are conceptualised as resulting from organisational systems that could be better designed to reduce the negative effects of stress. However, organisations more commonly attempt to lower the impact of workplace stress by providing employees with employee assistance programmes (EAPs) such as telephone help lines, stress management training, counselling and health promotion.

3.54   The evidence for the effectiveness of EAPs is mixed and generally points to improvements in mental health but little or no improvement in job satisfaction, productivity or accidents rates. Reynolds et al. (1993) found that stress management training lowered self-reported stress indicators but did not increase job satisfaction. Work counselling has been shown to reduce absenteeism and mental health symptoms and also show some increase in job satisfaction (Cooper and Sadri, 1991). Similarly, health promotion programmes that encourage employees to eat more healthily at work and attend health and fitness programmes tend to have few measurable organisational benefits. Worker health may increase significantly but much of this may be short-term if individuals do not make a commitment to maintain their new healthy lifestyle.

The risk-management approach to occupational stress

3.55   Human Resources professionals need to adopt a risk-management approach to reducing the negative effects of occupational stress, specifically by tackling the underlying causes of stress. That is, to identify stressors as occupational risk factors and redesign job/roles and the work environment to make them more efficient and, therefore, less stressful. Arnold et al. (1998) argue that 'employee assistance programmes present a high-profile means by which organisations can be seen to be doing something about stress'. They argued that EAPs merely assist employees to *cope* with the effects of inherently stressful work practices. In other words, they tackle the symptoms rather than the causes of work-related stress.

3.56   The use of EAPs has increased significantly in recent years as organisations have recognised the negative effects of stress on their workforce. Such programmes provide a reasonable precaution to safeguard employee health and are regarded as easier to implement and less expensive than engaging in organisational development. The evidence, however, is that the cost of *not* investing in the working environment is much greater in the long run. Inefficient systems and procedures that result in occupational stress are very costly as they inevitably result in greater absenteeism, greater employee turnover and the resultant cost of recruitment and training, losing experienced and valued employees to competitors and increased accident rates. The 'hidden' costs include the effects of low morale, lack of commitment and resistance to change on client/customer relations and on the overall image and status of the organisation. A risk-management approach to occupational stress is to view stress as an organisational risk factor that necessitates better management. Human Resources professionals can play an important role in initiating activities to change the culture of the organisation so that front-line and middle managers are made aware of their responsibility for identifying the causes of stress and to work with employees to remove or minimise them.

JOB/ROLE DESIGN

3.57   As knowledge and understanding of the factors that lead to organisational failure and loss have developed, so it has become increasingly clear that a vital component in creating a positive risk-management culture is to design job/roles that mitigate against the effects of human error. In a practical sense, this is largely about designing job/roles that reduce stress and increase job satisfaction. Inefficient systems and procedures are likely to cause stress and therefore error, as are boring, repetitive jobs that do not utilise the human potential to work together to achieve goals. This element is particularly relevant to risk management as it is intimately linked to organisational development, i e putting in place the organisational structure and processes that assist organisations to succeed by focusing on reducing the potential for loss. Although job/role design is a vital component in the management of risk, it must be supported by other organisational factors such as effective responsibility and communication frameworks and Human Resources functions such as learning and development, performance management systems and the development of work teams.

3.58   Until the latter part of the twentieth century, jobs became increasingly monotonous and controlled. Many jobs were designed to minimise skill requirements, minimise the time and mental effort to perform a task and maximise management control. Jobs designed in this way had a human cost in terms of poor job satisfaction and stress leading to poor mental and physical health. With the steady decline of manufacturing industries in the UK and the related disappearance of many manual and semi-skilled jobs, such work practices and thinking has diminished. The exponential increase in the numbers of knowledge workers has necessarily resulted in the evolution of different work practices that better utilise employees' skills and talents. However, the influence of antiquated ideologies, particularly with regard to management control, still persist in some quarters and need to be challenged if organisations are to effectively manage the risks associated with poor job/role design. Attempts have increasingly been made to redesign work to enable employees to use their skills and talents effectively and to improve the quality of working life; this usually involves increasing one or more of the following job/role characteristics:

- Variety of tasks or skills – increasing use of capabilities.
- Autonomy – more control over when and how jobs are done.
- Completeness – whether the job produces an identifiable end result that makes the task more significant and meaningful for employees.
- Feedback from the job – improved knowledge of the results of work activities.

3.59 Other characteristics that are believed to be important include the quality of social interactions with colleagues and line mangers, and job/roles that require some element of problem solving and the implementing of solutions.

The growth of work teams

3.60 As the economic environment has become increasingly competitive, fuelled by new communication technologies and consumer demand, so work teams have evolved as one of the most effective and flexible mechanisms to achieve organisational goals. Where individuals or small groups worked on limited tasks that were closely monitored, now work teams engage in bigger projects and are responsible for identifying, developing and implementing solutions to a much greater extent than in the past.

3.61 Work teams are effective because they contain many of the elements identified as increasing job satisfaction, for example greater task variety and autonomy, and an increased sense of ownership of tasks. Work teams bring together the skills, experiences and insights of several people so they tend to out-perform individuals or larger grouping without a specific function. High-performance teams invest much time and effort exploring, shaping and agreeing on a purpose that they feel belongs to them. Such teams are characterised by a deep sense of commitment to their growth and success as a team.

3.62 One of the most important aspects of work teams is that they more easily allow organisations to foster attitude change towards a new culture; this is because the internal dynamics of teams promote the development and adherence of group norms. Learning and development programmes for teams should therefore not only consist of the competencies required to carry out tasks and the interpersonal skills necessary to operate as a team, but also provide a mechanism for organisations to effectively promote the aims, attitudes and values they seek to create. The development of a risk-aware culture is best fostered by encouraging teams at all levels to be aware of the organisational factors that expose the organisation to unnecessary risk.

3.63 However, work teams are complex systems to manage because they involve greater interaction between members in an environment that is less clearly defined. Work teams are made up of individuals with their own attitudes, values, beliefs and agendas, therefore the effective management of work teams requires the selection, integration and shaping of these personal elements to achieve organisational goals. Human Resources professionals have a large part to play in creating and developing such teams.

Improving the effectiveness of work teams

3.64 At a strategic level, human capital management is concerned with managing employees to meet business objectives such as growth and profitability. Job/roles designed around work teams with specific responsibilities generally prove to be most effective in this regard. Although work teams are not appropriate for every type of job/role, organisations that think creatively about restructuring work processes to include work teams have found them very successful once teams have formed into cohesive groups. Human Resources professionals that see the potential benefits of developing work teams should consider a number of factors that can assist in their improvement:

- Select people who will fit the culture of the organisation and the team but are still capable of independent thought.
- Make use of personality inventories to identify personality types and ensure teams are made up of a mix of the appropriate types.
- Take particular care over appointing and training/developing team leaders, emphasising that their role is to work alongside team members to achieve results by collective effort, not to 'stand outside the team' and deliver instructions from the 'side-lines'!
- Emphasise constructive team work as a key core value of the organisation.
- Get work teams to determine and agree with their team leaders their own objective standards, eg standards associated with meetings, scope of projects, level of supervision, etc.

- Set overlapping or interlocking objectives for members who have to work together.
- Assess each member's performance not only by the results achieved but also on the degree to which they are effective team members.
- Clamp down on unproductive politics and confront disagreements openly and in a spirit of constructive feedback.
- Describe and think of the organisation as interlocking teams united by a common purpose.
- Devise and implement commitment and communication strategies that develop mutuality and team identity by developing cross-functional teams.
- Recognise and reward people who have worked well in teams.
- Introduce team rewards for achieving project objectives and commercial targets.

3.65   In order to be effective, work teams need a clear outline of their role and function, followed by a systematic approach to achieving their goals, ie identify needs, plan actions, decide responsibilities for actions, identify and obtain resources, carry out actions within agreed time frames, managers to provide effective support and feedback during tasks as required and a review of progress.

Limitations of teams

3.66   Of particular importance to the management of risk is the dangerous phenomenon known as 'groupthink'. Groupthink occurs when a group's need for unanimous agreement prevails over the need for careful consideration of the pros and cons of an argument and alternative possible actions. The need to maintain harmony and morale of the team supersedes the raison d'être of the team; that is, to meet organisational goals. Groupthink results in shutting out alternative views, exaggerating supporting evidence and suppressing dissent within the team. Janis (1972) points out that in the decisions preceding many disastrous business and political decisions, the risk of negative consequences could and should have been anticipated but were blocked by groupthink. The most recent case has been the global 'groupthink' about intelligence on weapons of mass destruction in Iraq, prior to the 2003 invasion. The term 'groupthink' was specifically mentioned in subsequent reports on intelligence failures.

3.67   The specific symptoms of groupthink are:

- Illusion of invulnerability – teams underestimate the likelihood of being wrong, especially if they have been successful in the past.
- Stereotyping – teams are quick to classify 'enemies', and do not notice discordant evidence.

- Pressure to conform – team pressure is put on dissenters.
- Pluralistic ignorance – because team pressure leads to no objections, this is seen as unanimous agreement.
- 'Mind guards' – canvass team members for support and keep bad or contrary news from leaders.

3.68 Autocratic leadership styles tend to encourage groupthink, and therefore a more democratic approach that encourages discussion and criticism is recommended. Simply being aware of the tendency to groupthink will allow team leaders and members to be cautious of such team dynamics and perhaps allow for one team member in rotation to play 'a devil's advocate role', specifically to make sure that groupthink does not happen.

COMMUNICATION FRAMEWORKS

3.69 Ensuring that communication systems are effective is a challenge for most organisations but the issue becomes particularly relevant when related to the management of risk. Effective communication is the foundation on which risk management systems are based. Embedding a culture of risk awareness requires risk to be managed in an organisation-wide, integrated manner. This process necessarily requires a high level of communication efficiency.

3.70 Human Resources professionals are ideally placed to plan, implement and monitor communication frameworks because of their organisation-wide remit and their involvement in processes such as performance management, reward and learning and development programmes. Human Resources professionals who are operating at a strategic level should also be involved in implementing the risk management strategy and be able to advise on how communication issues can impact on risk management and organisational effectiveness more generally. Effective risk management requires an effective communications framework. It is essential that Human Resources professionals ensure that the development of communication and dialogue is an integral part of the organisational strategy and for effective role models to be recognised, rewarded and celebrated. In addition, it will be necessary to invest in resources such as up-to-date communication technologies, learning and development programmes, the appropriate use of rewards and investment in time and resources in developing an effective communications framework. Such an investment is of course, also a key building block in the planned development of an organisation. Therefore the benefits of using the risk-management process to build a framework for communication will benefit the organisation in ways that go beyond the management of risk.

3.71 Because of the critical nature of communication, it is useful to think of communications as a specific management process in its own right, rather than being undertaken on an ad hoc basis to facilitate the development of other processes. When a framework for communication is developed, the following should be considered:

- It incorporates a common vocabulary.
- There are clear roles and responsibilities for ensuring that communication is adequate, appropriate and timely.
- It includes a list of all stakeholders and the information they require.
- Key elements of information to be distributed to stakeholders are identified, including when it is disseminated and received.
- A differential system of communication content and processes is in place, to ensure that only timely and relevant information is provided to any one group/person, so as not to create 'information overload'. Information overload is sometimes worse than no communication at all. So avoid communicating unnecessary information as this is likely to render the whole communication process ineffective.
- Specific methods to communicate certain information, e g email, newsletter, written reports, workshops, etc, and including the repetition of key information using different mediums.
- Encouraging individuals and teams to take responsibility for accurate communication, including confirmation, clarification and repetition.
- Including communication issues and the use of a communication framework in any risk-management learning and development programme.
- Setting up an independent audit to check that communication frameworks are in place, adequate and in use.
- Ensuring that responsibility for communication is included in people's objectives and that effective rewards and sanctions are applied.

3.72   Actions and decisions on risk management require multi-directional information flows between organisational levels and between and within functional areas. Information also needs to flow between the organisation and related external bodies. A focus on developing communication systems will ensure that risk-management strategies, goals and objectives are communicated and the methods, reasons and timings are understood and agreed by all involved in the process.

3.73   Clear top-down channels of communication serve to communicate the purpose of risk-management policies and the values and beliefs on which they are based. They also serve to reiterate the commitment of senior managers to its implementation and continuous development. Inadequate communication can result in risk-management projects no longer supporting the business direction or losing impetus.

3.74   Information that flows upwards from lower levels provides vital feedback to senior managers as to the organisation's risk status and progress in implementing the risk-management system. Therefore, this will influence senior-level strategic planning and decision-making. Inadequate feedback from lower levels can lead to unrealistic expectations from senior managers and to a disruption or breakdown in the implementation of the system. An important aspect of establishing clear channels of communication that flow upwards from operational levels is that it creates involvement in the process of risk management at all levels and helps to establish a culture of risk awareness and control.

3.75 The importance of effective communication extends to communicating with external stakeholders, such as suppliers, customers and investors. To ensure that costly misunderstandings are not created, communication with external stakeholders should be brought under the same communications framework as that operating within the organisation.

3.76 It can be argued that the reputation of an organisation depends to a large extent on what and how it communicates, therefore everything an organisation communicates (or does not communicate) in writing, verbally or via other mediums will affect how it is perceived. Mechanisms should be implemented to ensure that the risk of damaging communications leading to negative perceptions are minimised.

3.77 There is increasing pressure on organisations to communicate more fully and openly to stakeholders external to the organisation, for example to shareholders via the annual report. High-profile cases such as the collapse of Enron and WorldCom have resulted in the loss of confidence in corporate reporting and demands for evidence that the organisation has in place effective risk management programmes, particularly those that take into account non-financial risks such as organisational factors that are more difficult to quantify but are often the cause of failure. As has been discussed, organisational factors include communication and responsibility frameworks, job/role redesign to minimise stress and error etc. In addition, there are likely to be new legislative requirements placed on companies to report more fully. Recent developments on a UK initiative entitled 'Operating and Financial Review' are discussed in **Chapter 8**,

3.78 Effective use of external information and external communications is becoming increasingly important as organisations become aware that the business environment in which they operate is ever more sensitive to factors originating outside the organisation. The increasing interconnectedness of the marketplace, as a result of integrated global economies, communication systems and the media has brought huge business opportunities. However, socio-economic factors, market forces and the activities of external pressure groups can no longer be ignored if organisations are to survive and thrive. Consequently organisations can benefit in many ways by adopting the principles and practices of 'corporate social responsibility'. This is also discussed in **Chapter 8**.

3.79   A globally interconnected infrastructure also means that organisations are more vulnerable to distant events – economic crises on the other side of the world, catastrophic events such as those on 11 September 2001, virus attacks on IT networks, or competition from cheaper foreign goods and services. As a result of the above factors, organisations cannot afford to ignore external information and should seek out and engage with sources of information that may indicate how external factors can adversely or positively impact on their success, or perhaps even survival. The ability for organisations to examine and manage external risks as an integral part of the risk-management process will enhance organisational success.

3.80   The development of a common vocabulary of risk (see **Chapter 1**) and a framework for communicating risk-related issues should assist in evolving a culture of risk management and risk awareness, and also help to protect against human error that results from misunderstanding and miscommunication.

3.81   As discussed in other chapters, issues relating to risk have traditionally developed independently in different functional areas, ignoring the interconnected nature of risk and the possibility of learning from good practice in other areas. The systems necessary to manage risk are, however, the same across the organisation as risks have interrelated and accumulative consequences across functional areas. The development of a common language of risk is important in facilitating risk communications as different functional areas often give different meanings to key terms. A common vocabulary of risk will allow for a clearer identification of interconnected risks and, in addition, promotes better relationships between functional areas and improved problem solving. In **Chapter 1** we have included some examples of the definitions from two risk-management standards that can be used to develop a new vocabulary or review an existing one.

LEARNING AND DEVELOPMENT AND THE MANAGEMENT OF RISK

3.82   Risk management provides an effective mechanism for organisational growth and improvement. This is because uncontrolled risks result from inefficiencies that ultimately lead to an increase in error, loss and accidents. Implementing a risk-management system, as with any organisational change process, will require learning and development to provide employees with the necessary skills, knowledge and attitudes to achieve the organisation's new strategic goals. The lack of appropriate learning and development is a fundamental cause of loss and accidents in the workplace therefore learning and development programme initiated and implemented by Human Resources are seen as a key component in establishing a positive risk culture. Implementing a risk-management system will require employees at all levels and functions within an organisation to alter their behaviour and attitudes towards risk. The abstract nature of risk will also require changes in the perception of risk and the values that guide risk-related behaviour. Therefore, a coherent learning and development plan is necessary to achieve this.

3.83 A strategic Human Resources management approach to learning and development should clearly show how such activities will contribute to the management of risk. As discussed, risk-management goals could include minimising organisational failure and loss, enhancing performance or better controlling the uncertainties associated with new business development. Learning and development should therefore be considered an investment in human capital and not a cost. However, in order to justify the expense of these activities, they must be effective, and seen to be effective. Learning and development programmes that do not incorporate the intricacies and integrated nature of risk management are likely to cost less but not be very effective. Effective programmes necessarily view risk management as an organisation-wide, integrated process.

3.84 Because of the organisation-wide nature of risk management, learning and development plans should be part of, and not separate from, other Human Resources strategies such as personal development programmes, recruitment and reward strategies.

3.85 Learning and development cannot, however, create organisational change independently. Clear-risk management policies are essential, as is a commitment from senior managers to implement risk-management procedures. As discussed above, it is also important to develop organisational factors such as risk accountability frameworks, communication frameworks and job/role redesign; specifically, job/roles designed to minimise error and stress and increase job satisfaction.

3.86 At a fundamental level, any risk-focused learning and development programme is likely to operate on three levels:

1   Organisation-wide level.
2   Management level.
3   Job/role or task level.

3.87 The following processes form part of any learning and development programme, but their focus will vary depending on the organisational level at which they are being applied:

- The identification of risk.
- The assessment of risk.
- The development of skills, competencies and knowledge to make effective use of risk-control systems.

• Monitoring the effectiveness of learning and development programmes.

Developing knowledge and understanding of risk at the organisation-wide level

3.88 Organisational risk is not function-specific and often involves an interrelated set of circumstances across departments or organisational activities. Therefore, implementing a risk-management strategy will initially require an organisation-wide programme to raise awareness of the nature of organisational risk and the benefits of controlling risk. This should include the creation of a common risk vocabulary to facilitate communication as different functional areas often have different terms to express similar issues. Ideally, all managers and employees should undergo such awareness learning and development programmes. Managers and employees will also require specific knowledge and an understanding of risk-management policies and practices depending on their role or level within the organisation.

3.89 Human Resources professionals need to encourage the development and understanding of organisation-wide risk factors. This is best achieved by involving employees and managers in a structured process to discuss and analyse specific and relevant risk issues. Employees have a wealth of knowledge and experience of working in the organisation and should be encouraged to share this with others. Cross-functional and cross-level discussion groups will promote a greater understanding of how different organisational functions and levels of responsibility can impact on each other. This is necessary as latent failures are often due to organisational factors that are cross-functional, such as communication failures or unclear accountability for processes that continue across functional areas or that connect functional areas together.

3.90 The key objective of awareness programmes is to change attitudes and values about risk management by actively involving employees – and ideally other related organisations, such as those in the supply chain. Involvement results in ownership and therefore greater commitment to the risk-management process. It also enables the organisation to benefit from valuable expertise and 'local' knowledge that may otherwise be lost in a more top-down approach to training.

3.91 There are a number of tools and techniques available for communicating a corporate 'message' across the whole organisation. In our experience, a process entitled the OPC Process® has proved particularly effective in communicating the organisational and personal benefits of behaving in a risk-aware manner and in developing a sustainable risk-aware culture.

3.92 The OPC Process® is designed to communicate and engage large numbers of employees with any key corporate 'message'. It has been used successfully in many types of organisation, private and public, and in many countries. In the context of risk management, it is ideally suited for use by large organisations that wish to implement a risk-management system as part of their programme for organisational development.

3.93 The process is successful because it combines a sound understanding of how attitudes and behaviour can be changed to meet organisational needs with the effective translation of the organisation's 'message' into engaging workshops that internalise the 'message' for each participant.

3.94 A logical series of interactive and engaging tasks guide cross-functional teams to analyse and discuss specific risk-management issues. The process and materials are structured in such a way as to allow managers or employees without specific risk-related knowledge to act as facilitators. The team nature of the process means that a large number of managers/employees can be made aware of complex and interrelated risk-management issues in a focused and timely manner. Involvement and consultation also results in attitude change towards risk, and the identification of risk-related behaviours. It also results in a clearer understanding of how systems can be modified to control risk and provides the foundation on which to carry out organisational development.

3.95 In **Chapter 8**, a tool called 'RiskFrisk® – Human Resources Risk Management' is described. The tool can be used to identify the risk profile of an organisation and therefore assist organisations in identifying and understanding where risk management systems need to be enhanced, and where risk-taking behaviours need to be replaced by intelligent risk taking. The strategic risk goals identified as a result of a RiskFrisk® can be translated by the OPC Process® into a set of key messages to be communicated across the organisation and internalised by employees.

Developing risk-related competencies at management level

3.96 A number of factors will affect the type of learning and development necessary to imbed an integrated risk management system. Many of these factors have already been discussed but are summarised here from the perspective of learning and development for managers. Clear lines of responsibility and accountability for the management of risk should be established and the competencies necessary to carry out such responsibilities acquired through learning and development. A risk management competency framework for specific functions can be arrived at from an analysis of what risks managers are required to manage. A risk-profiling tool such as RiskFrisk® will identify specific functional risks and the behaviours and processes necessary to control such risks.

3.97　At the management level, the identification and evaluation of risk should form part of every learning and development programme related to the function for which managers are responsible. It should be imbedded into competencies that relate to actual behaviour in a specific setting rather than being bolted on as an independent unit on risk management.

3.98　It is necessary to monitor how effectively managers carry out tasks associated with competencies. Performance management systems that include risk management will ensure that it remains high on the agenda for managers. Reward systems that recognise effective risk management and intelligent risk taking will also make a significant contribution in encouraging managers to behave in accordance with risk-management policy.

3.99　Managers should be aware of their powerful influence as role models and seek to create a positive risk culture by maintaining a visible focus on the management of risk. This is often referred to as 'Walking the talk'. For example, managers should never allow risk-taking practices to be used arbitrarily under certain conditions, but not others.

3.100　Managers sometimes find it difficult to discipline employees for engaging in risky behaviour for fear of the effect it would have on their working relationship. In this way small offences become common practices and greater offences develop. Managers can be assisted in their role by unambiguous and transparent policies for deliberate transgressions of procedures likely to lead to error or loss. Managers can also benefit from learning and development programmes in how to give praise for intelligent risk taking and for enforcing risk-aware behaviour in a non-threatening but assertive manner.

3.101　If there is a clear and unambiguous commitment from senior managers to organisational development via risk management, there should be no conflict of interest for middle managers between their role in meeting 'production' targets and their role in managing risk. This should allow managers to seek to manage and improve organisational factors that can mitigate against risk-taking behaviour, e g poor communication systems and job/roles that result in job dissatisfaction and stress. Human Resources professionals operating at a strategic level should have the necessary expertise to assist managers in developing such organisational processes, especially when these processes are cross-functional and involve people management issues – for example, developing communication and accountability frameworks.

3.102　In order to help to maintain and improve the risk management process, it is important that managers are supported in this. A cross-functional forum to discuss issues relating to the management of risk and the exchange of good practice is therefore considered vital. Such a forum should include risk-management and Human Resources professionals, as they would be able to provide a broader, organisation-wide perspective. A valuable function of such a forum would be to co-ordinate and analyse the progress of risk management so that senior managers could be kept informed. The forum would also provide a mechanism for senior managers to communicate strategic risk management goals to those charged with implementing them.

Learning and development at the job/role or task level

3.103 Research shows that, at this level, risk-taking behaviour for routine tasks is largely habitual and occurs without conscious thought. The implications of this are discussed in greater detail in the section entitled 'The perception of risk', but the key point with regards to learning and development is that it is very difficult to change risk-related behaviour for routine tasks by simply attempting to change attitudes towards the perception of risk. An effective risk-management learning and development programme for routine job/roles and tasks will require the design and implementation of specific procedures that minimise risk- related behaviour in the first instance. Learning and development for new procedures is then best focused on behavioural change related to specific work situations.

3.104 Some key principles include:

- Behavioural change is best achieved via demonstration and practice of positive risk-related behaviours rather than simply through instruction.
- It is also necessary to alter perceptions as to the negative consequences associated with deliberate risk violations. This, however, is more effective for new employees than for those who have engaged in such behaviour without negative consequence in the past. Innovative communication methods that engage employees in discussing their perception of risk can be effective (see the section on 'The perception of risk', at **3.110**).
- Learning and development should make good use of the organisation's historical background on risk control. Operational feedback systems that collate data on human error, accidents and 'near misses' provide valuable sources of information that will place learning and development within the context of the organisation and specific functional areas.
- Learning and development should result in more than just being able to carry out or recite a series of complicated steps. It should provide the background contextual knowledge that allows individuals to evaluate the likely outcomes of their actions.
- There should be regular reminders as to what constitutes a positive risk culture.

INTRODUCTION TO HUMAN FACTORS

3.105 The term 'human factors' is increasingly being used in the organisational risk and safety literature. It is a useful concept because it draws attention to how people interact with organisational systems, procedures, tasks and equipment.

3.106 The term 'human factors' can sometimes include ergonomics, which is specifically concerned with matching human physical and spatial abilities with workplace practices to minimise physical fatigue, strain or injury. It is also sometime used to explain how organisational factors such as job/role design influences human behaviour. For the purposes of this chapter, a distinction is made between 'organisational factors', eg job/role design, communication and responsibility frameworks, etc, and 'human factors' that essentially describe intrinsic human characteristics such as cognitive abilities and attitudes that impact on human error and risk-taking behaviour. This perspective is derived from the work of organisational psychologists and utilises psychological theory and research methodologies to understand workplace error and risk. Human factors include cognitive abilities such as attention span, short-term memory capabilities, and problem-solving strategies, however almost any human characteristic will influence risk-related behaviour. Personality differences, cognitive style, attitudes, values and beliefs are just some of the categories that could be examined with regards to risk related behaviour.

3.107 This chapter focuses on higher order human factors that have a more consistent and generalisable effect on workplace risk-taking behaviour. They are:

- The perception of risk.
- Motivation and risk-related behaviour.
- The effects of stress as influenced by organisational factors.
- The nature of human error.
- Classifying and limiting human error.

3.108 Human Resources professionals involved in designing and implementing organisational factors such as responsibility frameworks or learning and development programmes need to be aware of how human factors can impact on the management of risk. Human Resources is ideally placed to provide input on these matters, and/or co-ordinate the input from other areas, for example operations management and health and safety management.

THE PERCEPTION OF RISK

3.109 The perception of risk is a human factor because, by definition, an individual's perception is not based on quantifiable evidence but on aspects such as previous experience, values, attitudes and personality characteristics. How risky a situation is perceived to be will, therefore, be different for different people. People tend to disagree about what is risky, dependent on how much control they feel they have over a situation or whether they have experienced any negative consequences in the past. Thus, experienced car drivers may feel less at risk driving their own vehicles than travelling by aeroplane, even if a more objective analysis of the risk of an accident would suggest otherwise.

3.110 Research into the perception of risk has attempted to identify and explain the factors associated with the perception of risk in the workplace and why people behave as they do when faced with situations that could have potentially negative consequences to themselves, to others and to the organisation.

3.111 One might assume that, before engaging in a potentially hazardous activity, an individual would make a conscious calculation as to how risky the situation actually is. For example, a decision to take a risk and bypass an established procedure because it is cumbersome or time-consuming would be weighed against the experience of having taken this risk in the past without negative consequences, and against the benefits of completing the task more easily or quickly. Research in this area suggests that, in fact, such conscious and rational decision-making rarely occurs, especially for routine tasks. It appears that much risk-taking behaviour in the workplace occurs out of habit, a habit that is shaped by a reality in which negative consequences rarely happen.

3.112 There are a number of implications that can be drawn from the above analysis. Firstly, if risk-taking behaviour, particularly for routine tasks, occurs without much rational consideration of risk, then risk taking cannot be attributed to a miscalculation or a misunderstanding of the risks involved. Rasmussen (1983) argues that, for this reason, when negative consequences eventually occur, blame should not reside with the individual but with senior managers whose role it is to consciously and rationally consider the possible causes of risk-taking behaviour and implement procedures and practices that minimise such incidents, particularly for routine tasks.

3.113 A second implication of the fact that work tasks are carried out largely without consideration of the risks involved is that it is difficult to cause individuals to consider the actual risks associated with their work and alter their perception of the risks involved. For this reason, despite millions of pounds spent on campaigns to make people more 'safety conscious' at work, the effects of such campaigns have only proved marginally effective, especially when introduced into areas where the 'risk taker' is already familiar with the situation and has decided the level of risk they wish to attribute to a particular task.

3.114   The extent to which risk is perceived to be associated with an action is dependent on a number of factors, including:

- The individual's perceived level of skill on a task.
- Past experience of negative consequences.
- The probability of detection and the types of sanctions applied for violating safety rules.
- Rewards for behaving safely such as praise or promotion.
- Rewards for violating safety rules such as more free time, kudos from less-experienced employees.
- Personality characteristics – research suggests that people vary as to how much risk they are prepared to take.
- Age – research shows that risk taking is greater amongst individuals aged under 35, especially for males.

3.115   The 'risk-homeostasis' theory (Wilde, 1982) suggests that people make use of the above factors to identify and maintain a personal level of perceived risk for a given task. Once this has been established, little conscious thought goes into re-examining the situation unless circumstances change – sometimes catastrophically. The risk-homeostasis theory postulates that if a task is made less hazardous by, for example, the use of better-designed equipment or less hazardous procedures, the person will continue to be motivated to maintain the same personal level of perceived risk as that previously established for the task. In effect, the individual takes greater risks to counter the effects of a more controlled working environment. To use a car analogy, as cars have become easier to handle and safer to drive, so speeds have increased and behaviour that would have been previously considered risky is now no longer thought of in that way. Indeed there is some evidence that, as cars have become safer, people take more risks, thinking that the safety features in the car will protect them or prevent negative consequences. For example, anti-lock brakes may have encouraged people to drive faster, thinking they can more easily avoid an accident. In reality, 95% of vehicle accidents are still caused by human error.

3.116   A second theory that can shed light on the perception of risk is the 'zero-risk' theory (Naatanen and Summak, 1976). It is related to the risk-homeostasis theory but suggests that individuals are motivated to seek situations in which risk is perceived to be minimal. In reality there may be considerable risk but this is not rationally acknowledged until safety rules are breached. Research shows that individuals are likely to operate at the outer limits of risk margins and to keep this margin as small as possible. To continue the driver analogy, the driver will only begin to consider the risk of such an activity if they are driving beyond the legal speed limit. The implication of this theory is that wide safety margins should be enforced to reduce the consequences of potential accidents and that the perception of risk results from the inculcation of habits brought about by the design of systems and procedures. This theory is clearly relevant to systems and procedures for managing risk at all levels and in all areas of an organisation.

3.117 The management of risk is therefore an ongoing process, and simply attempting to change attitudes towards risk is not very effective. A much more effective approach is to implement specific procedures and practices that cause individuals to behave in less risky ways. For example, in order to cause drivers to drive more safely, speed restrictions, traffic calming systems or speed cameras are more successful than advertising campaigns about the dangers of speeding.

3.118 In addition to restructuring work practices so that they result in less-risky behaviour, the perception of risk can be altered by increasing the benefits associated with behaving in an intelligent risk-taking manner. For example, management giving praise for working safely has been shown to be a strong motivator to comply with safety procedures. Publicly recognising and celebrating safe workers and safe managers also helps to alter the perception of risk taking as something that is undesirable within the organisation. Aligning intelligent risk-taking behaviour with performance appraisal reviews and promotion is perhaps the most effective way to use positive reinforcement as it is directly related to the individual's risk-taking behaviour and is continuously monitored.

3.119 The perception of risk can also be influenced by increasing the negative consequences of violating risk-management systems, for example by increasing the probability of detection via better monitoring and by creating a system of transparent and consistently applied disciplinary procedures with regards to dangerous or potentially harmful risk taking.

3.120 It is vital that effective learning and development programmes are used to ensure that employees know how to use equipment safely, know how internal controls on key business and operational processes need to be applied, and know how to carry out procedures so that the risk of error or accidents is minimised. However, it is also necessary to alter perceptions as to the negative consequences associated with deliberate violations of risk-management procedures. As has been discussed above, this per se is of limited effectiveness particularly for employees who have engaged in such behaviour without negative consequence in the past. This type of learning is more effective for new employees and should focus on the potential consequences of injury on family and career, effects on work colleagues, the extent of direct financial loss to both the individual and to the company, and the effects of less tangible losses such as damage to the reputation of the organisation.

3.121 Some ways in which Human Resources professionals can promote intelligent risk-taking behaviour are:

- Help to redesign job/roles, procedures so that barriers are placed against negative risk-taking e g signing-off or acknowledgement procedures. (see section on Classifying and minimising human error. 3.144)

- Instituting wider safety margins
- Effective recruitment and selection processes where the organisation's focus on risk management can be described and discussed.
- Induction and initial training on risk issues, where details can be provided about the organisation's vision, values and strategies with regards to risk management and internal control and how this is translated into individual responsibilities.
- Subsequent internal learning and development where appropriate elements about risk-management processes can be included on a regular basis.
- Introduce a strategic review and ongoing processes for job/role redesign and team development.
- Ensure that job descriptions contain specific responsibilities for risk management.
- Ensure that performance-management systems include a risk-management element.
- Ensure that sanctions and rewards systems include performance measures related to risk management.
- Establish systems to recognise good performance in risk-management compliance and intelligent risk-taking behaviour.
- Ensure that Human Resources systems operate in accordance with risk-management principles.
- Ensure that disciplinary procedures include examples of unacceptable risk-taking behaviour.

MOTIVATION AND RISK-RELATED BEHAVIOUR

3.122   Motivation is central to most human activities because it governs our choice of behaviour and attitudes. In order to understand how people behave with regard to taking risks in an organisational environment, it is necessary to understand what motivates such behaviour.

3.123   Motivation at work is a complex issue because it relates to a number of interrelated human and organisational factors. For example, human factors include individual differences in work competence, perceptions of the situation and self, differences in attitudes and values. Organisational factors include procedures, the design of job/roles and equipment, learning and development programmes, clarity of roles, accountability and communication frameworks, reward systems, etc.

3.124   A number of theories have been proposed to explain human motivation. Such theories have had considerable impact on attitudes towards work, job performance and the nature of work itself. No single theory can adequately prescribe how motivational factors can be utilised to manage employees. However, theories provide the best guide as to how motivation factors influences risk related behaviour in the workplace.

3.125 One of the main theories is *reinforcement theory* advanced by behavioural psychologists such as Skinner, (1938). He proposed that any behaviour that is rewarded would be repeated. This is known as *positive reinforcement*. In the workplace, this is could be any reward, praise, approval or money. However, it could also be greater responsibility, autonomy or access to decision-making processes.

3.126 *Punishment* is regarded as any unpleasant occurrence following a particular behaviour. This is likely to deter the behaviour in future. In the workplace, a strong 'punisher' could be a reprimand from a manager for not following agreed procedures. However, a punisher could also be something less dramatic, such as not having a suggestion for an improvement in risk management taken seriously, which would deter future initiatives or suggestions to improve risk management.

3.127 *Negative reinforcement* is described as any behaviour that results in avoidance or escape from a negative consequence. For example, an employee may agree to take on an increase in workload, not because it is rewarding but because they fear being negatively appraised for not doing so.

3.128 According to this theory, in order to cause behavioural change in individuals so that they do not engage in potentially risky behaviour, it is necessary to consider that individuals will balance the value of rewards for behaving in a intelligent risk-taking manner against the value of engaging in more risky behaviour. For example, getting the job done more quickly to increase leisure time, set against the probability of being caught or causing negative consequences. Individuals will be motivated to achieve the greatest reward; thus deliberate violations of known risk-management systems can be understood as the result of a 'rational' calculation that the benefits of such a violation will outweigh the likelihood of a negative consequence occurring. Once a decision has been made concerning a particular behaviour, it no longer receives much conscious thought and becomes routine.

3.129 The difficulty for risk managers is that the certainty of short-term rewards is set against punishers that may be weak, or may never occur. Thus, risky work practices persist because they are rewarding. In addition, the rewards for working in an intelligent risk-taking manner may be minimal. In some organisations, it is rare for anyone to get praise for working strictly to the rules.

3.130 Even if near-misses occur, the irony is that they may actually reinforce risk-taking behaviour, as success at avoiding a negative consequence may be perceived as skilled behaviour. To counter this, it is necessary to associate competence with taking intelligent action, rather than risk-taking action.

3.131   Reinforcement theory therefore suggests that, in order to redress the balance towards the avoidance of risk, there must be a relative increase in the benefits of adhering to risk management procedures as compared to the benefits of behaving in a risk-taking manner. Management giving praise to others for working to minimise risks has been shown to be a strong motivator to comply with risk-management practices. It is also the case that increased involvement and responsibility is, in itself, rewarding to most people, especially if it is associated with access to decision-making and supported by adequate learning and development programmes. The implementation of an organisation-wide risk management process will encourage involvement and responsibility and thus motivation to alter behaviour.

3.132   Effective learning and development is necessary in order to highlight the negative consequences associated with deliberate violations of risk-management procedures. For example, injury, effects on work colleagues, effects on family and career, financial losses both to the individual and to the organisation, and losses related to the reputation of the organisation, etc.

3.133   A related issue with regard to increasing negative consequences of risk-taking behaviour is to raise the probability of detection by better monitoring of adherence to procedures and by creating transparent and consistently applied disciplinary procedures.

3.134   Social Learning Theory contends that individuals are motivated not only by reward and punishment but by observing others receiving rewards and punishment. Individuals are motivated to imitate the behaviour of others if they observe that they are being rewarded for their behaviour. Any behaviour is more likely to be imitated if the 'role model' is perceived to be successful, charismatic or of a higher status. The implication of this is that managers, particularly senior managers, must lead by example if intelligent risk-based behaviour is to be improved.

3.135   Equally, such 'role models' can seriously undermine the development of a positive risk-management culture by showing less than total commitment to the process. Individuals perceived as high in status, although not necessarily of higher authority, will also act as role models. It is important therefore, that such individuals are identified and brought on board with regard to risk management. Giving high status to those who adopt a risk-aware and risk-management approach will also promote a positive risk-management culture.

3.136   Although it might be expected that incentive programmes such as receiving bonuses for reduced accident rates or wastage rate due to fewer errors would reduce risk-related behaviour, such reward schemes are, how-ever, only marginally successful. This is because rewards are given for *not* getting injured or *not* making errors rather than being rewarded for specific risk-management-related behaviours. Likewise, campaigns exhorting adher-ence to risk management procedures are not generally successful because motivation in risk avoidance appears to be highly situation-specific. Our experience is that it is much more successful to reward good behaviours, ie rewarding a manager for undertaking actions that improve the management of risk, rather than rewarding them for reducing the level of losses or other negative consequences.

3.137   *Goal theory*, usually attributed to Locke (1968), attempts to focus reward systems and involve the individual in personal goal setting. The basic concept is that employees are motivated to achieve specifically stated goals whereas simply urging people to 'minimise risk-taking' has little or no effect. Goals should also be perceived as personally achievable otherwise they are ignored. Goal theory has similarities to reinforcement theory in that motiva-tion is the result of rewards for achieving goals. However, goal theory states that employees should be actively involved in negotiating their own goals, therefore reinforcement does not come only from external sources (ie praise from line manager, bonuses, etc) but also from the satisfaction of meeting one's own goals. The following guidelines have been found to be useful:

- Risk-management goals should be challenging and SMART (Specific, Measurable, Achievable, Realistic and Time-framed).
- Support elements should be provided, ie resources as well as encour-agement, moral support, etc.
- Feedback en route to the goals should be provided in order to sustain and increase motivation.
- Risk-management goals should be negotiated with employees, as involvement will increase commitment and motivation.
- Individual performance on risk-management activities should be inte-grated with performance management, rewards systems and succession planning processes.

THE NATURE OF HUMAN ERROR

3.138   The study of human error has revealed a number of pertinent issues that have important implications for risk and Human Resources professionals engaged in the management of risk. At an organisational level, human error is considered to be largely the result of organisational factors that have not been controlled and therefore do not mitigate against this risk. An understanding of the concept of human error in an organisational context and how it can be classified in a generic sense will assist in the design of processes and procedures that reduce the likelihood of error and its consequences.

3.139 Human error has been defined generally as 'the failure of a planned action to achieve a desired goal' (Reason, 1990). This definition implies that there was an intention to achieve the correct outcome, but that the goal was unattained. The human factors approach to error does not therefore presuppose that someone is to blame because human error is, by definition, unintended. In other words, it does not make logical sense to blame an individual for an unintended act. For example, in the case of the Ladbroke Grove rail disaster or the *Herald of Free Enterprise* disaster, it was the person who triggered the incident who got the public blame, yet further scrutiny revealed a catalogue of organisation-wide system failures that were created or ignored over many years. Even deliberate violations of procedures can be seen as 'perpetrators' not clearly understanding the consequences of their actions. Such risk-taking behaviour is considered to be the result of ineffectively managed organisational factors such as poor learning and development programmes, ineffective procedures or the failure to enforce procedures.

3.140 It is a truism to say that 'to err is human' (A. Pope, 1711). Not only is error essential to learning but making mistakes is also a natural feature of human existence. Failure to acknowledge this in individuals or in an organisations, ie systems created by humans, is likely to lead to poor performance at best and disaster at worst because error feedback is not used to guide future behaviour.

3.141 One of the most enduring characteristics of human nature is the ability to solve problems. This involves utilising feedback from mistakes to continuously reinterpret the problem and eventually achieve the desired solution. Research has shown that 'trial and error' learning appears to be the most effective way to learn new tasks and, in fact, the propensity to make errors in order to learn is 'hard wired' into brain functioning as an evolved mechanism because it promoted the survival of our species. The importance of error feedback is recognised in safety-critical systems where simulations are used to allow operators to experience and therefore learn from the consequences of their actions in a safe environment. Simulated learning environments include the use of flight simulators in civil and military aviation, shutdown simulations in the nuclear power industry or practising emergency fire-exit drills.

3.142 Trial-and-error learning appears to be an enduring human characteristic. However, we are increasingly caused to interact with complex systems where the consequences of our actions may not be at all obvious. Therefore, although we may be intrinsically motivated to attempt new solutions to make procedures more efficient from our own personal perspective, the bending or breaking of established procedures may be entirely inappropriate in a modern working environment. It may also be true, however, that existing procedures are inappropriate given the nature of the task.

CLASSIFYING AND LIMITING HUMAN ERROR

3.143   It is difficult, if not impossible, to eradicate human error from organisational systems, although much can be done to reduce the risk of human error. An understanding of the types of errors employees are likely to make, and the circumstances in which they are likely to be made, provides a useful guide to designing organisational systems that seek to limit risk-related behaviour.

3.144   The term 'human error' describes occasions where the intention to carry out a particular sequence of actions or thought processes does not result in the desired outcome. The intention to achieve desired outcomes may fail because actions did not go as planned (called a slip), or because the plan itself was inadequate (called a mistake). This provides the basis for the distinction between two different categories of human error.

Slips and lapses

3.145   Slips typically occur when carrying out familiar tasks that do not require much conscious thought. They usually result from a lack of attention. Stressful circumstances such as having too much to do, having to work too quickly or simply feeling unfairly judged by colleagues or line managers can result in cognitive overload, which makes slips more likely.

3.146   Lapses are similar to slips in that the intention is correct but error occurs because of a failure of memory. Lapses result in a failure to carry out actions at the appropriate time or lose a place when carrying out a procedure or task. Like slips, lapses can be exacerbated by stressful circumstances.

Avoiding slips and lapses

3.147   Slips and lapses are not usually the result of ineffective learning and development programmes, yet they can sometimes lead to fatal errors. Workplace stressors leading to cognitive overload or stressful situations that originate outside the organisation in the home environment are likely to increase the probability of this type of human error at work. Slips and lapses can be minimised by designing procedures that are resistant to such errors.

This is particularly important for safety-critical procedures or when operating machinery. It is also important when designing risk-management systems to enhance internal controls.

3.148 The principles involved in reducing slips and lapses apply equally to carrying out procedures and operating machinery. They are presented here in some detail, but are not meant to be prescriptive, especially given the intricacies and pressures of business in the real world. Controls to minimise slips and lapses include:

- The use of checklists to ensure appropriate actions have been carried out or have been carried out in the correct order.
- Causing individuals to make some sort of positive acknowledgement at vital points in a procedure before proceeding further, for example, signing-off procedures.
- Procedures should be clearly and unambiguously named. Colour coding paperwork can help to differentiate specific procedural systems that are regarded as being particularly prone to error, or when the risk of such an error would result in serious consequences. Likewise, controls on machinery should be clearly labelled. Colour and/or different auditory markers can be used to differentiate key components.
- Cognitive overload can be avoided by presenting only the information that is necessary at the time. Long-winded memos and impenetrable text will lead to distractions caused by having to make too great an effort to access the required information. However, supplementary information should be provided at the point where it might be required.
- To avoid unnecessary cognitive effort, wherever possible, forms and paperwork should be designed so that recognition and confirmation of elements replaces the need for recall and extended writing.
- With regards to operating machinery, controls that are similar in design but that perform different functions should not be placed adjacent to each other as this could result in slip-type errors.
- Also with regards to operating machinery, input should result in immediate and unambiguous feedback as to what has been altered so as to allow the operator to undo any changes that have made.

Mistakes

3.149 Mistakes are errors that result from misunderstanding a process or situation. They are more common than slips and much harder to prevent because the perpetrator will believe that what they are doing is correct until the error occurs. Mistakes are also harder to detect because there are powerful psychological mechanisms that confirm our opinions once adopted, even in the face of contrary evidence.

3.150   A simple but important distinction can be made when analysing mistakes:

- **Errors of commission** are errors that result from action, for example, misunderstanding a set of procedures that results in confidential information being sent to the wrong people.
- **Errors of omission** are misunderstandings that involve a lack of activity when an activity is required.

3.151   Mistakes can be further divided according to work-based activities. Put simply:

- **Skill-based errors** are those that occur as a result of inappropriate application of learnt skills or where skills are not fully developed.
- **Rule-based errors** are those that occur as a result of incorrectly or inappropriately followed procedures.
- **Knowledge-based errors** are errors that arise through poor planning or misdiagnosis.

Avoiding mistakes

3.152   Vital to any process of organisational development is information about the state of the organisation. A key to avoiding mistakes, therefore, is to conduct a job/role analysis so that a clear idea is gained as to what job/roles and procedures actually entail. Job/roles described in concrete behavioural terms, ie terms that are observable, controllable and measurable, are far more useful than more abstract definitions. For example, a requirement 'to be responsible for monitoring risk related behaviour' is not as useful to the organisation or to the employee as a set of clearly defined behaviours that must be carried out. The more detailed and behaviourally based the job analysis is, the more useful it will be for a range of organisational improvements related to error reduction and the management of risk.

3.153   However, as the nature of the job/role becomes more complex or senior, and therefore less 'skills' based, so it becomes more difficult to describe 'behavioural' competencies associated with the job/role. For example, a senior manager may possess a wealth of knowledge and understanding that cannot be easily operationalised as a skill to be acquired or displayed.

3.154   A detailed job/role analysis will provide the basis for identifying where errors are likely to occur and the types of errors likely to be made. This can generate modifications in procedures and practices that mitigate against such errors.

3.155   Such a job/role analysis will, in conjunction with a 'skills' audit, also provide the basis for identifying a skills gap to be bridged by appropriate learning and development programmes. The term 'skills' is used in its traditional generic sense; however, as has been discussed, mistakes are not only due to a lack of technical expertise (skills) but also due to incorrectly followed procedures and a lack of understanding as to the nature of the task. While training can provide technical skills and knowledge of procedures, more senior-level jobs will require the ability to plan and diagnose situations that may not yet have occurred. Such higher-order cognitive processes result from 'education' and 'learning' and will include developing the appropriate attitudes and values that are necessary to carry out the job/role so that mistakes are not made. With regards to the management of risk, different aspects of learning and development will be required at the organisation-wide level, management level and job/role level (see section entitled 'Learning and development', at **3.103**).

3.156   It is possible to minimise human error by selecting the right person for the job in the first place. Careful selection procedures based on a job/role analysis to identify the required competencies will help to avoid the wrong person being selected. Selecting the wrong person, particularly in the case of managers, can result in costly mistakes that accumulate over time. From the point of view of human error, inefficiency is largely the result of low-level misdiagnosis and implementation of solutions to a problem. Indirect costs of poor selection processes are associated with a negative influence on morale and job satisfaction.

Latent failures

3.157   Latent failures refer to errors and violations of risk-related procedures that have no immediate effect but 'incubate' within the system until triggered. They are very difficult to prevent as it is not possible to foresee every potential error and how they might interact. Reason et al. (1988) distinguish between accidents caused by human factors and those caused by organisational factors. Human factors can be generally thought of as active errors or violations caused by an employee, while organisational factors are considered to be failures of systems and procedures. System failures are likely to be the main cause of latent failures. 'Rather than being the main instigators of accidents, operators tend to be inheritors of 'pathogens' created by poor design, incorrect installation, faulty maintenance, inadequate procedures and management decisions, and the like. The operators' part is usually that of adding the final garnish to a lethal brew that has been long in cooking.' (Reason et al, 1988)

3.158   Catastrophic organisational failures are often caused by latent failures. Turner and Pidgeon (1997) described the incubation period as the time during which there is an accumulation of unnoticed risk factors such as a lack of clear responsibilities for the management of risk, poor communication frameworks, or a poor learning and development programme. Avoiding latent errors is therefore primarily concerned with developing organisational factors so that organisations are resistant to the risk of error.

Deliberate violations

3.159 Deliberate violations of procedures or consciously behaving in ways that ignore the risk of error are not errors. However, violations are likely to increase and compound the consequences of error in organisations where the enforcement of risk-management rules has been allowed to drift.

3.160 Reducing deliberate violations of known risk-management procedures and encouraging the development of a positive risk culture is essentially what has been discussed in this chapter. In the first place, it is necessary to implement an integrated risk-management system that focuses on developing the organisational factors that minimise the risks of loss and accidents, and better control the uncertainties associated with being in business. These organisational factors include: senior management commitment to the risk management process, responsibility frameworks, communication frameworks, job/role design, and learning and development programmes.

3.161 Reducing deliberate violations and developing a positive risk culture also requires an understanding of what causes individuals to commit such actions in the first place, ie the human factors that result in risk-related behaviour. The perception of risk, motivation and the nature of human error have been discussed in this context.

REFERENCES

Arnold, J, Cooper C L, and Robertson, I T, *Work Psychology: Understanding Human Behaviour in the Workplace.* London: Financial Times/Pitman Publishing, 1998

Baker, E, Israel, B, and Schurman, S, Role of Control and Support in Occupational Stress: An Integrated Model, *Social, Science and Medicine,* 43, 1145–1159, 1996

Cooper, C L, and Sadri, G, The Impact of Stress Counselling at Work, in Perrewe, P L (ed), *Handbook of Job Stress (Special Issue), Journal of Social Behavior and Personality,* 6(7), 411–423, 1991

Fox, M L, Dwyer, D J, and Ganster, D C, Effects of Stressful Job Demands and Control on Physiological and Attitudinal Outcomes, in a Hospital Setting, *Academy of Management Journal,* 36, 289–318, 1993

Herzberg, F, *Work and the Nature of Man*. Cleveland: World Publishing, 1966

HSE, *The Draft Management Standards for Tackling Work-Related Stress* (www.hse.gov.uk/stress), 2003

HSE, *Real Solutions, Real People: A Manager's Guide To Tackling Work-related Stress*. Sudbury: HSE Books, 2003

Janis, I L, *Victims of Group Think: a Psychological Study of Foreign Policy Decisions and Fiascos*. Boston: Houghton and Mifflin, 1972

Jones, J R, Huxtable, C S, Hodgson, J T, and Price, M J, *Self-reported Work-related Illness in 2001/02: Results from a Household Survey*. Sudbury: HSE Books, 2003

Karasek, R A, and Theorell, T, *Health Work: Stress, Productivity, and the Reconstruction of Working Life*. New York: Basic Books, 1990

Kelly, J E, *Scientific Management, Job Redesign and Work Performance*. London: Academic Press, 1982

Locke, E A, Towards a Theory of Task Motivation and Incentives, *Organisational Behaviour and Human Performance*, 3, 157–189, 1968

Lord Cullen, The Piper Alpha Inquiry, 1990

Lord Cullen, The Cullen Enquiry. The inquiry into the Ladbroke Grove rail accident in 1999, 2001

Morgan, G, *Images of Organisations*. London: Sage Publications, 1997

Naatanen, R, and Summala, H, *Road-User Behaviour and Traffic Accidents*. Amsterdam: North-Holland, 1976

Pickering, T, Job Stress, Control, and Chronic Disease: Moving to the Next Level of Evidence, *Psychosomatic Medicine* 63, 734–736, 2001

Rasmussen, J, What Can Be Learned from Human Error Reports?, in Duncan, K D, Gruneberge, M, and Wallis, D (eds), *Changes in Working Life*. London: Wiley, 1980

Reason, J T, *Human Error.* Cambridge: Cambridge University Press, 1990

Reason, J T, Manstead, A S R, Stradling, S, Baxter, J, Campbell, K, and Huyser, J, *Interim Report on the Investigation of Driver Errors and Violations*. Manchester: Department of Psychology, University of Manchester, 1998

Reynolds, S, Taylor, E, and, Shapiro, D A, Session Impact on Stress Management Training. *Journal of Occupational and Organisational Psychology*, 66, 99–113, 1993

Schein, E H, Organisational Culture, *American Psychologist*, 45(2), 109–119, 1990

Shirom, A, Burnout in Work Organisations, in Cooper, C L, and Robertson, I (eds), *International Review of Industrial and Organisational Psychology*. Chichester, UK: Wiley, 1989

Skinner, B F, *Science and Human Behaviour*. New York: Macmillan, 1938

Turnbull, N, Internal Control – Guidance for Directors on the Combined Code, Report of the Internal Control Working Party, Institute of Charted Accountants in England and Wales, 1999

Turner, B, and Pidgeon, N, *Man-Made Disasters* (2nd edition). London: Butterworth Heinemann, 1999

Wilde, G J S, The Theory of Risk Homeostasis: Implications for Safety and Health, *Risk Analysis*, 2, 209–225, 1982

CHAPTER 4

Human Resources policies and procedures

A RISK-BASED APPROACH TO POLICY DEVELOPMENT

4.1 The question must initially be asked: 'Why have policies and procedures at all?' The answer to this question is fundamental to understanding the concepts in this chapter. From an organisational perspective, there needs to be a top-level strategy for managing risks within the organisation. This essential responsibility for the Board or senior management team not only protects the interests of the shareholders but also ensures a safe and effective working environment. In terms of assessing corporate risks, these are associated with a wide range of business activities such as buildings, plant and machinery, finance and, of course, people. Senior management have overall responsibility for ensuring that the risks faced by the organisation are managed and minimised.

4.2 The answer for Human Resources professionals is that the implementation of effective policies and procedures for Human Resources operational and regulatory requirements is key to managing Human Resources risks. As a result, not only will management fulfil this important part of their obligation to stakeholders, but they will also maximise the effectiveness of employees, thus maximising opportunities for the organisation.

4.3 Mention has already been made of the psychological contract as an unwritten set of expectations within an organisation. How Human Resources professionals write policies and procedures, determine the resulting practices and communicate them to employees can significantly shape the perception of the psychological contract for existing and prospective employees.

4.4 Where employees perceive that the psychological contract has been violated, they may react in a number of ways. They may merely put up with the situation, but in this case it is likely that future violations, however minor, may result in a more extreme response; they may voice their concerns; they may become negative and destructive and show their dissatisfaction with a downturn in performance; or they may choose to leave the organisation. Clearly, none of these responses are ideal.

4.5 Organisations need to maintain a constant focus to ensure that they are treating their employees fairly and are thus preserving the psychological contract. Human Resources professionals can support this focus by drafting policies that, whilst protecting the needs of the organisation, also respect the individual's position.

4.6 When new policies are introduced, Human Resources professionals need to ensure that the communication process is sensitive to the individual's position, whilst putting over the business case for the need for the policy. Both actions will help individuals feel respected and valued within the organisation and this will help to preserve the psychological contract which, as we have discussed elsewhere, is often very fragile. Where Human Resources professionals use this approach for the communication of policy and procedure, will have a strong influence on preserving the status of the psychological contract.

4.7 The key to effective policies is the approach used in their drafting. Human Resources professionals need to take a risk-based approach to such policies in order to ensure that the focus of the final version is appropriate for the culture and style of the organisation and that risks are minimised. This may require a change of approach for some Human Resources professionals. Policies and procedures are often drafted or redrafted based on the need to merely respond to legislative changes, from a desire to exert greater influence or increase the power of the Human Resources function, or to provide controls in situations where management is poor or weak. A risk-based approach to drafting policies and procedures should identify potential risks related to the policy issue, evaluate the impacts both in terms of addressing the risk and the risk of inaction, and demonstrate the need for action. The approach helps to gain commitment from all concerned, including senior management. Human Resources professionals can then draft policies/ procedures that fit the needs of the organisation to maximise opportunities and minimise Human Resources risks.

4.8 There is a need for Human Resources professionals to consult with managers and employees prior to finalising a policy/procedure. This will create an understanding of the need for the policy/procedure and ensure it is 'user friendly'. Once the policy/procedure is finalised, a formal communications process can be used, plus necessary coaching, education and training to ensure effective implementation and acceptance throughout the organisation.

4.9 In many organisations a major risk is the lack of involvement of managers in the drafting of the policy/procedure leading to poor communications. This results in managers and employees not fully appreciating the purpose and detail of the policy/procedure and, consequently, not building them into normal day-to-day business and operational processes.

4.10 The final stage in the process is to monitor, evaluate and amend the policy/procedure to ensure that it continues to meet organisational needs.

4.11 Figure 1 below shows the key stages in the process of policy/ procedure development.

FIGURE 1

Identify the potential risks related to the policy issue under consideration

Assess the risks and evaluate the impact of addressing or not addressing the risk

Identify risk treatment options and demonstrate the need for action

Gain commitment at the highest level to required risk control measures

Consultation with managers on draft risk control policy and procedure

Launch communication, education & training

Monitor, evaluate and amend

KEY RISKS OF NOT HAVING APPROPRIATE POLICIES

4.12   The key risks of not having appropriate policies in place are summarised below:

- The organisation's non-compliance with legislation.
- Lack of clarity of standards and behaviour for both managers and employees.
- Lack of workplace harmony and the risk of hostility from employees towards their employer.
- Inappropriately trained managers.
- Risk of claims, such as unfair dismissal, to the Employment Tribunal.
- Policies being inappropriate and not tailored to the culture of the organisation or the needs of the business.
- The organisation and Human Resources being reactive, rather than proactive, in the approach to employees.
- Risk of staff alienation, loss of productivity and profit.
- Increased employee turnover and, in particular, loss of key staff.
- Loss of clients, repeat business and damage to the organisation's reputation.
- Conflict between trade unions and the organisation.

- Breakdown of relations between employees and the organisation.
- The organisation and Human Resources professionals not being up to date with legislation, industry developments and developments in best practice.
- The interests of the organisation not being safeguarded. Instead, the organisation is exposed in many different areas.

4.13 This chapter and the following are closely linked. There is no value in having efficient Human Resources administrative procedures if the policies they underpin are not robust. The scenario works in reverse, as it will be pointless to have robust policies that are not supported by appropriate and effective Human Resources administration.

4.14 Once an organisation has understood the need for policies and procedures in relation to people risk the Human Resources professional can begin to consider what policies it needs to put in place, what are essential and what are 'nice to have'

WHY DO ORGANISATIONS DEVELOP SPECIFIC POLICIES?

4.15 There can be several reasons why organisations begin to develop and introduce policies.

1   Legislation requires it (e g disciplinary and grievance procedures).
2   An organisation buys an 'off-the-shelf', ready-made set of policies and procedures that they proudly put on a shelf in the MD's office or Human Resources office.
3   There is some incident or series of incidents within the organisation that prompts the Human Resources professional to develop a policy.
4   The situation is the 'flavour of the month' within the organisation or within that particular industry sector, or in the economy as a whole.
5   There is external pressure, pressure from a trade union or pressure from employees themselves to introduce a policy or policies.
6   Management or the Human Resources professional are enlightened and believe that implementing policies will promote better workplace harmony among employees.
7   Management or the Human Resources professional believe that implementing policies that are appropriate to the needs and culture of the business will actually enhance the working environment for both management and employees.
8   Reducing organisational risks and safeguarding the position of the organisation, helping it to achieve its business objectives and manage risks.

4.16 We will explore each of the above areas to consider the advantages and disadvantages to organisations of each approach. This will demonstrate the benefits to management of being proactive in this area to minimise risk, rather than letting other forces drive the introduction of new practices. We will then consider some specific policy areas where adopting a risk-based approach to policy is beneficial to all organisations.

Legislation requires it

4.17 The United Kingdom has comprehensive employment legislation that is continually changing and increasing with the impact of European Directives. Human Resources professionals must keep themselves up-to-date with forthcoming changes to legislation in order to identify possible risks and actions for their organisation. These would include, for example, changes to disability discrimination legislation introduced in October 2004 and age discrimination legislation due to be introduced in 2006.

4.18 Whilst the legislation covers all UK employees there are, however, few areas where a written policy is actually *required* to be provided. The two key situations where legislation requires an organisation to provide its employees with policies are in the area of disciplinary and grievance procedures.

4.19 There are minimum legal standards for disciplinary and grievance procedures. For example, in disciplinary situations organisations are required to write to an individual and inform them of the action they are considering taking, hold a meeting with them to discuss it and give them the right to appeal against the decision. Where an organisation does not follow these minimum legal standards when terminating someone's employment, and the employee complains to an Employment Tribunal, the Tribunal will find that the dismissal is automatically unfair. In this case the Tribunal can increase the compensation awarded by between 10% and 50%.

4.20 In recognition of the impact of this legislation, we spell out the particular requirement of the law below so readers are in no doubt how this relates to the management of key risks.

4.21 The law requires that any disciplinary rules that are applicable must be specified in the written terms of the contract of employment; or, if they are not explicitly stated, the document must point the individual to where they can gain access to such a document. The written terms of the contract of employment must specify who the employee should approach if they are not satisfied with any disciplinary decision against them. It must also state to whom the employee should apply if they have a grievance about their employment. Where there is a process in place, this must also be explained to employees.

4.22   Prior to October 2004, there was exclusion for employers with less than 20 employees. However, in October 2004, UK legislation changed with the introduction of minimum standards for disciplinary and grievance procedures and the exclusion for small employers was removed.

4.23   The minimum standards require that an employee must be notified in writing of the allegations against them. A meeting must be held to discuss the allegations before any action is taken. The employee has the statutory right to be accompanied at the meeting by a trade union representative or willing colleague. Following the meeting, the employee must be given the right to appeal against the decision. These provisions also apply to situations where employment is terminated by the employer, eg redundancy, retirement and expiry of a fixed-term contract.

4.24   The same process of written notification, meeting and right of appeal exists under the legislation for grievance issues. The employee must write to their employer to notify them of the grievance. The organisation must invite the individual to a meeting to discuss it and subsequently allow the individual the right of appeal if they are not happy with the outcome. As with disciplinary meetings, the employee has the statutory right to be accompanied at the meeting.

4.25   It is clear from the legislation that the intention is for employers to introduce appropriate processes for handling disciplinary and grievance situations and termination of employment. However, there are many other reasons for implementation of disciplinary and grievance procedures, that should persuade employers to have such policies, without the need for legislation. This clearly has not been taken on board by many employers in the past and has resulted in the need for the government to intervene and implement legislation to try to ensure that employers operate better practices in the future.

4.26   There are a number of reasons why an employer should want to introduce disciplinary and grievance procedures, irrespective of the legislative requirement:

1   Implementation of such procedures makes it clear to all managers and employees what standards the employer requires of them. This applies to how individuals conduct themselves within the organisation and what performance standards are required. If such matters are made evident to employees when they join the workplace, they will know how they should behave from the outset. They will also be aware of what conduct is and is not acceptable and this will have the effect of tailoring the conduct of employees and limiting the risk of individuals acting inappropriately. If there is an infringement, it can be picked up early on in the individual's employment, addressed and rectified.

2   Setting down the required standards in policies, on how to act in

particular situations so that individuals have access to them, allows employees and prospective employees to decide whether it is an appropriate working environment for them. For example, polices may detail what standards are required when driving company vehicles, what standards are expected about drinking alcohol on company premises and provision of a detailed list of what actions constitute gross misconduct. Individuals can read and consider the policies and procedures in place, which will give them an insight into the culture of the organisation, its values and methods of operation. It will also ensure that they are aware of the practices that the organisation requires.

3   Such procedures also promote workplace harmony and ensure fair and equitable treatment of employees. They will ensure that an incident or problem is handled in a similar manner in different parts of the organisation. Human Resources professionals need to minimise the risk of ineffective or inconsistent application of the procedures.

4   In addition, having an effective and appropriate disciplinary procedure will protect the organisation against the risk of an employee making a claim to an Employment Tribunal. The Tribunal will look to the employer to have behaved reasonably, for example, making it clear to employees what standards of conduct and performance that are required, ie the policy, will demonstrate reasonableness. The employer being able to show that not only do they have a policy/procedure, but that it is complied with when dealing with situations covered by the policy/procedure, can demonstrate further reasonableness.

Buying an 'off-the-shelf' package

4.27   There are many 'off-the-shelf' handbooks and packages that provide guidance and give examples of policies/procedures to cover those situations that most frequently occur. Some of these areas may be key risk areas, others may just focus on the legislative requirements. These 'off-the-shelf' packages will normally cover holiday entitlements and management, working time, maternity, other family-friendly policies, sickness procedures and disciplinary and grievance procedures.

4.28   There are risks in buying such packages. An organisation may purchase a package, but take no action to communicate it or promote its use withing the organisation believing that the contents of the package will provide a safeguard against all aspects of employment legislation. There are many packages available and most form a sound basis for the development of policies/procedures that will be appropriate to the culture and nature of an organisation. However, if the contents are not tailored to an organisation, then many of the policies/procedures and practices will be inappropriate, and potentially more risky than not having any policies/procedures in place – but not in all circumstances. For example, within a disciplinary procedure it is essential to determine which level of manager will have responsibility for which aspects of the procedure, who is responsible for dismissals and how appeals will be held. It is impossible for an 'off-the-shelf' package to be able to accommodate the complexities and differences of a particular organisation or to anticipate the changes required as the organisation changes. The risk of buying an 'off-the-shelf' package' and leaving it unchanged is that, should an unfair dismissal claim be taken to an Employment Tribunal, the Tribunal will look to establish whether the organisation has followed its own policy/procedure. If the organisation cannot actually follow the policy/procedure that is in use because, for example, the organisation is not structured in the manner described in the policy/procedure, then the non-adherence will not be a defence against the claim. The Tribunal will expect the organisation to have followed its own policy/procedure and for that policy/procedure to be appropriate and relevant for that organisation.

4.29   The purchase of an 'off-the-shelf' package can save valuable time in drafting required policy/procedures, as the contents can provide valuable guidance to the policies/procedures required and essential content.

4.30   In addition, policies/procedures are ineffective if managers are not trained to use them and employees are not made aware of them. Additionally, as we will see in **Chapter 5**, it is essential for Human Resources professionals to understand the background to the policies/procedures and the way that they need to be implemented and monitored.

4.31   This is an opportunity for the Human Resources function to make an impact on the business by providing policies procedures that make sense to managers and employees; that are drafted in terminology commonly in use within the organisation and that are realistic in terms of the actions recommended, bearing in mind the operational and business characteristics of the organisation.

A particular event prompts introduction

4.32   It is unfortunate that often, within organisations, managers will allow difficult situations to get out of hand before dealing with them. There is a desire in most people to be 'nice' and, unfortunately, the role of manager does not always allow the manager to be nice all the time!

4.33   A situation may have been bubbling under the surface as an issue for many months when an extreme situation occurs and it is only at this point that

Human Resources are contacted. Set out below is a case study that gives an example of such a situation.

Case study

4.34   An employee in a customer services team was repeatedly five or ten minutes late for work. This was a small team and the lateness had an impact on the other members of the team and on the department's ability to provide service to customers for the full range of the opening hours. The manager, however, did not take any action to address the situation.

4.35   Within time other members of the team began to come in late and were often late back from their lunch break. The situation went unchecked and this level of poor time-keeping became the norm. Some members of the team began leaving work about five minutes before the finish time. The manager still did not take any action to address the situation.

4.36   The Chairman of the organisation received a letter from a prominent customer complaining that he had tried to telephone the customer services department on a number of occasions either early in the morning or towards the end of the day, but had received no reply. He had been planning to place a big order with the organisation but, as a result of being unable to make contact, had placed his order elsewhere.

4.37   This resulted in a number of reactions by the organisation. The Chairman made contact with the customer to try to recover the business. There was a disciplinary investigation concerning the actions of the manager. There were also investigations surrounding the employees. Disciplinary hearings resulted.

4.38   Once these situations had been resolved, the Human Resources professional worked with the manager to develop a procedure on time-keeping and attendance. The procedure had to be implemented quickly by all staff in the organisation with special meetings held with the customer services department in particular.

4.39   In addition, management guidelines were written and managers had to receive in-depth training on how to operate the guidelines.

4.40   The risks of not having an appropriate policy are evident in such a situation -- the organisation lost a prestigious client; the Chairman had to spend time and effort trying to recover the position; there was potential for the reputation of the organisation to be severely damaged within the industry; time had been taken to undertake disciplinary investigations and meetings; a policy has been drafted hastily as a 'knee-jerk' reaction with little thought to the outcome or practicalities; a huge learning effort had been expended and employees, particularly in customer services, were demotivated because they perceived they have not done anything wrong since nothing was made clear to them about working hours when they joined the organisation.

4.41   This shows the risk of Human Resources professionals not being in tune with the issues in their client groups. There may also be the risk that they are not proactive in working with managers to address potential issues in implementing, or allowing to be implemented, policies and procedures that are not fitted to the culture and needs of the business.

4.42   Contrast this with the situation where Human Resources professionals have been proactive. A well-thought out and well-written policy already exists when a new customer services representative joins. Managers have been involved in the writing of the policy and understand the implications of bringing it to the attention of employees and of dealing with problems as they occur. As part of the induction the manager talks through the policy with the new employee. The employee knows from the outset what standards are required in respect of time-keeping and attendance.

4.43   Thus, if an employee is late back from lunch on two consecutive occasions, the manager takes them to one side and reminds them of the requirements of the policy and the reasons for it. The employee's time-keeping would, hopefully, return to normal and there are no further impacts on the business.

'Flavour-of-the-month' policies

4.44   This situation is similar to the one above in that, within a particular sector, sometimes policies are introduced because of a particular problem that has arisen in one organisation. The situation is communicated to other organisations within the same sector and organisations then panic as they think the same thing can happen to them. A policy is developed and implemented, often as a 'knee-jerk' reaction to this sector-wide bad publicity. Often little attention is paid to how this particular organisation operates in that type of situation and whether there is really a risk.

4.45   It is essential that when policies are written for an organisation they take account of the culture and operating practice of that organisation. This is an area where the Human Resources professional can really add value. Putting in place appropriate policies procedures will ensure employees and managers know what is expected of them and often prevents problems before they occur.

Pressure to introduce policies and procedures

4.46 There may often be pressure on organisations to introduce policies of a certain type or style. Pressure may come from employees or from external sources such as trade unions or employee professional bodies, for example as a result of 'full employment' where individuals will come to expect the same practices and standards in all employment sectors. These expectations may have resulted from publicity on certain issues in the press.

4.47 Trade unions may have a general concern about the lack of policies and procedures in an organisation. Employees may have heard publicity about particular cases in the press. Such situations often lead to unease amongst a workforce, particularly where the trade union or employees have identified the need for a particular policy and requested it from the employer but the employer has not responded. The risk if this situation recurs is that the relationship between the employees and the organisation may break down and become one of lack of trust and co-operation.

4.48 Again the Human Resources professional can be proactive here by keeping up-to-date with developments in employment legislation, with developments in Human Resources best practice and with developments in the sector in which they are currently working. They can also ensure that they are tuned-in to the issues and needs in their client groups.

4.49 By keeping abreast of topical issues the Human Resources professional can recommend introduction of appropriate measures and policies in advance of changes in legislation and before they become an issue within the organisation or in the press. This will create a better working environment where employees believe that the organisation is protecting their best interests. The converse being suspicion of the employer's motivation. Even if the organisation has inadvertently omitted to introduce a particular policy, it would be difficult to publicise this fact to employees because of adverse external publicity. The employees are therefore likely to think that the organisation is not protecting their interests in having not introduced such a policy. Distrust develops in the organisation, leading to demotivation, downturn in productivity and attrition.

4.50 Additionally, where an organisation is unionised, by Human Resources taking the above proactive approach to the implementation of policies, good relations with the trade union will be maintained. It is much better to consult the trade union on a policy from a position where the organisation has instigated it than from a position where the trade union has demanded it. The latter position will result in suspicion from both sides as to the motivation of the other party; it can result in time delays to the implementation of the policy, and the organisation being driven to agree to measures that it would not otherwise have had to take had it been in 'control' of the consultation process.

Enlightened managers and Human Resources professionals

4.51   The situation in many organisations is not always as bad as has been painted above. Many managers and Human Resources professionals are enlightened to the benefits of introducing of appropriate policies and procedures.

4.52   Where the Human Resources professional is in tune with the needs of their organisation and up-to-date on future legislative changes and changes to Human Resources best practice, they will raise issues long before any of the issues mentioned above arise.

Enhancing the working environment

4.53   In some situations it may be necessary for the Human Resources professional to recommend the introduction of a particular policy/procedure to benefit the organisation. Some advantages of this include the management of employee expectations and performance; good employee relations in the organisation; good and open channels of communications and a caring approach by the employer to the employees. These will all influence employee motivation and change productivity and attrition rates for the better.

Safeguarding the interests of the organisation

4.54   It is hoped that organisations will be persuaded of the benefits of introduction of new policies. However, where they experience one of the situations mentioned above, Human Resources professionals will need to be persuasive in demonstrating that a proactive approach for the future would actually prevent the problems and have a more positive effect on the organisation. Sadly, in many cases it is all too easy to believe that the situation will not recur again and that there is therefore little point in taking action.

4.55   There is clear evidence that proactively writing policies/procedures so that they fit the needs of the organisation will lead to a better working environment. Managers and employees who are clear on expected standards can be in no doubt what action should and will be taken if these are not followed. In addition, Human Resources professionals can take a proactive approach in adapting and amending policies/procedures in the future. This will help to keep the employee relations climate positive within the organisation and reduce risks.

THE LINK BETWEEN EMPLOYMENT LEGISLATION AND POLICIES

4.56   In **Chapter 5**, we will mention the potential impact of employment legislation on the recruitment process, primarily in the area of discrimination legislation. It must also be noted, however, that discrimination legislation has an impact on the whole sphere of employment and is not just restricted to recruitment. We have also seen that employment legislation can impact on other policy areas such as disciplinary and grievance procedures.

4.57   There are, of course, other specific aspects of legislation that could require the development of policies. For example, such areas as the family-friendly policies introduced as a result of the Employment Relations Act 1999 and modified by the Employment Act 2000, redundancy, working time and holidays.

4.58   An organisation may take the view that there is no need to develop a policy since it will always operate in line with the statutory requirements. However this approach is not without risks. We will see in **Chapter 5** how relatively complex the maternity leave and pay regulations are, with requirements for different actions on particular dates, otherwise employees lose entitlements.

4.59   Having no policy written down for maternity or other family-friendly policies leaves an organisation in a situation where employees may know that there is a statutory provision, but have no idea of the requirements. It is important for organisations to make their obligations and those of their employees clear. This will result in management of the individual's expectations and ensure workplace harmony. Where an employee is not made aware of the legal and policy provisions they may believe their entitlement is greater or different and could potentially alienate themselves from the organisation when they find out the situation is different.

4.60   In addition to stating the law, policies and procedures, if accurately and effectively written, will give guidance to managers on what is the best way to operate in practice. It will also set the expectations of employees entitlements in particular circumstances. Setting the expectations of the employee in advance will reduce the risk of conflict and confusion when dealing with what may be a difficult or sensitive situation.

4.61   The risks of not having policies that demonstrate a reasonable approach may be far reaching for an organisation. For example, many disciplinary procedures, it is hoped, will be written in line with the Advisory, Conciliation and Arbitration Service (ACAS) Code of Practice on Disciplinary and Grievance procedures. The Code indicates what is best practice in disciplinary and grievance situations. Failure to observe the recommendations of the Code would not, in itself, render an employer liable to Tribunal proceedings. However, the risk arises for employers if they do not follow best practice guidelines in dismissing an employee and the employee subsequently makes a claim of unfair dismissal to a Tribunal.

4.62   The Employment Tribunal, when considering an unfair dismissal claim, will look at whether an employer has behaved reasonably towards the employee. If the employer has not behaved in accordance with the ACAS guidelines, it will be more difficult to demonstrate to the Tribunal that the approach taken has been reasonable. The risk to the organisation is the Tribunal finding that the dismissal was unfair. The current upper limit on the compensatory award for unfair dismissal is £56,800 (February 2005 and reviewed annually) and there is no upper limit in successful discrimination claims.

4.63   Clearly this is a huge risk for employers, not only in financial costs – which could break smaller organisations – but also in the cost of adverse reputation since Tribunal cases are in the public domain.

4.64   Human Resources professionals can achieve positive benefits for the organisation in developing a disciplinary policy that is in line with the recommended best practice from ACAS, complies with the legal requirements and works for the organisation. However, the Human Resources input does not end there, because Human Resources professionals have a role in training and educating managers in how best to use the policy in order to protect the organisation's position. Subsequently there is also a role to ensure that managers operate in accordance with the policy. By the organisation achieving all of these aims, employees will know what to expect in a disciplinary situation; and the organisation will be protected from a Tribunal finding that a claim is unfair on the grounds that the disciplinary procedure was not followed.

4.65   This situation has become more important for all organisations, no matter what their size, since the legislation on minimum standards for disciplinary procedures was introduced in October 2004.

Employment legislation and recruitment policies

4.66   We will now look at the specific impact of employment legislation on recruitment policies and the risks of not developing appropriate policies procedures. We will also link this to **Chapter 5** and the need to ensure robust, efficient and accurate record-keeping and administrative practices to underpin the policies.

4.67   In **Chapter 5** we will see that there is a wide range of employment legislation that impacts on the recruitment process. Although the list is given here, detailed information on what each piece of legislation covers and the potential risks can be found in **Chapter 5**.

- Equal Pay Act 1970.
- Rehabilitation of Offenders Act 1974.
- Sex Discrimination Act 1975 (amended 1986) and the Race Relations Act 1976 (amended 2000).
- Employment Equality (Sexual Orientation) Regulations 2003.
- Protection from Harassment Act 1997.
- Disability Discrimination Act 1995.
- Asylum and Immigration Act 1996.
- Human Rights Act 1998.
- Data Protection Act 1998.
- Part-Time Workers (Prevention of Less Favourable Treatment) Regulations 2000.
- Employment Equality (Religion and Belief) Regulations 2003.

Primary risks in the recruitment process

4.68   The primary risk to organisations of ineffective recruitment policies is the risk of discrimination claims. Secondary or supplementary risks in the process are appointing an inappropriate candidate, i e a 'square peg in a round hole' and an employee subsequently not being productive.

4.69   We will consider here how, in practice, Human Resources professionals can develop effective policies to minimise the possibility of such claims, as well as, in the event of a discrimination claim, how Human Resources professionals can best demonstrate, on behalf of the organisation, that there has been no discrimination in any part of the recruitment process, particularly as this is now a requirement under the Sex Discrimination (Indirect Discrimination and Burden of Proof) Regulations 2001, in the event of such a claim.

4.70   There are a number of stages in the selection process and we will examine each of the following stages to determine what the Human Resources professional can do to minimise the risks to the organisation.

4.71   Stages in the selection process:

- Selection criteria.
- Sourcing candidates.
- Shortlisting.
- The Interview:
    - Questioning techniques.
    - Questions that should not be asked.
    - Note taking and evaluation.
- Other recruitment activities.
- Making an offer.
- Giving interview feedback.
- Other considerations:

- –   Overseas candidates.
- –   Photographs.
- –   Email and phone calls.

Selection criteria

4.72   Discrimination can be avoided at all stages in the selection process by applying selection criteria that are relevant to the job and by making decisions based only on these criteria. Selection criteria may be determined from the following:

- Job description.
- Person specification.
- Competencies.

4.73   Human Resources professionals must ensure that, for each recruitment process, a detailed job description and person specification are compiled. The job description defines the overall purpose of the role and the main tasks. From the job description and knowledge of the requirements of the role, a person specification can be determined that gives details of the qualifications, personal qualities and experience that are required to perform effectively in the role.

4.74   In addition, competencies may be used to determine the knowledge, skills and behaviours that are required for effective performance in the role. A competency-based approach recognises that past behaviour is the best predictor of future performance. Using competency-based selection is now widely recognised as an objective mechanism for gathering information about what a candidate has actually undertaken or achieved.

4.75   Before starting a recruitment exercise, Human Resources professionals should work with the manager to determine the selection criteria. It is important to set the requirements at the level that is necessary for effective performance of the role, no lower and no higher. Once these criteria have been determined, they should be used at all stages of the recruitment and selection process to ensure a fair and objective approach.

4.76   By adopting such an approach, the organisation will be able to demonstrate objectivity and thus there will be less likelihood of a discrimination claim succeeding. The Human Resources professional is faced with challenges during this exercise, as managers are not always responsive to such measures, seeing them as needless bureaucracy imposed by Human Resources. The Human Resources professional can overcome this situation by delivering appropriate training to managers and describing the business, financial and risk management benefits of a robust process.

4.77 If at any stage in the process, the job description changes or it is necessary to make changes to the selection criteria, these must be agreed by those responsible for making the selection decisions. In order to demonstrate fairness it will be necessary to advise all applicants of the changes and, if these are extensive, it may be necessary to re-advertise the position.

Sourcing candidates

4.78 There are many possibilities for sourcing candidates for vacancies:

- Advertising in local or national press.
- Advertising in professional or technical journals.
- Internet recruitment web sites.
- Agencies and head-hunters.
- Job centre.
- Radio and television advertising, both local and national.

4.79 The main risk associated with many of these methods results from writing unfocused copy for the advertisement, which will produce an inappropriate field of candidates. In addition, inappropriate media may be chosen, which again will produce inappropriate candidates. An associated risk of such problems is the financial cost to the organisation where the cost of placing the advertisement may be wasted and has to be repeated again with a more objective focus or better media choice.

4.80 Human Resource professionals must ensure that care is taken in the drafting and placing of the advertisement to ensure that it is not potentially discriminatory. An advertisement itself cannot be held to be discriminatory. However it may show an intention to discriminate in the future. In addition, what is written in the advertisement may in future be construed as part of the contract of employment.

4.81 The advertisement text should follow the job description in describing the role and should detail the selection criteria that have already been determined. This will enable possible applicants to decide whether to apply for the position. Including detailed selection criteria in the advertisement will also discourage applications from those whose backgrounds differ widely from the stated criteria. This will also help in the shortlisting process when applications are received.

4.82 Careful thought should be given to placing of advertisements so that this cannot be perceived as discriminatory. Does the make-up of the workforce represent the local ethnicity profile? Does the advertising campaign attract a full mix of candidates or is there a need to focus the advertising to a local or specific publication? In particular, by only advertising jobs internally or on the Internet limits the opportunity for some people to submit an application.

4.83   Careful thought to the wording and placing of advertisements will reduce the risks to the organisation of possible claims of discrimination.

Shortlisting

4.84   Applications may be received in a number of ways, e g by post on an application form, by post by CV, via the Internet. At this point in the process, the Commission for Racial Equality and the Equal Opportunities Commission recommend gathering information on sex and ethnic origins of candidates. However, it is recognised that this information could potentially be used to discriminate. Human Resources professionals therefore need to determine appropriate mechanisms for gathering this information, retaining it for monitoring purposes, but not passing it on to managers. It may be possible to send out a self-classification form to individual applicants asking them to classify their own ethnic origins. Completion of the information on candidates is optional but, by collection and analysis of this data, an organisation could potentially demonstrate that they have not discriminated, because of the range of different origins of applicants. What is important is that this information is either collected on a separate document or on a part of the application form which is detached before shortlisting commences.

4.85   Selecting candidates for interview should always be done against the selection criteria that were determined at the start of the process. Each applicant must be assessed against the criteria and a record kept on how closely they match the criteria. It is essential that this assessment is carried out and the result recorded and retained for each candidate. In the event of an Employment Tribunal claim, the manager or Human Resource professional would be required to prove that they have been objective in determining a shortlist. If they are unable to produce a detailed and objective shortlisting record, a Tribunal would be open to construe that they had discriminated in the shortlisting process.

4.86   The importance of good record-keeping can be seen here, and organisations should devise their own form to record shortlisting decisions. It is preferable to complete the form by hand and it should be signed and dated on the date the shortlisting was done. Human Resources professionals or managers should keep these shortlisting records for six months.

The interview

4.87   We will look at the various aspects of the selection interview and ways of reducing the risk of possible discrimination claims.

Questioning

4.88   To avoid possible discrimination and to ensure an objective assessment, all questions should seek information about the agreed selection criteria and the same general line of questions and question areas should be used for all candidates.

Questions that should not be asked

4.89   It is essential to ask questions that cannot be construed as discriminatory and to use the same line of questioning for all candidates.

4.90   Questions that are unrelated to the selection criteria must not be used, for example personal questions about marital status or childcare arrangements. Questions about whether a disabled candidate is able to perform the job as described, with or without adjustments, are allowable, as are questions as to the nature of any adjustments that may be required.

4.91   Care should be taken in asking questions related to hobbies and interests as these could be construed as infringing an individual's right to privacy under the Human Rights Act 1998.

4.92   It is important to be aware that matters discussed at interview can be construed as part of the offer of employment. Therefore it is essential that if a candidate asks a question about salary or benefits, to which the answer is not known, that no answer is given. It is better to check the answer and go back to the candidate than to promise a salary or benefit to the candidate that the organisation is not in a position to meet.

Note-taking and evaluation

4.93   It is important that notes are taken during the interview so that, when an assessment is made of the candidate, there will be an accurate record. Notes should be taken against questions asked that relate to specific areas of the agreed selection criteria. Human Resources professionals can assist managers by providing standard formats for note-taking and evaluation. There may also be benefit in developing a ranking or scoring mechanism that becomes the norm in the organisation.

4.94   After each interview, time should be set aside to review the notes taken at the interview and objectively assess the information that has been gathered against the agreed selection criteria. Assessing against the agreed selection criteria will allow objective selection decisions to be made and candidates to be evaluated on the same terms by all interviewers or recruiters who have been involved in the process. Following such mechanisms will enable the Human Resources professional to defend the interview process should this become necessary.

4.95 It is important to record interview assessments following interview. If a round-up meeting takes place where the views of several interviewers are shared, a record of this discussion should also be made, with objective reasons for selection/non-selection of candidates. In the event of an Employment Tribunal claim, the organisation would be required to prove it had been objective in determining which candidate to select. If a detailed and objective record could not be produced, a Tribunal would be open to construe that an organisation had discriminated in its selection. As with shortlisting records, interview assessment records should be signed and dated and retained for six months.

4.96 The Human Resources professional can add further value to the organisation by providing comprehensive training in all aspects of the recruitment and selection process. This should cover legislative and process aspects as well as interviewing and selection techniques. It will be particularly important for managers who have never carried out workplace interviews, or as refresher training for those who have not interviewed for a long time, or those who have not previously recruited under a formal process.

Other recruitment activities

4.97 Organisations may also plan to use other recruitment activities such as meals on the evening prior to the interview, tours, presentations and tests.

4.98 Activities such as meals and tours should not form part of the selection process and the recruiting manager should not be present. This is because at such a forum it is not advisable for participants from the organisation to use the forum to make judgements, as the performance of the candidate does not form part of the agreed criteria. These events should be seen as purely informative, for the candidates to gain information about the organisation and meet representatives of the organisation. Candidates should be made aware of this.

4.99 Where candidates are required to give presentations or take tests, these must be related to the job requirements and be assessed against the agreed selection criteria to ensure that they are valid and not open to discrimination. Candidates should be notified in advance if presentations or tests are to take place. The Human Resources professional can again add value here by recommending appropriate tests and by providing information on the validity and legality of various tests.

4.100 Risks associated with using such tests are that the test may not have been validated. Care should be taken with some psychometric tests, for example, that have no validity studies and, as such, are not robust as predictors. Care should also be taken if the Human Resources professional or recruiting manager are developing the test themselves to ensure its validity and that it does not discriminate. If developing a test internally, it would be wise to use the team with whom the candidate will be working as the test group. If a test has been validated, it is essential to ensure it has been validated against an appropriate control group. For example, a test may have been validated on a group of white females aged between 35 and 45. Such a test may not be appropriate for a candidate of a different ethnic origin who is aged 55.

4.101 Use of an unvalidated test or in inappropriately validated test could result in recruitment of an inappropriate employee or could result in a discrimination claim.

4.102 Examples of some types of tests are:

- Psychometrics – to gain an insight into the personality profile of the candidates.
- Computer aptitude tests.
- Numeracy.
- Verbal reasoning.
- Language/translation/interpretation.
- Driving assessments – for example, for forklift truck driving or general work-related driving.
- Assessments for other manual skills – e g machine operation.
- Typing and shorthand tests.

Making an offer

4.103 Verbal offers of employment are legally binding. It is therefore essential that, before any offer is made, the terms are agreed between the Human Resources professional and the appropriate manager, otherwise this puts the organisation at risk of claims if they have offered something that they cannot later support. It is advisable to make the offer subject to references and many organisations will also make it contingent on medical clearance. This allows the organisation to withdraw the offer if an adverse reference is received, or a medical problem is discovered.

Taking up references

4.104 References should normally only be taken up by a Human Resources professional. They should only be taken once the candidate has given their permission to contact their referees, normally after an offer of employment has been made. Adopting this approach ensures that the process is under control and avoids the risk of previous employers being contacted before the employee has handed in their notice or notified their current employer that a reference request will be made. It is advisable to warn the candidate not to resign from their current position until satisfactory references have been obtained.

4.105   As will be seen in **Chapter 5**, there is also a need to check eligibility to work in the UK in line with the Asylum and Immigration Act 1996 and this would normally be undertaken by checking passports and work permits and also requesting a National Insurance number.

4.106   At this stage in the process it will also minimise risks if checks are made for specific qualifications where these are either required by regulation or organisational policies/procedures, eg clean driving licence, forklift truck licences. It is not good practice to subsequently discover that, after an employee starts work, they cannot work as a delivery driver because they had been disqualified from driving.

Pre-employment medical clearance

4.107   In order to protect the organisation from recruiting someone who, subsequently, is unable to do the job for health reasons, Human Resources professionals can introduce pre-employment medical screening. Many organisations, particularly larger ones, that have their own Occupational Health Department require the completion and satisfactory review of a medical questionnaire or satisfactory passing of a medical examination before a prospective employee may commence employment. This avoids appointing new employees with long-term sickness problems and also highlights people who might be at risk in certain work situations, eg individuals with a respiratory restriction being required to work in an area where respiratory protection is required – even if a last resort control – or an individual with 'tunnel vision' may not be able to undertake a role that requires driving a forklift truck.

Making other checks

4.108   Depending on the nature of the job it will be necessary for Human Resources professionals to check qualifications, particularly where these are necessary for the performance of the role, or are perceived appropriate for a particular work environment.

Case study

4.109   An organisation whose employee population was made up of highly qualified employees, many with postgraduate and Doctorate qualifications, recruited a Human Resources Director. One of the selection criteria was that this individual should also have a Doctorate or postgraduate qualification. A suitable individual was identified whose CV stated that the candidate had carried out PhD research at Cambridge.

4.110   When the individual joined the organisation it was discovered that whilst this was actually the case, the individual had never actually written up their PhD thesis and had therefore not achieved their Doctorate.

4.111   The result was significant embarrassment of the Human Resources function and a lack of acceptance of the Human Resources Director by many of the senior managers within the organisation.

Providing interview feedback

4.112   Some candidates may request feedback following an unsuccessful interview. In order to protect the organisation's position it is important that the Human Resources professional ensures that management are aware how this feedback should be handled. Where feedback is given, it must be objective and relate to the agreed selection criteria. Particular care should be taken where feedback is given verbally and a detailed record of the conversation should be kept. Adopting this approach is the only sure way to defend successfully against any future claim. Feedback given any other way could prejudice the position of the organisation were a claim to be made.

Other considerations

Overseas candidates

4.113   Current legislation provides that candidates from any European Community (EC) countries may work freely throughout the EC. It is therefore important to ensure that candidates from other EC countries are not treated differently from UK candidates.

4.114   With the enlargement of the EU on 1 May 2004, there are currently transitional requirements for workers from the ten accession states. Apart from Cyprus and Malta who are exempt, workers from the other new member countries are required to register with the Home Office as part of the Workers Registration Scheme. This registration gives them the right to work legally in the UK for twelve months. After that date, provided they have continued to work legally, they can work freely in the UK with no further registration requirement.

4.115   Organisations should check with employees within the first month of employment that they have registered and should obtain a copy of the registration document. The risk to the organisation of not doing this and allowing an employee to continue to work illegally is criminal prosecution.

4.116   Where a candidate is selected from a non-EC country, a work permit application will be required. The process for obtaining work permits is very rigorous and the organisation would need to be able to demonstrate why an EC national could not do the job, as well as what is unique about the skill set of the desired candidate. Detailed shortlisting records and interview assessment records will form part of any work permit application, in the same way that they form part of a discrimination defence. It is therefore essential to ensure that all the administrative processes are adhered to, otherwise it may be found that, although a non-UK national is the most appropriate candidate for the role, the organisation does not have the evidence to support this. The risk then is that the organisation will not be able to obtain a work permit for the individual and will therefore not be able to offer the job. The whole cost and time of the recruitment process will then be wasted and the process will have to begin again.

Photographs

4.117   Candidates should not be asked to produce a photograph of themselves, neither should managers take photographs of candidates. This practice is unlawful and could be construed as an intention to discriminate.

Email and phone calls

4.118   Care should be taken in the wording used in emails and phone calls with candidates. Information given, either by phone or on email, may be construed as part of an offer of employment and, if information is misrepresented, could put the organisation in a difficult position.

Defending a discrimination claim

4.119 In order to prevent any discrimination claims, it is essential that the Human Resources professional makes sure that all who are involved in the interview process familiarise themselves with the job description, know the agreed selection criteria and select against them. Use of agreed selection criteria applies not only to the interview but also where assessment centres are used. The more people who are involved in the process, the more it becomes essential to the defence of a claim to be able to demonstrate that all were aware of, and were selecting against, the objective and pre-determined criteria.

SUPPLEMENTARY RISKS IN RECRUITMENT

4.120 It is clear that the legislative risks around the recruitment process are extensive. However, these are not the only risks of using a non-robust process. Following the guidelines, detailed above, will help to ensure the selection of an appropriate candidate based on job-related criteria. Failure to do this could result in no candidate being found and the process having to start again. Even worse, it could result in the appointment of an inappropriate candidate who is unable to do the job effectively.

4.121 The recruitment process is lengthy with the time from initial identification of the need to job offer often being three months or more. In addition advertising costs are significant. For example, the cost of local press advertising (2004 costs) for a single advertisement is likely to be in the region of £500. For a larger advertisement for three vacancies the cost could be as much as £1,000. Advertising in the national press is even more expensive, whilst advertisements in specialist publications could also be up to £3,000 depending on size. Some companies use recruitment agencies that normally charge a percentage of starting salary, typically between 20% and 30%. However, they can provide services in specialist areas and situations where the resource is scarce in the employment marketplace, eg particular disciplines or skills.

4.122 Human Resources professionals need to help minimise the cost of advertising, and minimise the risk of repeat advertising time and costs, as there are not only these direct costs but the loss of productivity in the team and the impact on team members of having to perform tasks for a colleague who has long since left the organisation.

Employment Legislation and redundancy policies

4.123 The benefits of writing policies and practices will ensure equitable treatment for all employees. The organisation may have a policy that determines the redundancy terms and approaches. However, particularly if a large redundancy exercise is being planned, it will be essential for Human Resources functions to have a procedure to ensure that each Human Resources representative behaves in the same way with employees and that the legislative requirements are each followed.

4.124   In order to minimise the risks if there is an unfair dismissal claim, it is essential to ensure that the process includes a reasonable consultation period and that this is with employee representatives if the workplace recognises a trade union or with specially appointed employee representatives. In order to comply with the minimum standards for dismissal procedures, there is the need to invite the individual to a meeting to discuss the situation and to allow them the opportunity to be represented at that meeting by a work colleague or trade union representative.

4.125   In addition, it is essential to use objective selection criteria and select each candidate for redundancy against these criteria. This will help the organisation should an unfair dismissal claim to an Employment Tribunal result.

4.126   It is important to minimise the risk that key employees may leave the organisation as soon as a redundancy situation is announced, because they recognise that their skills are marketable elsewhere. In order to achieve this, the process should be carried out reasonably quickly. However, there should not be undue haste, as the Tribunal could consider this unreasonable.

4.127   It is difficult to determine how long the process should take. For large-scale redundancies, there are legal requirements as to how long the redundancy consultation process should take. Where an organisation is likely to make 20 or more employees redundant at one establishment within a period of 90 days, the consultation must begin at least 30 days before the first dismissal. If the number is over 90 employees, the consultation must begin at least 90 days before the first dismissal. For smaller-scale redundancy exercises, the organisation must try to determine what is a reasonable approach.

Case study

4.128   An organisation announced likely redundancies of 10–15 employees. They launched a redundancy consultation period of two weeks, during which time they consulted with both employee representatives and individual employees likely to be affected. At the end of the redundancy exercise, the feedback from all concerned was that two weeks had been too long and had caused considerable stress to those whose roles were at risk of redundancy.

4.129   The organisation underwent a subsequent redundancy exercise some time later and decided on a consultation period of one week, as a direct result of this feedback.

Case study

4.130 An organisation launched a redundancy exercise with a group meeting at 4 pm on a Tuesday evening. One employee was not in the office and, although a telephone call was made to the individual to advise them of the situation, they did not receive any face-to-face consultation until the following morning.

4.131 The redundancy decisions were made first thing on the following Monday morning and the individual who had been absent was advised of their redundancy at 9.30 am that day.

4.132 The individual's claim to an Employment Tribunal succeeded and the Tribunal found that three working days was insufficient time for consultation on redundancy.

4.133 The Human Resources professional needs to ensure that the organisation can demonstrate it has taken all necessary steps to ensure that the approach was reasonable.

WHAT POLICIES ARE REQUIRED?

4.134 The above situations show that the arguments for having appropriate policies to minimise all the above risks are compelling. However, how does an organisation decide which policies it should have?

4.135 Following the pattern described earlier, in order to minimise risks it is a good strategy to develop policies in all areas where legislation makes particular requirements on employers. This will ensure that all employers, employees and managers know what to expect and preserve the position of the organisation against possible claims against it.

4.136 The following is a checklist of policies that may be introduced, with some comment on the risks of not implementing each one in line with the above recommendations. We will consider which policies are *essential* and which are *desirable*.

Essential policies

Family-friendly policies

4.137 Such policies may be drafted, even if the decision has been taken to adopt the statutory minimum requirements. The publication of policies/procedures will ensure that employees are aware of their entitlements and provisions in the following areas:

- Adoption leave and pay.
- Maternity leave and pay.
- Paternity leave and pay.
- Parental leave.
- Right to request flexible working.
- Time off for emergencies related to dependants.

Disciplinary procedure and grievance procedure

4.138   Given that minimum standards are a legal requirement, it is essential for the Human Resources professional to develop robust and appropriate policies in these areas. This will ensure that the organisation complies with the legislative requirements and that employees understand the conduct and behaviour expected of them within the organisation and the risks of non-compliance. Putting in place appropriate disciplinary policies and ensuring managers are trained in their best use will minimise the risk of a claim to a Tribunal for Unfair Dismissal succeeding against the organisation.

Equal opportunities and diversity

4.139   Given the risk of Tribunal claims and the fact there is no upper limit on the compensatory award for such claims organisations should have such a policy.

Dignity in the workplace

4.140   Organisations should aim to provide a workplace free from conduct that harasses, disrupts or interferes with an individual's work as a consequence of an intimidating, offensive or hostile environment. Such conduct is not acceptable for organisations from their employees. It may be unlawful and may result in a legal liability on individuals as well as the organisation. It may cause demoralisation, stress, anxiety and sickness amongst employees and may lead to poor morale, high employee turnover and, ultimately, reduced organisational effectiveness. Organisations should aim to provide a workplace free from these issues to enable employees to contribute more effectively to the success of the organisation and thus achieve greater job satisfaction.

4.141   The aim of such a policy is to clarify the standards of behaviour expected of employees and to provide guidance. This will ensure that, as far as is practicable, both individuals who make complaints and individuals about whom claims of harassment are made are treated sensitively, fairly and objectively. It will also ensure that any complaints are dealt with promptly.

Holiday entitlement and working for another employer

4.142 The Working Time Regulations 1998 provide legal provisions about holiday entitlement and about working hours. To ensure that employees understand the legal position, the organisation's position and their joint responsibilities, Human Resources professionals should develop policies in both these areas to prevent misunderstandings and ensure motivation levels of staff.

Health and safety

4.143 The Health and Safety at Work etc. Act 1974 places obligations on employers who must recognise their responsibilities for the health, safety and welfare of their employees at work and that this duty of care extends to other people potentially affected by the organisation's activities.

4.144 Organisations should aim to provide working conditions that comply with the relevant statutory requirements and officially approved codes of practice that are designed to ensure good standards of health and safety. Health and safety arrangements should be designed to ensure that health and safety factors are fully taken into account at all levels of the organisation's operations. The overall responsibility for health and safety rests at the highest level of management, generally the 'chief executive', often referred to as the 'designated person'. All employees have an obligation to safeguard the health and safety of themselves and fellow employees. It is of paramount importance that Human Resources professionals implement effective health and safety policies that are supported and communicated from the highest levels throughout the organisation.

Data protection

4.145 As we will see in **Chapter 5**, there are complex and rigorous recommendations as a result of data protection legislation and the Employment Practices Data Protection Code. As these provisions are so complex, organisations cannot afford not to have a policy. Human Resources professionals must ensure that all responsibilities are clear in respect of the use of personal and sensitive data. In particular, it will be necessary to issue computer-held personal information to individuals on an annual basis so that they can check the accuracy of the records held on them.

Drug and alcohol abuse

4.146 An organisation's policy should be to employ a workforce free from the illegal use of drugs either in or out of work and the influence of alcohol while at work. Organisations can develop policies that state employees shall not use illegal drugs or abuse legal substances or report for work while under the influence of such substances or alcohol. Possession of and dealing in illegal substances should be reported immediately to the police. The organisation will have no alternative but to take this course of action.

4.147 Human Resources professionals may experience some resistance from managers in implementing such a policy, particularly where it impacts on the individual's life outside work. However, since such behaviour is illegal and could adversely affect the safety and welfare of other employees, the organisation will have little alternative but to implement such a policy.

Sickness reporting and managing absence

4.148 Given Statutory Sick Pay and record-keeping requirements, organisations must have policies to ensure that they do not infringe Inland Revenue Regulations.

4.149 Organisations will need to produce guidelines for managing absence to ensure that management are aware of how to deal with such situations effectively and in the best interests of the organisation.

Redundancy

4.150 It is not essential for an organisation to have a redundancy policy from the outset. However, when the pressure of a redundancy situation arises, it will probably be too late for the Human Resources professional to discuss and agree with senior management and Trade Unions where recognised, the essential elements of a policy, draft it, get approval and launch it along with training for managers. We therefore recommend that all organisations should have a redundancy policy in place. This will ensure that employees are handled equitably and fairly at a sensitive time. Having effective systems in place should minimise the risk of more adverse reactions to these difficult situations, for individuals leaving the organisation, for managers who have to deal with the situation and for those who are left behind in the organisation.

Termination procedures

4.151 With the implementation of the minimum standards on disciplinary and grievance procedures in October 2004, organisations now have to introduce termination procedures that comply with the minimum standards. These standards require that when employment is to be terminated, an employee must be notified in writing and must be able to attend a meeting to discuss the situation. At that meeting the employee has the statutory right to be accompanied at the meeting by a trade union representative or willing colleague. Following the meeting, the employee must be given the right to appeal.

Email, the Internet and use of company computer systems

4.152   Given the ever-increasing use of technology in the workplace, plus personal computing and wireless technology, it is essential for most organisations to have a clear policy that guides managers and provides 'rules' for employees. The policy needs to highlight what is considered to be appropriate use of the technology and Internet. This needs to be made clear to all employees from the start of their employment to prevent abuse. Management must monitor this and take action where inappropriate use is found. This is necessary both to protect individual employees from conduct that harasses and also to protect the organisation from abuse of its systems and disclosure of confidential or market-sensitive information.

PAY AND BENEFITS POLICIES AND PROCEDURES

4.153   In Chapter 5 we will look at the implications of inefficiencies in the administration of pay practices and also the introduction of new pay mechanisms and benefits policies. Where a new payment mechanism, practice or benefit is introduced there are several steps the Human Resources professional can take to ensure smooth and effective introduction.

4.154   The first stage is to undertake pay and benefits research in the area that is under consideration; suppose, for example, that the organisation is looking to introduce cafeteria benefits for employees. Cafeteria benefits are a benefits system where each benefit is given either a monetary or points value. Each employee is allocated points or cash values for their benefits, depending on their position or level in the organisation. They can then choose which benefits out of the whole range they would like, up to the value of their points or cash.

4.155   Introduction of such a system will be a major change within an organisation and it will be vital for the Human Resources professional to have undertaken the research into how other organisations have operated such systems, how they have been communicated, how they been received and the extent to which they have been successful. The same applies to the introduction of any new benefit or policy.

4.156   The Human Resources professional needs to develop the business case for the introduction. Having benchmarking information will allow the organisation to explain its decision to employees, by giving positive examples from other experiences. Without this information the organisation risks being unable to demonstrate the benefits of the new scheme and the potential then is that implementation will not be welcomed by employees and may be unsuccessful.

4.157   The next phase for the focus of the Human Resources professional is to consider the planning of the communication process. For any major change it will be necessary to gain the commitment of the workforce. Failure to do this will result in lack of interest and the potential that the new system may fail, resulting in the organisation having a direct loss in the time expended in the preparation and an indirect loss as a result of a downturn in productivity and morale.

4.158   Once the policy has been developed it may be appropriate to consider a trial within a discrete area of the workplace. The benefit will be that if it is a success, the organisation will have champions who can support the wider introduction. If the trial is not completely successful, the failure will be contained in a small area of the business. If the communication of the trial is successful, the views of the trial group can be incorporated and their input can be sought on what needs to be changed to improve the policy. The risk will therefore be restricted to the trial group and the policy can be revised before wider communication to the rest of the organisation.

4.159   The above are the most important policy areas for Human Resources professionals to implement. Implementation of robust policies in these areas will help to minimise the risks to the organisation, as discussed above.

Desirable policy areas

4.160   The following areas may also be appropriate for policies to be developed, depending on the culture and nature of the business of the particular organisation.

- Compassionate leave – where an organisation wishes to be specific about leave entitlements, eg following death or serious illness of a relative, rather than relying on the legal provisions in respect of time off for emergencies to look after dependants.
- Share dealing, covering internal access to sensitive information and individual restrictions on share dealing as a result.
- Expenses – the organisation's approach to reimbursement of money which the individual has spent on behalf of the company during the course of their employment.
- Jury service – the approach the organisation takes towards payment for jury service.
- Mobile phones – in relation to the legislative provisions about non-use

of mobile phones while undertaking work-related driving, or when driving a vehicle provided by an organisation. The organisation may also wish to specify their stance on use of personal mobile phones during working time and on the organisation's premises.

- Retirement – such policies will normally state the provisions in respect of normal retirement age and may also mention such special leave as retirement rundown and also whether any particular training is given for retirement adjustment.

- Learning and development – the organisation's approach to learning and development of its employees. This may also include the approach to further education, ie in what circumstances the organisation will support further education, either financially and/or with paid or unpaid time off.

- Employee concessions – where an organisation sells products or services and these are available at a discount to employees.

- Trade union membership – whether the organisation recognises trade unions, what is the nature of that recognition, and whether deduction of trade union subscriptions can be made via the organisation's payroll system.

- No smoking – the organisation's approach to smoking in the workplace.

- Relocation – the organisation's policy on contributing to the expenses of employees where they are required to move home at the request of the organisation.

IMPLICATIONS FOR HUMAN RESOURCES PROFESSIONALS

4.161   The key implication for Human Resources professionals is that the implementation of effective policies/procedures for Human Resources purposes is a key element in the management of Human Resources risks. Where Human Resources professionals can persuade senior management to take a proactive approach, not only will the organisation fulfil its obligation to stakeholders, but it will also assist in maximising the effectiveness of employees and organisational opportunities.

4.162   Human Resources professionals need to take a risk-based approach to the drafting of policies/procedures in order to ensure that the focus of the final version is appropriate for the culture and style of the organisation and that they minimise potential risks. A risk-based approach to drafting policies/procedures identifies the potential risk related to the policy issue, evaluates the impacts both in terms of addressing the risk and the risk of inaction and demonstrates the need for action. The final stage in the process is to monitor, evaluate and amend any policies/procedures that do not meet the needs of the organisation.

4.163   Human Resources policies/procedures cannot stand in isolation. In order to provide a full range of operational functions, Human Resources professionals must ensure the consistent application of policies/procedures, consistent accuracy of administration and effective manager and employee communication. Human Resources professionals must combine Human Resources polices/procedures with effective and efficient performance of administrative tasks to provide best value to the organisation. In **Chapter 5** we explore the risks associated with ineffective and inefficient Human Resources administrative functions and consider how some of these risks may be removed or reduced.

CHAPTER 5

Human Resources administration

INTRODUCTION

5.1 In this chapter we demonstrate that whilst Human Resources administration is considered the routine side of Human Resources work, it is essential that such administrative tasks are planned and performed with complete accuracy. There are three main reasons for this. Firstly, the Human Resources professional will never be able to move away from the routine administration and add greater value to the organisation if this is not the case. Secondly, there are potential legislative risks. Thirdly, there is a risk of lack of confidence in Human Resources administration that may lead to lack of confidence in the organisation as a whole, demotivation of employees and possible loss of a key resource.

5.2 The chapter highlights some of the key tasks associated with Human Resources administration, identifies possible risks and looks at mechanisms for avoiding these pitfalls.

5.3 To look at how Human Resources may add greater value to the organisation, it is important to go back to basics. To consider the topic of Human Resources administration, we need to understand what Human Resources administration is and then consider the potential risks if these tasks and functions are not performed effectively.

5.4 Clearly the administrative functions associated with Human Resources are wide reaching and can involve significant risk to the organisation. Human Resources professionals can add value to the organisation by eliminating these risks, first by highlighting the areas of risk exposure and the potential impact of not taking action. Existing processes and systems may need to be reviewed but Human Resources professionals will need to work with the organisation to understand where priorities for action lie and gain agreement to taking whatever action is necessary. A process is discussed in detail in **Chapter 8**. Human Resources professionals will be instrumental in establishing how the risks can be minimised and can add further value by establishing measures for monitoring future performance in such areas. Value will also be added by establishing the cost of taking the corrective action in comparison with the potential cost of the activity going uncorrected. By putting an appropriate action plan in place, ensuring the corrective action is taken and monitoring the results for the future, Human Resources professionals will add significant value to the organisation by minimising the risks associated with Human Resources administrative processes and procedures.

RECORD-KEEPING – THE IMPORTANCE OF ACCURACY

5.5 At its most simple level, the Human Resources administration function focuses on keeping basic employee records and making sure people are paid accurately and on time. In any organisation, no matter what its size, these types of records are fundamental not only to good administration but also to employee harmony. Where people are not paid, are paid incorrect amounts, where incorrect deductions are made for tax and National Insurance, this can lead to demotivated employees and a lack of confidence in administrative processes. There is also a need to ensure that the organisation complies with the basic legislative requirements for deduction of tax, payment of National Insurance and other statutory provisions such as sick pay, parental leave entitlements, maternity leave and payments and also deductions from payroll, for example county court judgements or trade union subscriptions. All organisations have a duty both legally and morally to ensure that these aspects are carried out correctly, accurately and efficiently for all of their employees.

5.6 For smaller organisations, keeping employee name and address details, dates of birth, bank details and pay information may be all that is necessary. Systems are often paper-based or use a simple stand-alone PC-based spreadsheet. Organisations may contract out their payroll administration to an external organisation. However, more complex organisations with more employees and more complex structures will require enhanced administrative systems and more comprehensive payment mechanisms. There may be more complex working arrangements such as shift systems, part-time and full-time employees, a mix of categories of employee all with a different basis for their pay calculations. Smaller organisations that have grown into larger corporate organisations, either by organic growth or by mergers and acquisitions, often ignore the need for additional accurate record-keeping. This means that larger organisations may still have the need to evaluate their Human Resources administrative systems to ensure that they are robust and meet the current and future needs of the organisation.

5.7 For example, as organisations grow they may introduce share option schemes, bonus arrangements, annualised hours, cafeteria benefits – the more complex the scheme and the bigger the organisation, the more there is a need for accuracy in administration.

5.8 There is also a need where organisations are making job cuts. When making employees redundant, for example following a merger, it is essential to know age, length of service and pay details to accurately calculate any redundancy entitlement. At such a sensitive time, organisations cannot afford to get it wrong. Accurate administration is the difference between employees leaving the organisation with dignity or leaving full of resentment because 'Human Resources couldn't even get my payments right'.

5.9 Recruitment is usually the first contact a potential employee has with an organisation. Inefficient recruitment administration, such as a delay in responding to applications, slowness in scheduling interviews or inaccuracies in job offer letters, give a very bad impression of the organisation to applicants. It may result in the loss of good applicants to other organisations.

5.10 Those responsible for Human Resources administration need to ensure that they are 'one step ahead' in terms of basic record-keeping, and that administrative systems adapt to the changing needs of the organisation. Paper systems may need to evolve and will eventually need to be computerised in some form.

5.11 As organisations grow, the record-keeping requirement also develops. For example, as more employees are recruited there is more necessity to monitor and manage attendance. Unplanned absences are disruptive to any team. It often falls to those with responsibility for the people issues in organisations to keep the holiday and sickness records, and this is inevitably Human Resources.

5.12 How this information is used is also crucial to the success or otherwise of the organisation. Human Resources may often keep the records, which 'gather dust' and are not utilised elsewhere within the organisation. It is not surprising, therefore, that Human Resources is often seen as the administrative function that does not add value to the organisation. A more proactive approach using an analysis of the data and providing feedback on trends, etc, to managers will provide them with concrete evidence with which to address such matters, and will add value to the organisation, particularly where poor attendance is an issue.

5.13 Human Resources administration covers a very wide range of issues and situations. The risks of either not undertaking an administrative task at all, or of doing it but not getting it right, can be far reaching. In terms of the profile and reputation of Human Resources, the difference is marked. Getting the administration right probably means that no one will actually notice! Getting it wrong will result in complaints and lack of credibility of the Human Resources function if errors are repeated or are significant. Ultimately this could lead to adverse reactions from employees and managers, demotivation and potentially even attrition if the situation is extreme.

5.14 The situation to which Human Resources must aspire is one where no one notices the administrative processes. It really has to be about getting the administrative processes so slick that they virtually run themselves, with the result that Human Resources professionals have more time to focus on other issues within the organisation, adding additional value rather than just performing administrative roles. The risk to Human Resources professionals, weighed down by cumbersome administrative tasks and queries, is that they will never be able to grow and develop their personal profile or that of the Human Resources function. These aspects of managing Human Resources risks are covered in more detail in **Chapter 8**.

5.15   In addition, it is essential that Human Resources administration is carried out effectively and efficiently so that, if there should be a challenge, there is an audit trail to explain what has been done, why and by whom. Such an audit trail may protect an organisation in the event of a legal challenge, eg to an Employment Tribunal, or in the event of an Inland Revenue investigation.

5.16   The following table gives some examples of Human Resources administrative tasks and the potential risks associated with not performing these tasks effectively and efficiently. This list is not intended to be definitive or exhaustive and Human Resources professionals should think carefully about their own Human Resources administration activities when thinking about operational risks in this area. Each item in the table is discussed in more detail later in the chapter when we will also look at how to reduce or remove these risks.

	Administrative task	Potential risks
1	Employee records	Lack of confidence in administrative processes. Employee disharmony. Lack of accurate records prevent or hinder the change within the organisation. Records are not held and data not managed in line with data protection principles set down in the Data Protection Act. Not complying with the Data Protection Codes on: ● Recruitment and Selection. ● Records Management. ● Monitoring at Work. ● Medical Information. Not complying with the requirements of the Health and Safety at Work Act for retention of data where health surveillance may be necessary.
2	Payroll and payment mechanisms	Lack of confidence in administrative processes, resulting in employee disharmony and potential high employee turnover. Lack of compliance with legislative and Inland Revenue requirements. Possible poor publicity if the matter is publicised in the press. Additional administrative resource is required to correct errors or rectify problems.

3	Organisational growth with no review of administrative processes	Systems and processes no longer appropriate to the scale and complexity of the organisation. Errors in processing leading to demotivation among employees, non-compliance with legislative or Inland Revenue requirements. Potential increased employee turnover.
4	Pay and benefits administration	Incorrect payments contrary to Inland Revenue rules, leading to fines and interest payments. Perceived inequity between employees. Demotivation. Potential increased employee turnover. Ensuring that pay and benefits measures are appropriate to the needs of the organisation.
5	Redundancy administration	Perceived unfairness amongst all employees, not just those who are being made redundant, leading to poorly motivated employees. Employees leaving without dignity and with resentment against the organisation. High-fliers leaving the organisation because of perceived lack of stability.
6	Paper-based versus computerised records	Paper systems not being translated into effective computerised systems soon enough or accurately, will lead to employee suspicion of such systems and eventually to mistrust in Human Resources. This could lead to demotivation and potentially to employees leaving if the situation is not put right. Inaccurate data held in paper systems translated to computer systems. Input errors.
7	Intranet-based systems	Inappropriate communication and training and fear of technology among managers and employees could produce a lack of use and therefore inaccurate records. Human Resources administrative employees may fear losing control, and concern themselves about their medium-/long-term employment position.

8	Managing attendance	Disruption to the work team or activity, where attendance, e g sick pay, holiday and other absence, is not managed. Where records are kept by Human Resources but are not analysed or made available to managers, the organisation can be unaware of serious attendance problems. This can result in a reduction of productivity or level of service and impact on the morale of those employees who are at work. Lack of compliance with Inland Revenue requirements, record-keeping, reporting and payment. Claims in respect of the Working Time Regulations. High costs from lack of control of attendance and absence.
9	Pay review administration	Internal impact on employees' confidence in the Human Resources function and possible demotivation of employees. Internal systems not being adequate to accurately calculate pay awards. Perceived lack of parity or equity amongst employees as a result.
10	Recruitment administration	Non-compliance with legislative requirements leading to potential Employment Tribunal claims for discrimination (e g race, sex, disability). Contravention of equal-pay legislation. Non-compliance with the Rehabilitation of Offenders Act 1974. Employing an individual who is not legally entitled to work in the UK. Damage to the reputation of the organisation. Failure to issue a written statement of employment particulars within eight weeks of the individual joining.

| 11 | Administration of family-friendly policies | Inaccurate records of start dates to ensure correct service requirements being adhered to and incorrect statutory and company payments (if applicable) are made. Incorrect processing can result in stress to the mother and unborn child at a time when this should be minimised. Inaccurate mechanisms to ensure correct return to work dates and correct return to work arrangements. Inaccurate records for parental leave so that inaccurate information is passed on to a future employer if the employee leaves. Inaccurate record-keeping or inaccurate processing of data in these areas could result in an employee believing they have been discriminated against and making a claim to an Employment Tribunal. Inaccurate record-keeping, which allows employees to take unfair advantage of the provisions in respect of time off to look after dependants. |
| 12 | Administration of flexible working arrangements | Flexible working requests, particularly if these are turned down, need to be recorded in the event of a claim against the employer. If new working arrangements have been agreed, they need to be implemented and administered in accordance with what has been agreed to ensure that the individual is not demotivated where problems arise. |

| 13 | Termination of employment | Ensuring that records are kept about termination arrangements so that the organisation could prove that it had complied with the statutory minimum standards for disciplinary procedures in the event of a claim against the employer. Ensuring payment or reclaiming of holiday entitlement in line with the requirements of the Working Time Regulations to prevent employee claims. Preventing employees leaving with a bad impression of the organisation by getting the terminations procedures effective and efficient. Inaccurate calculation of termination payments, preventing correct amounts being paid and Inland Revenue requirements being met, in respect of taxation or the tax-free nature of some payments. |
| 14 | Internal and external communications | Poor internal and external relations where, e g applications are not acknowledged in a timely manner, employees are unaware of policies, procedures and entitlements. Risk of inconsistency of message communicated either internally or externally. |

5.17   In the following sections we look in more detail at the above administrative tasks, examine potential risks in more detail and recommend ways of managing the risks.

Employee records

5.18   There are two main areas where Human Resources professionals or administrators can put their organisations at risk in respect of employee record-keeping. The first is the accuracy of record-keeping. It may be that records are so inaccurate or inadequate that they prevent or hinder the development of new practices and processes. The second case is not respecting the confidentiality of information. Employees working in Human Resources must respect and maintain confidentiality of employee data and records. In addition, employers have basic obligations in respect of the Data Protection Act 1998.

5.19   Maintaining the accuracy of employee data held within an organisation underpins the success or otherwise of all Human Resources administrative systems and processes. As an organisation grows and develops, it will inevitably become more complex. As more complex structures develop, more complex payment mechanisms are introduced. As this growth takes place, Human Resources systems will also need to develop and change to accommodate the changing needs of the organisation. Fundamental to the successful implementation of, for example, a new payment system is the accuracy of the data that is input into the system. Thus employee records need to be kept up to date and verified regularly for accuracy.

The Data Protection Act 1998

5.20   The Data Protection Act 1998 gives employers two basic obligations in respect of employee personal data.

1   They must comply with the eight 'data protection principles' detailed in the Act. The risk of not complying with the principles is a financial penalty, with no upper limit.
2   They must comply with Data Protection notification requirements if applicable. Section 17 of the Act states that an employer must be registered to process personal data where there is computerised processing of the data or where the Secretary of State specifies that certain types of processing must be notified.

5.21   The eight data protection principles require that personal data will be:

1   Processed fairly and lawfully.
2   Processed for limited purposes.
3   Adequate, relevant and not excessive.
4   Accurate.
5   Kept only as long as is necessary.
6   Processed in line with employees' rights under the Data Protection Act.
7   Secure.
8   Retained within the European Economic Area unless a country outside that area ensures an adequate level of protection in respect of processing the data.

5.22   In addition, the UK Information Commissioner has introduced an Employment Practices Data Protection Code. This Code of Practice covers the following four main areas:

1   Recruitment and selection.
2   Employment records.
3   Monitoring at work.
4   Information about workers' health.

5.23   The Data Protection Code only applies to information held on an electronic filing system or other organised filing system. This obviously has significant implications for Human Resources administration, as these provisions will cover much of the information held.

5.24   There are specific rights of workers under the Code. A worker is described as any individual who might wish to work for, currently works for, or has worked in the past for, an organisation. The Code applies to a wide range of employees and workers in the following categories and also applies to former workers as well as current ones:

- Applicants (successful and unsuccessful).
- Employees.
- Agency workers.
- Casual workers.
- Contract workers.

It may also apply to volunteers and those on work placements.

5.25   All these individuals have the right to have a copy of any information held on them. They also have the right to have inaccurate data held on them corrected. This obviously has far-reaching implications for Human Resources administrators.

5.26   All personal data is covered by the Act, including automated and computerised records, data held on paper or microfiche in a relevant filing system. If an employee or worker wishes to have access to the data this should be requested in writing and employers may charge a fee of up to £10 to comply with the request and should respond to it within 40 days.

5.27   Employees have a responsibility under the code for protection of data and no worker should disclose personal data outside their employer's procedures or use personal data held on others for their own purposes. Serious breaches of data protection rules should normally be handled under the disciplinary procedure and may also render the employee liable for prosecution.

5.28   All organisations should aim to follow the principles outlined in the Data Protection Code of Practice. The risks to an organisation of not doing so are that, whilst the Code does not contain legal requirements, it is recommended best practice. Therefore an Employment Tribunal would be open to construe that an organisation would be at fault if the Code had not been followed.

5.29   The main features of the Code are listed below.

PART 1 – RECRUITMENT AND SELECTION

5.30   The Act provides that an employer is able to collect and use personal data in connection with the recruitment and selection process. This may include the following:

- To ensure health, safety and welfare at work.
- To select safe and competent workers.
- To ensure a safe working environment.
- To ensure it does not discriminate.
- To ensure the reliability of workers with access to personal data.
- To protect customers' property.
- To check immigration status before employment.

5.31   The employer should ensure that personal details that are kept as part of the recruitment and selection process are relevant to and necessary for the process itself and that this could be justified. It is also appropriate to keep information in order to defend the process if it is challenged.

Part 2 – Employment Records

5.32   Under the requirements of the Act, an employer should nominate an appropriate person within the organisation as the one responsible for ensuring employment practices comply with the Data Protection Act 1998. There is an onus on the employer to ensure that managers and workers understand their responsibilities for complying with the regulations. Organisations may use employee data to ensure:

- The health, safety and welfare of workers.
- A safe working environment.
- They do not discriminate.
- They accommodate workers with disabilities by considering reasonable adjustments to the workplace.
- They keep accurate statutory records, e g Statutory Sick Pay, Statutory Maternity Pay and disclose these records where there is a legal requirement, for example to the Inland Revenue or Child Support Agency.
- That workers are not dismissed unfairly.
- To supply information on accidents where industrial injury benefit may be payable.
- The protection of customers' property or funds in the Company's possession.
- Continuity of employment for employees transferred under the Transfer of Undertakings (Protection of Employment) Regulations 1981.

5.33   In adhering to these requirements, organisations should ensure that records are accurate, that they are stored securely and safely and that employees who have access to those records protect their confidentiality. It is also important to keep sickness and accident records separate from absence records and not to disclose sickness, accident or absence records to other employees. However, such information may be disclosed to managers about employees who work for them so that they can undertake their managerial functions.

5.34   Organisations should also ensure that information is collected only for a specific purpose and is used only for that purpose and that, for example, data held for employee schemes, e g pensions, are only used for the purposes for which they were collected. The Code recommends that, each year, employers should provide employees with a copy of personal information that may change, e g name or home address, so that records can be kept up to date.

5.35   Employers should also undertake to keep information collected on ethnic origin, disability and religion confidential and to a minimum. The final recommendation of the Code is that employers should only disclose or publish confidential information to a third-party where they have been given express permission and where the third-party undertakes to treat this information confidentially.

PART 3 – MONITORING AT WORK

5.36   This part of the Code makes provision for monitoring the workplace. The Code provides that employers may monitor workers when the advantage to the organisation outweighs the intrusion into the workers' affairs. Examples of such monitoring might include CCTV, email usage and telephone call monitoring. Generally covert monitoring should only be undertaken in extreme circumstances where it is necessary for the prevention and detection of crime and where there is a risk that notifying workers of the monitoring would frustrate the purpose of the monitoring. Such monitoring should normally be authorised at a very senior level in the organisation.

5.37   In other circumstances where monitoring is found to be necessary, an employer should also consider other factors. For example, what use is to be made of the information or data, which information is gathered, and what will be the impact on the individuals who are the subject of monitoring. Monitoring should not be considered in areas that employees could reasonably expect to be private. This is in addition to comparing the impact of the advantage to the organisation with the potential intrusion to the individual(s). Ordinarily employees should be informed if monitoring is to take place. Where information is discovered as a result of the monitoring, it should only be used for the purpose for which it was sought. Any information discovered should be kept secure and access should be restricted as appropriate. In addition, it is important to exercise caution when monitoring potentially personal communications.

PART 4 – INFORMATION ABOUT WORKERS' HEALTH

5.38   This part of the Code recommends good practice organisations should adopt when obtaining and handling information about workers' health. It covers such information as might be sought or acquired through the following:

- An employee questionnaire to detect health problems.
- Information about disabilities or special needs.
- The results of eye tests.
- Records of blood tests.
- Results of alcohol or drugs tests.
- Genetic test results.
- Assessment of fitness for work or eligibility for benefits.
- Records of vaccinations and immunisations.

The Code confirms there are limits on how much an employee's consent can be relied upon as the basis for processing information on workers' health. Consent must be explicit and freely given – ie they must have been told how the information would be used and the worker must have a real choice whether or not to give consent.

The employer must assess the impact of collecting and using the data and look at possible alternatives to establish whether the course of action chosen is justified.

5.39   Clearly the Employment Practices Data Protection Code has far-reaching implications for Human Resources administrative functions. It sets guidelines on what information may be kept, how it may be used and what it may be used for. There is a risk to all organisations of not complying with the recommendations of the Code and potential claims from employees and workers against organisations for the abuse or misuse of their personal data. In a situation of non-compliance, the Information Commissioner has recourse to three types of action:

- An enforcement notice requiring the data to be handled in the correct way.
- Criminal prosecution for an offence of misusing personal information.
- Warrant for entry to a premises to obtain information on whether information has been incorrectly used.

5.40   Human Resources professionals should also be aware of the requirements of the Health and Safety at Work Act for retaining records for extended periods (eg 40 years) where health surveillance has taken place. For example, the increase in incidence of asbestosis, caused by exposures to asbestos many years ago, may result in claims against the organisation, which would have to show it had returned such records for the required period.

Payroll and payment mechanisms

5.41   There are three main risk areas: that of the individual within the organisation, the possibility of internal systems being inadequate for the transmission of payroll data and the legislative and regulatory risks.

5.42   The likely problem areas in respect of employees personally are self-evident. Employees may be paid incorrect amounts, may not be paid on time or, worse still, not paid at all. The individual may be understanding on the first occasion since most people will accept that mistakes do happen. However repeat that error again and again and an understanding employee will quickly become one who is angry and upset. Individuals often have complex personal financial situations and if the organisation cannot pay on time or pay the correct amounts this may add stress to an already anxious employee.

5.43   An individual who is underpaid or not paid at all will be quick to complain. Compare that with an individual who is overpaid. An unscrupulous or disloyal employee may well take the view that if the company cannot get it right it is not their problem and say nothing, in the hope the mistake is not discovered. It may be that the error never comes to light, in which case there is the risk of financial loss to the organisation, which may be significant if the error recurs with each payroll run.

5.44   Any error that is subsequently discovered requires more administrative effort to redress. In addition there may be a need to placate the individual. If the error has resulted in a significant loss to the organisation or the error appears to be due to negligence, there may even be a need to investigate with a view to possible disciplinary procedures.

5.45   The result of repeated errors will be a lack of employee confidence in the Human Resources function. If the problems become chronic this is likely to manifest itself as a general sense of dissatisfaction with the organisation as a whole. There may also be a drop in motivation amongst the Human Resources administrative team. The situation could lead to valued employees in either Human Resources or elsewhere leaving the organisation, resulting in the time and cost of recruiting and retraining.

5.46   The second area, that of internal practices and processes not being appropriate or efficient enough to ensure that payment mechanisms work, was explored in **Chapter 4**.

5.47   In respect of pay and benefits matters, the requirements of employment legislation and rulings by the Secretary of State are implemented by the Inland Revenue and the Department for Work and Pensions. There are clear rules on deduction of tax and National Insurance, on payment of benefits such as Statutory Sick Pay (SSP), Statutory Maternity Pay (SMP), Statutory Paternity Pay (SPP) and Statutory Adoption Pay. Where the Inland Revenue makes a compliance visit (to check that the organisation is correctly following the requirements) they may find that there are no problems, in which case an organisation may then be free from a further visit for as much as three or four years. If problems are found but it is determined that this is an innocent error – say, for example, National Insurance or tax has been under-deducted – the Inland Revenue will be likely to expect payment of the amount of the underpayment from the date due, plus interest. Where an innocent error is found they are unlikely to impose any penalties, but such a situation is likely to result in more frequent compliance visits to ensure that the situation has been accurately corrected and does not occur again.

5.48 Where the error or errors are not found to be innocent, the Inland Revenue will expect the underpayment to be paid from the date due, plus interest, and they may also impose penalties that can be up to 100% of the amount owing plus interest. Thus the organisation could be facing a significant financial penalty.

5.49 In addition, it is worth noting that if an employer sends in a year-end return with 5% or more of National Insurance numbers incorrect or missing, this is also likely to trigger a compliance visit.

5.50 In respect of the penalties imposed, the pressure to get the system right at the outset is therefore very significant.

5.51 In addition, there are legal requirements for payroll additions and deductions such as attachment of earnings orders for such items as non-payment of council tax and payment of family credit. Incorrect payments or deductions result in additional administrative effort to correct, as detailed above. In addition, there is the possibility of an Inland Revenue investigation into the practices within the organisation. If this investigation finds that the organisation deductions or payment mechanisms are incorrect, the result could be a significant fine for the organisation. The cost to the organisation is not the only risk. The matter may be publicised in the press, giving the organisation a poor reputation – not only as an employer, but also with the public as a whole, potentially influencing sales and profit.

5.52 In respect of all of these situations, there will be a need for additional administration to correct the problems, putting a strain on Human Resources or payroll administrators to duplicate tasks that should have been correct initially. It is vitally important for the reasons above for the employer to ensure that payments and deductions are correct and made on time. The key is to ensure that appropriate policies/procedures are put in place at the outset. This point has been covered in **Chapter 4**.

5.53 In addition, Human Resources and payroll administrative employees need to be appropriately trained and need to understand the reasons for a particular process or way of working. Any organisation may consider it appropriate to buy in payroll expertise or to outsource the payment of employees to a payroll bureau, to ensure the legislative changes and Inland Revenue rules are adhered to.

Organisational growth with no review of administrative processes

5.54   Where organisations have grown and have not undertaken a review of administrative processes, it is often the case that the processes have become inadequate or inappropriate to the changed needs of the organisation. If the organisation has grown both in size and complexity, the systems may simply no longer be sophisticated enough to cope.

5.55   Where errors occur as a result, or where there are frequent processing errors, employees will swiftly lose faith in the ability of the Human Resources function to process any information effectively or efficiently. This will result in dissatisfaction but, in extreme circumstances, could also eventually result in individuals leaving because they no longer wish to work for an organisation that is unprofessional in its approach to maintenance of employee data. As has been discussed earlier, errors in the systems can also lead to non-compliance with Inland Revenue regulation, which can lead to significant fines for the organisation.

Pay and benefits administration

5.56   As organisations grow and develop, their complexity also develops. This is also true in the area of pay and benefits administration. Growing organisations will be continually looking at mechanisms for attracting and retaining top-quality employees. It may be the introduction of bonus arrangements, company car schemes and share schemes. The type and level of pay and benefits being offered is crucial to the success of this attraction and retention exercise. Here we are focusing on the administrative aspects and the possible risks for the Human Resources professional and the organisation as a whole.

5.57   We have already talked about the importance of accurate employee records and payroll and this importance is heightened as the organisation introduces more complex and detailed pay and benefits. As we have already seen in **Chapter 4**, getting the level and type of remuneration and benefits correct is vitally important. However the success of the introduction of a new benefit is only as good as the administrative processes that support it.

5.58   Employees are often suspicious about the introduction of new benefits and new types of benefit and, as we discussed in **Chapter 4**, how the change is communicated and sold to the employees is vital to the success of the introduction. However, imagine a scenario where there has been a huge effort in the communication process, but no attention has been paid to the resulting procedures that need to support the change. The new arrangement is introduced, but the administration fails and individuals are not paid or do not receive the benefit at the correct time. The risk is that all credibility for the communication process is lost and employees will return to suspicion and doubt about their employer's motivation for the change.

5.59   The end result could be serious demotivation and thus attrition where employees seek employment elsewhere in order to find an employer who looks after their interests better. The psychological contract between employer and employee is much weaker now than it was in the past. With increasing rounds of 'right sizing' in organisations leading to frequent redundancies, employees recognise that there is no guarantee from an employer of a 'job for life'. The response to this is that employees are more likely to seek employment elsewhere if their current employer cannot get it right.

5.60   In addition, there could be other financial losses to the organisation if effective administrative systems and processes are not put in place to cover pay and benefits. As we have already seen, if appropriate systems are not in place there could be overpayments, underpayments and incorrect tax and National Insurance deductions. Such problems could potentially result in Inland Revenue investigations and fines.

Redundancy administration

5.61   It is important to ensure the accuracy of Human Resources administration in redundancy situations. There may be heightened emotions of anger, resentment or lack of understanding. Where the organisation does not manage the termination payments accurately and on time, these feelings will be exacerbated and it will result in a poor reputation for the organisation in the mind of the leaving employee and those that remain. Organisations should always bear in mind that the way in which they treat the 'casualties' in these situations says more about them than the way they treat their successful employees, or those who are not leaving, during a redundancy situation. Those employees who remain after the redundancy exercise will be concerned that a poor process and less-than-generous payment levels could be applied to them next time. So those with transferable skills and knowledge often leave, rather than wait for the next round of 'cuts'. This often results in the organisation losing the very employees that they wished to retain.

5.62   In addition, it is essential to ensure effective administrative process so that appropriate tax payments are made. At the present time there is an Inland Revenue tax-free limit on redundancy payments of £30,000. For pay in lieu of notice, either in redundancy or disciplinary situations, where the contract allows the employer to make payments in lieu of notice the payment is taxable. Where there is no contractual provision, payments are tax-free within the £30,000 limit as stated above. Clearly it is essential for Human Resources administration to process these amounts accurately to ensure that individuals have the correct tax treatment on leaving.

Paper-based versus computerised records

5.63   Many small organisations only operate paper-based Human Resources administrative systems. However, as organisations grow, these become more and more cumbersome. Eventually it will become impossible to operate efficiently without some kind of computer-based system. This may only be simple and enable the organisation to produce a mail merge of documents. However, this will be much more accurate and quicker than a manual system.

Case study

5.64   A small production company grew from 50 to around 200 employees. During the period of growth, because the market forces dictated it, the company had introduced share options and share save schemes, a new company pension scheme, bonus arrangements and had moved its production department to a 24/7 shift operation. All employee records were paper-based and, although the company had a Human Resources manager and administrative Human Resources support, the bulk of their time was spent recruiting and there 'just wasn't time' to take a wider view.

5.65   Some time later, the company was the subject of a take-over by a larger organisation and, during the process of integration, the Human Resources function struggled to provide the information that was needed to ensure a smooth hand-over of information. When the organisation came to issue bulk communications to all employees, it turned out to be a cumbersome process. With all employee data retained on paper, it was not even possible to set up a simple mail merge to send letters to all employees' home addresses. One of the Human Resources team had to input all the data to a spreadsheet before the letters could be produced. When the organisation came to make redundancies some time later, it was again time-consuming and cumbersome to produce figures and information accurately and quickly, since no information was held in a computerised format.

5.66   Implementation of some simple computer-based record systems early in the company's development would have greatly facilitated the provision of statistics and information requested by the new parent company and eased the employees through the integration process.

5.67   Introducing Human Resources administrative systems is not without risk. There are many 'off-the-shelf' packages that offer the possibility for maintaining employee records, training records, absence recording and recruitment administration. However, the risk in buying an 'off-the-shelf' system is that it may be inflexible and unable to do what you need it to do.

Case study

5.68   An organisation had a large number of casual employees who were paid on an ad hoc basis. The pay rates differed for each category of employee and they did not work fixed hours. In addition, the organisation had a number of 'add-on' items to its payroll that had developed historically. The organisation was growing and the small Human Resources function bought an 'off-the-shelf' package for employee record-keeping and payroll processing. The criterion for selection of the package was purely cost. They bought the cheapest package available with little consideration of its functionality. When the package was installed and the Human Resources team were trained in its use, it was found that it could not accommodate the ad hoc nature of the employees' hours and payment systems. In addition, it was not possible to make adjustments to the package to allow it to accommodate these categories of worker. As a result, the package was never used and the cost was not recovered.

5.69   It is, of course, possible to buy systems designed to meet an organisa-tion's own requirements. However, it is important to specify precisely what is required for the current situation, as well as looking at future requirements. Care must be taken to ensure that costs of implementation and subsequent operation of the system are controlled.

Case study

5.70   A large organisation took the decision to update their Human Resources administrative systems. They decided to buy an 'off-the-shelf' package that could be tailored to their needs. They set up a working group whose remit was to determine the specification for the new system and liaise with the provider organisation. Unfortunately the group was so large that they were unable to reach agreement on a realistic specification. The size of the system being introduced grew and grew – as did the costs of implementation! The result was that implementation was delayed by over twelve months, which caused significant demotivation amongst the Human Resources function. It also caused lack of support for the system amongst line managers in the organisation who were sceptical about repeated delays in the introduction of the new system.

Intranet-based systems

5.71   In many large organisations it is becoming more popular to develop intranet-based employee-record systems. These systems allow not only Human Resources administrators, but also managers and employees to access and update certain aspects of their own or their employees' records via a personal computer.

5.72   Human Resources professionals need to ensure that, when such systems are set up, access and security procedures and control systems are effective and include such matters as varying security access levels. This can enable Human Resources professionals to have wide, general access, with managers having restricted access to authorised parts of the records of employees in their department. Their access may be to view certain parts of the data and update others, e g holiday and sickness records or pay data at pay review time. It should also provide for individual employees to have access to their own data and allow them to update personal information, e g home address, telephone number or holiday requests.

5.73   Where such a system is introduced, Human Resources professionals will need to take particular care with the communication and training process. Failure to do this may result in lack of use of the system due to fear and suspicion. The end result of this will be that records are out of date and inaccurate.

5.74   Careful communication and training will be particularly necessary in organisations where not all employees have access to the system, for example in a non-office environment. In such an environment, Human Resources professionals will need to be aware that employees may have a fear of technology, which may restrict their inclination to use such a system. This can be overcome if PC terminals are provided in communal areas such as reception, restaurant areas, conference rooms, libraries and rest rooms.

However, consideration will need to be given to ensuring privacy of the terminals, otherwise individuals may not use them for fear of being over-looked.

5.75   A further risk associated with the introduction of such systems is that Human Resources administrative staff will fear a loss of control over the administrative systems. This may result in demotivation and loss of productivity. Human Resources professionals must take care to include the administrative employees in the communication and training process and to highlight the business benefits so that Human Resources administrators are supportive of the system even before it is introduced, and can actively support the new 'users'.

Managing attendance

5.76   With holiday, sickness and other absence records, the key risks are a lack of compliance with legislative, ie Inland Revenue, reporting and payment requirements. In addition, ineffective monitoring and thus lack of attention to absence can lead to poor efficiency, low morale and therefore a reduction in productivity or profit.

5.77   At the most basic level, the focus on attendance monitoring, if there is any at all, is for payment of Statutory Sick Pay. There is a requirement for Statutory Sick Pay purposes to maintain records of sickness absence and what Statutory Sick Pay payments have been made. Failure to keep accurate records could result in a significant fine from the Inland Revenue if an investigation takes place.

5.78   Regarding the general recording of absence, in some instances managers may record or monitor holidays taken, although most employees will know their own entitlement down to the last hour, half-day or day and will know whether their employer is not complying with the requirements of the Working Time Regulations 1998 for provision of a statutory 20 days of paid holiday. In some instances, record-keeping will fall to the Human Resources function simply because historically that has been seen as one of their functions. In some cases, organisations have chosen to address this by devolving the responsibility for record-keeping to line managers.

5.79   However, in many cases records do not begin to be formally maintained until a problem arises. Such a problem may be persistent or repeated intermittent sickness absence by one individual, which causes strain and demotivation among the rest of the team. It may be that there is excessive sickness absence in the organisation as a whole causing a downturn in productivity or profit. Alternatively, a department may experience a clash of holiday dates for key personnel because no one has monitored when employees have requested to be away.

5.80 Once such a problem does occur, however, it will fall to Human Resources professionals to work with the manager to deal with the situation. Following the resolution of the problem, the Human Resources function should put effective record-keeping mechanisms in place. These may be either centrally held record-keeping systems or systems developed at line-manager or departmental-manager levels to assist managers in monitoring such situations.

5.81 Whatever type of system is developed, there will be a need for careful planning and communication of the aims and functions of such a system. The Human Resources professional must carefully assess with the management team the key objectives of the recording system. If this assessment is not undertaken, there is a risk that any system implemented will not be used by management. Often in such a circumstance 'less is more' and the provision of some basic data, eg numbers of days sick per month per line manager or department, will be better than an in-depth statistical analysis.

Pay review administration

5.82 There are three main areas where risks may be created:

1   Incorrect processing of data for individuals within the organisation.
2   Inadequacy of internal systems for the calculation of pay increases.
3   The possibility of lack of parity of any system developed that may lead to equal pay claims.

5.83 Human Resources professionals will need to ensure that whatever pay review process is put in place is objective and equitable. It is therefore essential that administrative systems allow ease of processing and show records of the decisions that were taken and on what basis.

5.84 For individual employees this is essential since the concept of awarding increases in pay, particularly when these are related to performance-based mechanisms, are potentially very emotive.

5.85 If the system cannot demonstrate that each individual has been treated in exactly the same way as another, it will be very difficult to defend decisions taken on pay increases for individuals if they are not happy about the level of increase awarded.

Recruitment administration

5.86 One of the key areas where an organisation may unwittingly place itself at risk is that of recruitment administration. The areas of risk are wide ranging, and the key problem areas include possible discrimination claims and damage to the organisation's reputation.

5.87 There is significant employment legislation that impacts on the recruitment process. However the Sex Discrimination (Indirect Discrimination and Burden of Proof) Regulations 2001 place the burden of proof in sex discrimination cases on the defendant. In cases related to recruitment, this means that the recruiter must be able to show that they have not discriminated in any part of the recruitment process.

5.88 Employment legislation makes discrimination unlawful and recruiters must be aware of this. It is essential that recruitment administration systems and processes are robust so that, should the employer have to defend a claim, the evidence is already collected and collated in an objective format. Recruitment administration systems should be able to show that the organisation is following the principles of the Equal Pay Act 1970 that provides for equal pay for women and men in the same employment, where they are employed in like work, work rated as equivalent or work of equal value. Human Resources administrative systems should be able to demonstrate that the organisation has complied with the requirements of the Rehabilitation of Offenders Act 1974 in demonstrating that, where a criminal conviction is regarded as spent, there is no requirement for an individual to declare it to an employer or prospective employer and therefore the organisation has not taken this into account in the recruitment and selection decision.

5.89 The Sex Discrimination Act 1975 (amended 1986) and the Race Relations Act 1976 (amended 2000) both provide that it is unlawful for a person to discriminate against another person in the arrangements made for determining who should be offered employment, in the terms of offer, or by deliberately omitting to offer employment on the grounds of race (including colour, nationality or ethnic or national origins) or on the grounds of sex (including marital status and gender reassignment). In addition, the Employment Equality (Sexual Orientation) Regulations 2003 make it unlawful for employers to discriminate on the grounds of sexual orientation and the Employment Equality (Religion and Belief) Regulations 2003 make it unlawful for employers to discriminate on the grounds of religion or belief.

5.90 Recruitment administration systems can provide an effective defence to a claim by recording information on sex, race and ethnic origin. Such systems need to ensure that this information is kept separate from the information used to select. By the provision of statistics the systems can help to demonstrate that no particular group has been treated any differently from any other?

5.91 The Protection from Harassment Act 1997 provides that a person must not pursue a course of conduct that alarms another person or causes them distress and this applies equally in the recruitment process.

5.92   The Disability Discrimination Act 1995 has a big impact on recruitment administration. The Act makes it unlawful to discriminate against a person who has a physical or mental impairment that has a substantial or long-term effect on their ability to carry out normal day-to-day activities. The Act requires employers to take reasonable steps to accommodate a disabled person. In recruitment this includes arrangements to ensure that a disabled person is not disadvantaged in the selection process. This may include adjustments to the premises or making arrangements for a helper to accompany the candidate. Recruitment administration systems should also be in place to ensure that candidates are asked at the time of invitation to interview whether any special requirements or adjustments are necessary.

5.93   The Asylum and Immigration Act 1996 makes it an offence to employ a person who does not have authorisation from the UK immigration authorities to work in the UK. This means that recruitment administration systems should put in place nationality checks, eg passport and work permit checks to ensure that the organisation is complying with the legislative requirement. However, care should be taken so that in recruitment any checks that employers put in place for potential employees are applied to all applicants and do not contravene the Race Relations Act 1976.

5.94   The Data Protection Act 1998 provides an employee with the right to consent to the gathering of information about them during the interview process. It also controls the scope of monitoring systems that the employer can use in the workplace. In reality this means that the candidate could require the organisation to provide them with copies of any notes that have been taken as part of the interview process. Recruitment Administration systems must therefore make provision for effective note-taking and for retention of such notes for a period of time that is relevant to the organisation – as a minimum, three months or, ideally, six months.

5.95   The Part-Time Workers (Prevention of Less Favourable Treatment) Regulations 2000 make it unlawful for employers to treat part-timers less favourably than a comparable full-timer. As regards recruitment administration, the government best practice guidelines recommend that employers should periodically review whether a post on offer can be undertaken by a part-time worker. When approached by an applicant who wishes to work part-time, employers should give consideration to whether part-time arrangements could fulfil the requirements of the post and will need to establish an organisational need in order to justify turning down such a request.

5.96   In addition, the Human Rights Act 1998 puts an emphasis on an employee's right to privacy and freedom of expression and, as a result, recruiters should consider carefully the interview questions they ask and ensure that they are objective and based on job-related criteria.

5.97 In addition to UK legislation, there is significant impact from European directives. For example, the EC Equal Treatment Framework Directive requires all member states to prohibit age discrimination in employment by 2006.

5.98 The risks of discrimination claims are associated both with recruitment administration and with the robustness of the recruitment processes. The impact of employment legislation on the recruitment process was covered in **Chapter 4**.

5.99 Assuming that an organisation has robust recruitment processes in place, good record-keeping will be essential to enable the recruiter to demonstrate that no discrimination has occurred if a claim is made. The risks of a discrimination claim succeeding are extremely high, as can be seen from the examples below. The need to put mechanisms in place to reduce the risk has an impact for individual recruiters as well as the organisation as a whole.

5.100 Individuals may claim to Employment Tribunals about possible discrimination in recruitment. Any unlawful act of discrimination by an employee will be treated as if it was an act of discrimination by both the employee and employer. For example, in *Johnson v HM Prison Service* (1996) an award against the employer of £28,000 was made to a black prison officer who had been repeatedly discriminated against. In addition, an award of £500 was made against each of the two prison officers who were responsible for the discrimination.

5.101 Where an employee or prospective employee is successful in making a claim to an Employment Tribunal, there is no ceiling on the potential financial award that can be made in claims of race, sex or disability discrimination. The following are examples of recent compensation awards to individuals against their organisations:

- £103,000 against British Sugar for disability discrimination.
- £358,000 against the London Borough of Hackney for race discrimination.
- £234,362 against the London Borough of Southwark for sex discrimination.

5.102 All managers and employees within organisations have a responsibility to ensure that recruitment and selection decisions are not the subject of discriminatory practices, are based on organisational needs and on the individual's ability to do a job. However, it often falls to Human Resources professionals to ensure that these responsibilities are upheld. The best method of managing the risks in this area is to implement and maintain efficient and rigorous record-keeping.

5.103 Potential damage to the organisation's reputation may also arise as a result of ineffective processes or poor administration. An organisation may not acknowledge applications at all, or the time delay for acknowledgement may be extended. This could result in bad publicity for the organisation with applicants reporting to their friends that it is not a good organisation to apply to since no response is ever received. It is recognised that the burden on organisations for acknowledging applications is potentially great. There are some alternative mechanisms to reduce or remove this burden.

- Many organisations using e-recruitment often acknowledge applications via email, with emails being automatically generated.
- It is possible to use pre-printed acknowledgement cards to avoid the expense and time of producing individual acknowledgement letters.
- Where the response to an advertisement is predicted to be high, organisations may put a statement in the advertisement such as:

'We expect the volume of applications for this position to be high and we will therefore be unable to acknowledge each application individually. However we would like to thank you in advance for your application. If you have not heard from us within 4 weeks of applying this means that we have received applications from other candidates whose profiles more closely match our needs.'

5.104 Whilst this may appear a little harsh on first reading, it does serve the purpose of managing the expectations of the candidates and thus protecting the reputation of the organisation.

5.105 Human Resources professionals should also be aware of the legal requirement under the Employment Rights Act 1996 that a written statement of employment particulars must be given to all new employees within eight weeks of their joining the company. To qualify for a written statement under the legal provisions, an employee must be employed for one month or more. However many Human Resources professionals, when setting up recruitment systems, will actually arrange for the written statement to be issued with all offers of employment to ensure that the new employee is fully aware of the terms and conditions of employment before joining the organisation.

Administration of family-friendly policies

5.106 With the changes in employment legislation introduced in the Employment Relations Act 1999 and modified by the Employment Act in 2000 a number of family-friendly policies have been introduced into UK employment law. Such regulations place an onus on Human Resources functions to ensure that proper processes are in place to allow individuals their legal rights. Legislation now exists to make provision for maternity leave and pay, paternity leave and pay, adoption leave and pay, parental leave, time off for emergencies relating to dependants and for individuals to make a request to work flexibly.

5.107   Looking first at maternity rights, Human Resources administrative functions will need to have accurate records of employee start dates in order to ensure the correct maternity leave and pay provisions are afforded to pregnant employees. The regulations are specific in terms of numbers of weeks of entitlement, when eligibility for various aspects starts and when maternity leave can commence.

5.108   For example, all pregnant employees, irrespective of their length of service or hours of work, are entitled to a statutory 26 weeks' maternity leave known as the 'ordinary maternity leave period'. All employees must take a minimum of 2 weeks' maternity leave after the birth, and this is known as 'compulsory maternity leave'. However, employees with more than 26 weeks' service at the end of the fifteenth week before the Expected Week of Childbirth (EWC) are able to take an additional period of maternity leave that starts at the end of ordinary maternity leave and lasts for up to 26 weeks. This is known as 'additional maternity leave'.

5.109   By the end of the fifteenth week before the expected week of childbirth, an employee is required to notify her manager that she is pregnant, provide evidence of the expected week of childbirth in the form of a certificate from a GP or midwife and provide written notification of the date on which she intends to start ordinary maternity leave. The earliest date on which maternity leave may start is eleven weeks before the expected week of childbirth. The start date of maternity leave will be the earlier of:

- The date notified to the company as the start date of leave.
- The first day after the beginning of the fourth week before the EWC where the employee is absent from work as a result of a pregnancy-related illness.
- The day the baby is born.

5.110   The situation in respect of Statutory Maternity Pay is somewhat different as employees with at least 26 weeks' service by the end of the fifteenth week before the expected week of childbirth will be entitled to the following 26 weeks' Statutory Maternity Pay (SMP):

- Six weeks' pay at 90% of average earnings.
- 20 weeks at standard-rate SMP.

5.111   Payments are subject to tax and National Insurance. The UK government sets the rates of SMP.

5.112   Clearly the situation is quite complex. It can be further complicated where organisations have maternity provisions that are more beneficial than the statutory requirements.

5.113   It is clear that dates must be accurately calculated to ensure that the employee gets the appropriate entitlement and also provides notification to the organisation on time. The potential risk in not keeping these records accurately is an employee not receiving her legal entitlement, either to maternity leave or maternity pay. In practice should this be the case it would be hoped that this would be easily rectified through discussion with the individual concerned, although it could result in demotivation and possible stress for the employee at time when the organisation should be minimising the risks to the mother and her unborn child.

5.114 The worst-case scenario is that an employee makes a discrimination claim for unfair treatment as a result of her pregnancy. As we have already stated earlier in the chapter, there is no upper limit on the compensation payment for discrimination claims.

5.115 Thus it is vitally important to ensure that dates are accurately recorded and that diary notes or 'bring forward' notes are kept so that it will be evident what the applicable dates are and no important aspect will be missed. A solution to reduce the risk of data being recorded incorrectly or dates being forgotten or missed is to introduce a Notification of Maternity Leave form that an employee can use and that will capture all the relevant dates on one document. Use of such a document will ensure that all parties are working to the same information and that the information used complies with the legislative and Inland Revenue requirements and that employees are treated fairly. Once the organisation has received this notification, an acknowledgement must be issued to the employee within 28 days indicating the date on which the organisation will expect the employee to return to work.

5.116 Similar provisions apply for adoption leave and pay and thus the potential risks are similar to those that might be experienced if accurate maternity records are not maintained. Therefore the necessity for accurate record-keeping is the same. The provisions, however, apply only to employees who have worked continuously for the employer for 26 weeks leading into the week in which they are notified of being matched with a child for adoption. They must have been newly matched with a child for adoption by an approved adoption agency to be eligible for adoption leave.

5.117 Adopters are eligible for 26 weeks' Ordinary Adoption Leave (OAL) followed by 26 weeks Additional Adoption Leave (AAL). Leave may start from the date of the child's placement for adoption or from a fixed date up to 14 days before the expected date of placement. Adopters taking Ordinary Adoption Leave will be eligible for Statutory Adoption Pay (SAP) for 26 weeks on the same basis as the standard rate of Statutory Maternity Pay (SMP).

5.118 Adopters should notify the Company of their intention to take adoption leave within seven days of being notified by their adoption agency that they have been matched with a child for adoption. Employees should advise:

- When the child is expected to be placed with them.

- When they want their adoption leave to start.

5.119   Employees will have to provide a 'matching certificate' from their adoption agency as evidence of their entitlement to adoption leave and Statutory Adoption Pay.

5.120   There are also provisions that apply to paternity leave and statutory paternity pay, although the leave period is much shorter. The differences make the requirements more acute for accurate records to ensure the legislation is complied with. Employees who have worked continuously for their employer for 26 weeks up to the fifteenth week before the EWC or 26 weeks leading into the week in which they are matched with a child for adoption, will be eligible for up to two consecutive weeks' paternity leave if they meet the following conditions:

- They are the biological father of the child or the mother's husband or partner.
- They will have responsibility for the child's upbringing.
- They have recently been matched with a child for adoption.

5.121   Paternity leave may only be taken as complete weeks, not odd days, and employees may choose to take one week, or two consecutive weeks. Leave must be taken within 56 days of the actual date of the birth of the child. However, if the child is born early the leave must be taken within the period from the actual date of the birth up to 56 days after the EWC. Leave may be taken as follows:

- From the date of the child's birth.
- From a chosen number of days or weeks after the child's birth.
- From a chosen date.

5.122   Only one period of leave will be able to be taken at one time, irrespective of how many children are born as a result of the same pregnancy. Employees need to inform the organisation by the end of the fifteenth week before the EWC that they intend to take paternity leave. Again many employers use a standard form to ensure accurate data, but if a form is not used, the following information should be provided:

- The Expected Week of Childbirth.
- Whether they wish to take one or two weeks' leave.
- When they want their leave to start.

Employees should also confirm they meet the criteria stated above.

5.123   Employees may change the date they wish to commence their paternity leave by giving the organisation 28 days' notice. Employees will normally be eligible for Statutory Paternity Pay (SPP) at the prevailing rate, set by the government and reviewed from time to time. The rate of Statutory Paternity Pay (SPP) will normally be the same as the standard rate of

Statutory Maternity Pay. Employees whose average weekly earnings are below the Lower Earnings Limit for National Insurance will not qualify for SPP, but may be able to get Income Support. Information is available from the local Benefits Agency office.

5.124   So far, the risks we have considered with administration of family-friendly policies are primarily focused on internal problems or non-compliance with the legislation. Parental leave is interesting in that the entitlement is personal and travels with an individual from employer to employer. Parental leave is defined as leave taken to look after a child or to make arrangements for the good of the child. Employees with one years' continuous service have the right to parental leave provided they:

- are the parent (named on the birth certificate) of a child, or
- have adopted, a child under the age of 18, or
- have acquired formal parental responsibility for a child who is less than five years old.

5.125   The employee is entitled to take up to 13 weeks' parental leave, however the legal provision is *for each child.* The leave must be taken before the child's fifth birthday, hence the possibility that leave entitlement is carried over from one employer to another. Human Resources Administrators have to develop a mechanism for ensuring this information is passed on to the prospective employer and also that they have received this information from the previous employer of any new employee. If this is not undertaken, the organisation will not be complying with the legislative requirements. A possible mechanism for avoiding this risk is to request this information when taking up references for new employees and to pass this on when giving references. Whilst this mechanism can work, it is clearly not foolproof since the employee may not necessarily give their previous employer as a referee.

5.126   Unless there is a negotiated agreement in the workplace, there is a fallback scheme for parental leave entitlement that makes the situation reasonably simple to administer. A maximum of four weeks' parental leave can be taken in any one year, which must be taken in blocks of at least one week. Employees who work less than full-time hours will be entitled to leave on a pro-rata basis. Parental leave is unpaid. As with all employees who abuse the absence entitlements within organisations, there will be a need to monitor the taking of parental leave. If the situation is abused, the risk of implementing disciplinary procedures arises.

Administration of flexible working arrangements

5.127   Other risks with family-friendly policies could arise where an individual requests flexible working arrangements. For a number of reasons this is an area where there is a particular requirement for the administration procedures to be robust.

5.128 An employee who has 26 weeks' service and has a child under six or a disabled child under 18, has the right to request flexible working. In order to be eligible to make such a request, they must be mother, father, adopter, guardian or foster parent of the child or be the spouse or partner of the mother, father, adopter, guardian or foster parent. They must have, or expect to have, responsibility for the upbringing of the child and be making the application to enable them to care for the child. The request for flexible working must be made no later than two weeks before the child's sixth birthday (or eighteenth birthday if a disabled child). Only one request for flexible working may be made in any twelve-month period.

5.129 Already there is confusion here for administrative purposes since it will be noted that the other family-friendly policies have the cut-off at the child's fifth birthday, whereas for flexible working the cut-off is the child's sixth birthday. Effective practices and record-keeping mechanisms need to be in place to ensure that the correct details are retained.

5.130 If a request for flexible working is accepted, this will present administrative challenges for organisations, firstly in compiling the contract or confirmation letter that will need to accurately reflect the agreed flexible arrangement. A further administrative challenge arises if an employee does not work fixed hours, or works annual hours. It will be necessary to ensure that pay, holiday and attendance records are accurately maintained.

5.131 Flexible working arrangements might include:

- A change to the number of hours an employee works.
- A change to the times when an employee is required to work.
- Working from home.

5.132 Among the working patterns that may be considered are annual hours, flexible working, home working, job-sharing, staggered hours, shift working and term-time working. All such arrangements need adequate administrative support to ensure that they work both for the employee and the organisation. The possible risk of inadequate records in this area may mean that, for the organisation, the flexible arrangement does not work.

5.133 It is important when talking about family-friendly policies to mention the legal right to time off to deal with emergencies involving dependants. In principle this should be easy to monitor and control since time off should be only for emergencies and therefore by its nature should be relatively short in its duration. However, there is a need to ensure that employees do not take advantage of this provision. This will mean Human Resources professionals putting in place adequate procedures and guidelines to ensure that managers can effectively manage the situation.

Administration on termination of employment

5.134   There can be many reasons for an employee leaving an organisation and these will either be their own choice or the organisation's choice. When an individual leaves it is essential to ensure that the Human Resources administration associated with their leaving is performed accurately.

5.135   Where an employee leaves of their own accord, there is a need to ensure that the final salary payment is accurate and that any holiday entitlement not taken is paid in accordance with the requirements of the Working Time Regulations 1998, or the organisation's holiday entitlement. Where an accuracy of administration is achieved on the processing of a termination of employment, the employee will leave with a positive perspective. This will ensure a positive reputation outside the organisation for the future. Where an employee is asked to leave the organisation, for example as a result of a disciplinary hearing, it is vital to ensure that notice and other final payments are accurate as it may otherwise be impossible to recover these.

5.136   There is also a need for systems to allow for production of employee P45s as soon as possible after leaving. Where an employee moves to a new employer without a P45, they are likely to be placed on an emergency tax code in the new employment. Invariably this will result in them paying more tax than they need to and this may take some time to resolve. Again this could affect the reputation of the previous employer with the employee who has left, and others in the job market.

Internal and external relations

5.137   The internal impact for employees of the efficiency and accuracy of any administrative system used in Human Resources is paramount. Otherwise employees will lose motivation and key employees may leave the organisation.

5.138   The same goes for information provided internally by Human Resources functions. When a manager seeks information, timeliness of response is key, as is the accuracy of the information provided. If Human Resources functions are providing advice and guidance to managers on policies and procedures, there needs to be a consistent approach that portrays a consistent message. This will ensure that all parts of the organisation are operating in the same way and there will be no risk of incorrect actions. It will also avoid the risk of two parts of the organisation operating in different ways in the same situation, resulting in a poor reputation for the Human Resources department as being unable to provide appropriate administration or consistent advice.

5.139 However, there are also potential external risks associated with Human Resources Administrative systems. Any contact with the external environment could affect the external reputation of the organisation as whole. We have already seen that organisations should respond to job applications in a timely and efficient manner. Inefficiency and tardiness can cause any organisation, no matter what its size or prestige, to gain a poor reputation. Information on poor recruitment responses spreads more quickly than that of good processes.

WHAT CAN EMPLOYERS DO TO MINIMISE THE RISKS?

5.140 The risks associated with poor and inefficient Human Resources administration are numerous and varied. Impact can be felt inside an organisation with demotivated employees, plus potential legislative and Inland Revenue risks.

5.141 Set out below is a checklist that can be used by Human Resources professionals to identify and avoid or reduce some of the risks. Not all suggestions will be appropriate for all organisations and, in addition, at certain times in the development of an organisation, different approaches will be necessary.

Risk area	Risk treatments
Record and administrative systems	Introduce effective and appropriate systems as soon as possible to avoid future problems. Ensure systems are streamlined, ie that they are appropriate for the processes and policies they support, and are accurate, effective and efficient.
Accuracy of records	Ensure that accurate employee records are maintained from an early stage in an organisation's history and are checked and updated regularly with employees. Include an annual issue of computerised personal data to employees so that they can confirm its accuracy and request any changes.
Policies and procedures	Ensure that policies and procedures are linked to the administrative support systems.

Learning and development	Provide effective learning and development for Human Resources administrators so that they both understand the actual operation of the policies/procedures and also legislative and policy related reasons that created the need for the policy/procedure. This will avoid the mentality of 'It's always been done like this' and will also promote a culture that generates improvements to systems and practices.
Computerised systems	Introduce computerised record systems that are appropriate for current needs, but that will allow some flexibility for adaptation and change for the future. Ensure that a thorough process is used to identify the organisation's needs before a purchase decision is made. Do not allow the implementation team to 'get carried away' and enlarge the system beyond the actual need.
Maintaining quality	Introduce quality standards that assist the Human Resources function to internally monitor its own performance.
Systems reviews	Review such systems regularly to ensure their continued appropriateness and effectiveness. Such reviews might be incorporated as part of an employee satisfaction survey to gain a view on what those who experience the systems actually feel about them (see **Chapter 2** for details of 'Employee sensing surveys'). Feedback should also be obtained from those maintaining the systems.
Focus on internal administration	Consider outsourcing some Human Resources administration functions, so that Human Resources professionals can focus on activities that add greater value to the organisation.

The implications for human resources

5.142   We have seen in this chapter that the risk management implications for Human Resources administration are significant. The main implications are:

1   Administrative tasks must be performed efficiently and with complete accuracy. There must be checks in place to ensure accuracy and consistent robust systems.

2   Administrative systems must be appropriate to the profile, organisational culture and structure of the organisation and appropriate for the policies/procedures and processes they support. It is essential that

Human Resources administrative systems be reviewed on a regular basis to ensure that they continue to meet the needs of the organisation.

3 Human Resources professionals must have a detailed knowledge of the legislative areas that can be impacted by poor or inefficient administrative systems to ensure that there is no risk of non-compliance or incorrect interpretation of Inland Revenue regulations. In particular such areas as payroll, pay review and pay and benefits administration, administration of termination procedures including redundancy, managing attendance and administration of family friendly policies, including flexible working.

4 The importance of effectively communicating changes in administrative systems to all likely to be affected. In particular the communication will need to highlight the business justification and/or legislative impact that has brought about the change. There is also the need to provide timely, appropriate and effective learning and development for those working in Human Resources functions, line managers and, where they are directly involved, for employees.

5 Human Resources professionals should introduce quality standards and introduce monitoring mechanisms to ensure those standards are being met. There should also be an effective review mechanism that will enable Human Resources professionals to anticipate necessary administrative changes before the impact on the organisation is too great.

5.143 Where Human Resources professionals are aware of these implications and act on them positively, they will protect the organisation by minimising non-compliance with legislative and Inland Revenue provisions. They will also positively affect morale in the organisation by minimising the risk of lack of confidence in the Human Resources function as a result of poor administration. Human Resources professionals will therefore be able to move away from the routine tasks and add greater value to the organisation.

CHAPTER 6

Business transformation

INTRODUCTION

6.1   The old cliché, 'the only constant in organisations is change' is as true today as it has ever been. Although the volume of mergers and acquisitions has decreased somewhat in the early part of the twenty-first century compared with the late 1990s, business reorganisations, outsourcing and downsizing have continued to occupy many strategic Human Resources professionals. The signs are in 2004 that merger and acquisition activity is now on the increase again. Both types of activity require a high level of risk-awareness and risk management capability on the part of Human Resources professionals to navigate them successfully. A number of studies have indicated that about 70% to 80% of mergers actually destroy value when the new organisation is compared to the constituent organisations; that in 50% of mergers there is a drop in productivity during the first year following the merger; and that less than 25% of acquisitions earn their cost of capital. British businesses undertake major reorganisation on average once every three years. A recent report from the Chartered Institute of Personnel and Development, 'Reorganising for Success', (CIPD, 2003), indicates that around half of reorganisations fail to achieve their objectives, take longer to implement than planned and cost more than budgeted. In some cases, reorganisations have no positive impact, or even make matters worse.

6.2   It would appear, therefore, that some people in these organisations are not identifying and evaluating the risks appropriately, or, if they are, their implementation capabilities are less than required. This is not to suggest that it is possible to analyse and strategise so carefully that risk can be eliminated. Unknown factors, that the best-laid plans will not be able to circumvent, will frequently arise in implementing change in complex, large organisations. But we argue that Human Resources practitioners need to improve their capability of risk-assessment and risk management in planning for major change activities. There are two separate stages in major change programmes that need to be addressed separately, but in an integrated manner for risk assessment:

1   Assessing the need for, and planning, the change.
2   Implementing the change.

RISKS ASSOCIATED WITH ASSESSING THE NEED FOR, AND PLANNING, THE CHANGE

6.3　In the past, a major factor contributing to problems with mergers and acquisitions has been the failure to address the people issues early in the process. One of the most common causes quoted for failures of mergers is a mismatch of cultures. The Watson Wyatt (1999) survey on mergers and acquisitions (M&A) covering 165 top managers with global M&A experience found that cultural incompatibility was consistently rated as the most serious impediment to successful integration.

Case studies

6.4　In the late 1990s, the two pharmaceutical companies, GlaxoWellcome and SmithKline Beecham failed to agree on merger conditions due to a clash of cultures at the senior management level, which led to a breakdown of trust between the negotiating teams. Fortunately, this happened before, rather than after, the merger. In 2001, following senior management changes, new market pressures, further consolidation in the industry and shortcomings in their product pipelines, the two companies finally agreed merger conditions. Although the senior management had changed, the differences in the cultures of the two companies led to a painful transition period of several years before the merger was successfully completed.

6.5　Another example (*Journal News*, 2004) is the acquisition of Snapple by Quaker Oats for $1.7 billion that ended with its sale for $300 million three years later, due, it is suggested, to a clash of the two cultures.

In **Chapter 2**, we mentioned the impact of the differences in culture that slowed down the realisation of some of the savings from the integration of the Morrisons and Safeway retail organisations.

6.6　Often the focus of the due diligence process is very narrow, being led by legal and finance staff whose remit is to check that the finances and legal affairs are sound. A recent report of research carried out by the CIPD, Bacon & Woodrow and PricewaterhouseCoopers (CIPD, 2000) indicates that there are encouraging signs that Human Resources due diligence is increasingly performed well during deals. But the same report, disappointingly, shows that Human Resources professionals are less involved in the post-transaction integration activities. Involvement of Human Resources in the due diligence activities, however, does not always happen. According to the Watson Wyatt mergers and acquisitions survey (1999), Human Resources professionals are in many cases only involved in the latter stages, often after the merger has been announced. Lessons learned in the 1980s and 1990s indicate that it is essential to assess the people risks and to ensure that there is value to be realised from the Human Resources dimension of the merger.

6.7   One of the challenges for Human Resources professionals is to prove that they have the capability to add value to the pre-merger activities and to argue the case for the importance of the people issues that are often less tangible than the financial and legal issues. Incomes Data services (IDS), in conjunction with Watson Wyatt, have published *The International Human Resources Due Diligence Checklist* to give guidelines to Human Resources professionals on how to go about the pre-merger Human Resources due diligence (IDS, 2000). They argue the case for broad Human Resources due diligence that is not only directed at risk assessment in the legal sense, but is required to let the deal proceed. It should be sufficiently wide to find value and ensure that the subsequent integration of the acquired entity can proceed rapidly. This provides a challenge for many Human Resources professionals for whom this would be a venture into uncharted waters. If Human Resources professionals and the Human Resources function are to be recognised as strategic contributors, then they must be able to identify people risks and opportunities associated with the proposed merger or acquisition:

- They need to understand the strategic rationale for the deal, together with the constraints and opportunities.
- They need to be able to identify how the deal might create value – if at all – and identify specific Human Resources components that will add value. For instance, does the target organisation bring new skills that will complement existing skills or, indeed, open up new opportunities in research and development, technology, marketing or manufacturing that are in line with the merger or acquisition strategy?
- They need to provide a picture of the current state of the target organisation from a human resources perspective – with a balance sheet of risks and sources of value.
- They need to evaluate the cultural similarities and differences, so that effective integration programmes can be implemented rapidly once the deal is signed off.
- They must identify people issues that might prejudice a successful integration and the degree and nature of such risk.
- They will be required to develop contingency and action plans to ensure risks can be managed effectively and rapidly – possibly even changing the nature of the deal.
    - How do the salary policies and grading structures compare and what will be the costs of moving employees to a common salary structure? How do the pension and benefits policies compare; what will be the costs of harmonising policies; are there funding issues with the pension plan?
    - Are there risks of retaining key talent – either of executive

management or of specialists – and what would be the cost of implementing retention plans, say, through long-term incentives?

– What is the most effective way of involving employees at all stages in the merger process by establishing a comprehensive communication and involvement plan? What skills do the managers have for leading and communicating the change process and how can any gaps be filled by appropriate short-term training activities?

– They need to establish a flexible integration plan and project management process in advance, to ensure that senior management understand the time, resources and processes required to manage the transition.

6.8 The following are some of the risks identified in the IDS guidelines that Human Resources professionals need to address:

- Strategy attainment risks:
  - Loss of key staff.
  - Organisational mismatch – loss of synergies.
  - Communications failures.
  - Due diligence fails to create the basis for integration.
- Non-compliance risks:
  - Employment law on hiring, consultation, termination, terms and conditions.
  - Collective agreements on pay, hours of work, health and safety.
  - Adequate reserves for pensions.
- Business/operating risks:
  - Risk to continuity of activities (poor communication, poor integration plan).
  - Loss of key staff.
  - Risks to contracts.
  - Disruption caused by acquisition.
- Cultural risks:
  - Different values and cultural norms.
  - Ego clashes between top managers.
  - Different ethical standards.
  - Unconscious assumptions about power, status and decision-making.
- Financial risks:
  - Pensions and benefits.
  - Severance liabilities.
  - Loss of staff – retention costs.
  - Provisions for litigation.
  - Relocation costs.
  - Health and safety.

6.9   Once they get involved in the cut and thrust of merger discussions and negotiations, many senior managers find dealing with people issues too difficult or time consuming, or consider them irrelevant. It can be a real challenge for Human Resources professionals to gain their attention and to get them to focus on some of the people issues that could make or break the deal. Acquisitions can often run into difficulties because the decision-makers have not paid attention to relocation and redundancy costs or factors such as pension liabilities, long-term incentive plans or costs of integrating salary schemes. Failure to take into account the cost of losing key people, not only in terms of loss of expertise, business continuity and morale, but also of using search consultants to hire replacements, can seriously undermine the rationale for a merger or acquisition. Often the reason key people leave is that no one has taken the trouble to identify them and to talk to them about their future in the new organisation. Good people frequently do not wait to find out how things will pan out. They know their market value and are not prepared to wait around until someone more senior deigns to dispel the darkness of non-communication and offer them a position in the new organisation.

Case study

6.10   Valerie Garrow (*People Management* (2003)) reviewed the successful merger between the oil companies Total and Elf. Although both oil companies were French-owned, with head offices in Paris and global operations, their histories and ways of working were very different. Elf, state-owned until 1994, was seen as less flexible and dynamic than its rival, though its oil exploration business was recognised as more efficient. Also, shortly before acquiring Elf, Total had taken over the Belgian oil company, Fina. Employees who were already living with uncertainty faced more of the same.

6.11   In spite of these potential problems, the merger met many of its business objectives. The enlarged Total group had the critical mass to compete head-to-head with Exxon, Shell and other major oil firms. It achieved synergies in the form of productivity gains, asset sales and organic growth worth €4.8 billion (£3.3 billion) in 2003.

6.12   The Group Head of Job Evaluation said that early attention to people issues made a big contribution to the success of the merger. Initial decisions about the make-up of the new company's top teams and how the merger would be handled were made soon after Elf and Total reached agreement in September 1999. Dealing with such decisions quickly gave the group a head start when it came to explaining to employees why the merger was taking place and what would be involved. They learnt that concentrating on those issues from day one positively influenced the performance of the business and avoided any detrimental effect on the morale of employees.

6.13   By the end of 1999, the six-strong top team, 50 senior directors and around 300 other senior people had all been appointed. Most other appointments were made by the end of 2000. At the same time, large numbers of working groups were set up to recommend new structures, operating methods and ways of driving costs out of the group's diverse businesses. In the exploration and production business alone, there were more than 500 working groups, each based on a job family such as geophysics, Human Resources or finance, and including people from all levels of the organisation. As well as involving a wide cross-section of the workforce in creating the group, top management announced early on that it would try to appoint people from both Elf and Total to every team. Logistical difficulties, including some people's refusal to relocate, meant it wasn't always possible to achieve this. But top-level commitment to the principle of parity was important.

6.14   It also helped that the group promised to reduce headcount through voluntary early retirement, rather than compulsory redundancies, for at least three years. So the process of cutting the workforce from 132,000 worldwide to around 122,000 was a relatively painless one. That, along with a massive communications drive, minimised uncertainty throughout the group. It is uncertainty that hits employee morale and performance in many merged organisations – and can lead to failure to realise the benefits of the merger.

RISKS ASSOCIATED WITH IMPLEMENTING CHANGE

6.15   In this section we consider some of the potential risks in implementing major change and what the Human Resources professional can do to manage this risk. The changes can be in the form of mergers and acquisitions or major organisational changes, such as reorganisations, downsizing, changes in core business processes or introduction of new technology. Some specific changes currently affecting the workplace include:

- Traditional organisational structures are becoming more fluid: teams, often multi-disciplinary, are increasingly becoming the basic building block; new methods of managing are required.
- Changing employment contracts: more employees are on part-time and temporary contracts, more jobs are being outsourced, tight job definitions are being replaced by flexible role descriptions.
- Organisations have downsized and delayered: the common parlance is to run 'lean and mean' organisations through rigorous cost cutting, which means that individual employees have to carry more job responsibilities and heavier workloads and work under more pressure.

- Markets, technology and products are constantly changing: customers are becoming ever more demanding, quality and service standards are constantly going up.
- Outsourcing, to reduce the workforce to match the core competencies: many organisations have contracted out some of their services, including exporting jobs to low-cost areas such as the Far East. This includes professional services such as information technology and Human Resources in addition to the traditional areas such as catering, payroll and security.
- Technology and finance are no longer the primary sources of competitive advantage: human capital is becoming more critical to business performance in the knowledge-based economy.
- Over the past ten years, the constant theme has been consolidation through mergers and acquisitions. Although this has slowed in the most recent years due to the economic downturn, signs are that activity is picking up again.

6.16 Many books have been written on change implementation. This section is not intended to be a comprehensive guide for change implementation. It addresses the role Human Resources professionals can play in the identification, assessment and management of some of the major risks associated with major change programmes.

Planning, communication and participation

6.17 The belief that the senior management team can lead and drive the change completely from the top is a major risk in implementing major change programmes. One of the reasons why Human Resources professionals are not brought in to the discussion from the start is the belief that the primary objective is to drive for the business or financial objectives for the change. This can result in failure to recognise that without the energy, drive and commitment of the employees, the degree of achievement of the required outcomes from the change is likely to be less than desired. This belief and leadership behaviour is frequently reinforced by the justifiable concern for confidentiality and the need to prepare, plan and consider contingencies before embarking on the change or making it public. The end result is that the implementation of the change commences before a coherent communication and participation programme has been prepared and all the building blocks put in place. Or, alternatively, that the communication is all about what needs to be done rather than involving people in discussions about the reasons for the change and allowing time and space for them to make comments and express concerns and anxieties before commencing the change. Human Resources professionals need to be courageous in getting in front of the change steamroller and ensuring that the risks of a poorly thought-through communication and participation strategy are thoroughly reviewed with the senior team – and that options and alternatives are put in front of the team for consideration. It is a challenge for Human Resources professionals to move the senior team's thinking from the command and control perspective to understanding that the way they lead the change initiative will influence the culture of the organisation and the way that people view their roles and responsibilities, along with their commitment to the overall organisational goals.

Case study

6.18   This is an example of how not to manage change. We recently held discussions with Human Resources professionals in a business unit of a major corporation about a project to improve the quality of their performance-development process. The history of the organisation was that middle managers felt disempowered and that they took a very mechanistic approach to performance-development discussions with their direct reports. They demonstrated the belief that these discussions were of limited value and were just something that needed to be done to keep the Human Resources functions 'off their backs'. One of the objectives of the proposed project was to encourage and support these managers in changing the way that they interacted with their direct reports in these discussions and to build trust and openness from both participants in the discussions – with the aim of achieving higher levels of performance and commitment. Early in the discussions it was discovered that the corporate compensation group was planning to introduce a new job grading and performance-related pay system for middle managers. This was designed entirely by the corporate compensation team, who planned to launch the new salary plan on the middle-management group throughout the business at the same time as the performance development change programme started in the business unit. The compensation team were very concerned that nothing should be leaked to the managers prior to the launch. Human Resources professionals in the business unit felt that they were powerless to influence the way in which the pay programme was introduced. They were unwilling to recognise that the way in which the pay programme was being introduced reinforced the perceptions of the middle managers that they were disempowered and that the company merely required them to be obedient messengers and implementers of senior management actions. Our recommendations, that middle managers should be involved in the design of the new pay programme and that the aims and objectives should be discussed with them in advance, were rejected. Consequently, we declined to proceed with involvement in the performance-development project, as it was felt that the actions of the corporate compensation group and the senior management belied the professed aims of the changes to the performance development process.

Change and complexity

6.19   Another risk is the perception that change is a linear process and that a major change programme can be designed from start to finish and driven through the organisation single-mindedly. Of course any change programme needs careful planning and project management. But change in a large organisation, which is a complex system, is not necessarily a linear and predictable process. It is complex and difficult to implement with any degree of certainty. The change may be initiated, driven, controlled and managed from the top of the organisation or by a small chosen group but, for successful accomplishment, there will need to be active engagement and involvement of people involved in the change process to assist in influencing the change process itself. There will often be unexpected outcomes or 'side effects'. The risk for the organisation is that the change process is seen as a failure in some respects if it does not progress remorselessly from start to finish in the predicted manner. Human Resources professionals need to manage expectations of the senior team to regard the change programme as, to some extent, an experiment in progress and for the senior team to be prepared to respond positively to unexpected events in order to influence the outcome, rather than looking for someone to blame because the programme has 'gone off course'. This again emphasises the importance of involving employees in the process, as they will often be able to influence the course of events when the unexpected occurs.

Short-termism

6.20   Another risk of change is short-termism. It is a sobering fact that the average tenure of Chief Executive Officers in large corporations is three to five years. Given that this is the case, is it a surprise that so many corporate plans are, in fact, short term, even though they may argue that they have a long-term perspective? We discussed in **Chapter 2** the PricewaterhouseCoopers survey in 2002 that established that senior managers were making short-term cuts to please shareholders, not implementing long-term strategies to build businesses. What can the Human Resources professional do to ensure that the longer-term, as well as the short-term, effects of changes are properly considered? Often the longer-term effects of changes are on people issues, which Human Resources professionals are uniquely qualified to highlight, as we argue in **Chapter 2**. One approach is to build long-term incentives into the reward programme. But the trouble with many of these so-called long-term incentive plans is that they effectively have a three-year perspective. Share option plans often encourage managers to focus on activities that have short- to medium-term effects on the share price. Often when there is a pressing financial or business problem, the only option considered is the direct route to cutting costs urgently. The key contribution of the Human Resources professional is to evaluate carefully and thoroughly the people risks and benefits of the short-term plans, to develop otpions and alternatives for minimising the risks which also enable the achievement of the business objectives and to engage their senior colleagues in discussions on the benefits of these options. Who said the role of the strategic Human Resources professional was an easy one!

Psychological contract

6.21   The psychological contract is an area of high risk for the company in times of change – a risk that Human Resources professionals play an important part in managing.

6.22   The psychological contract refers to the perceptions of employees and employers of what their mutual obligations are towards each other. These obligations are often informal and imprecise and usually unwritten. They are built up from custom and practice and from expectations that have been built up from the recruitment and induction processes and from management communications over the years. From the employees' viewpoint, the psychological contract reflects what they are required to do, how they are required to behave and how they expect managers and the organisation to behave towards them. It affects the way they behave from day to day, influences their commitment to the job and the company and has a profound impact on job satisfaction and morale. It is based on a sense of what is 'fair and right' in terms of what the employee receives from the organisation and also on the quality of trust that exists between managers and employees. These two elements have been referred to as the *transactional* and *relational* elements of the contract. The Human Resources policies/procedures and the way that line managers implement them will influence the state of the psychological contract. Clearly, the importance of the psychological contract is its power to influence negatively or positively the performance of the employees and the business.

6.23   The psychological contract needs to be distinguished from the legal contract, which is a statement of the requirements of the job and the terms and conditions of employment. This is something to which the employee has probably contributed little, other than to sign when he or she was recruited.

6.24   The term 'psychological contract' was first used in the early 1960s, but it became more common in the 1990s, in large part due to the economic downturn with the consequent increase in downsizing and consolidation of organisations. At that time employers, recognising the impossibility of guaranteeing security of employment, instead began to talk to their employees about offering 'employability' by providing learning and development to enable employees to be more effective, and therefore more marketable. An unexpected outcome – to the organisation – was that employees increasingly recognised that their relationship with their organisation had changed and that if the organisation no longer felt an obligation to protect their jobs, then long-term loyalty from them towards their organisation was not something that they considered obliged to offer as their part of the contract. Employees, particularly professionals whose skills and talents were in high demand, became more mercenary in negotiating personal pay packages and moving to other organisations if their employer did not meet their expectations. Organisations found that the challenge of retaining these knowledge workers had greatly increased, that payroll costs escalated and that the complexity of incentive plans increased. This reflects the complexity of the psychological contract and its fragility at times of change, unless line managers exert effort to understand, honour and manage the contract, and, indeed, are prepared to discuss it openly and continuously with employees at times of change. The dip in performance or in employee motivation and morale that often follows mergers and acquisitions or major changes in organisations can often be due to the employees' response to perceived one-sided changes to the psychological contract by organisations.

6.25   To some extent, each person's psychological contract is specific to them, although there are elements that are common to many employees in an organisation. The relational elements of the contract are based on trust and loyalty and the transactional elements are based on expectations about reward and benefits for effort, commitment and performance, both in relation to individuals and groups inside and outside the organisation as well as in absolute terms. When an organisation is going through change, both the relational and transactional elements of the contract are likely to be affected, which could have positive or negative effects on performance and the ability to deliver the change effectively. Human Resources professionals, in conjunction with line managers, need to address both elements of the contract at a time of change. The risk is that workload invariably increases at a time of change and managers may feel that they need to focus on their tangible deliverables and targets, rather than on something as intangible as the psychological contract.

6.26   Research carried out by Roffey Park (2003) suggests that transactional contracts should be dealt with in a transactional way with clarity on short-term, quid pro quo economic arrangements. But where previous psychological contracts were relational, resorting to short-term bonuses and rewards may signal to employees that the relationship no longer operates on trust. While relational contracts are more complex, they may be less expensive. The Roffey Park research identifies the following principles for managing the psychological contract in the wake of a merger or acquisition:

- Recognise that a breach of the psychological contract presents a serious business risk.
- Post-merger strategy should be viewed as an opportunity to lay the foundations for new relationships. Acquirers of an organisation in a merger or acquisition should assess whether the predominant psychological contract is 'relational' or 'transactional' and plan their strategy accordingly.
- Early communication at a time of change is the foundation stone for a new psychological contract. Organisations should be cautious when making promises, as if they do not deliver, the perceived breach of the contract will have serious consequences.
- Good Human Resources practices can oil the wheels when organisations are negotiating a new 'deal' with employees.

6.27 A factsheet published by the Chartered Institute of Personnel and Development (CIPD, May 2003) also summarises some key insights and lessons for managing the psychological contract:

- Avoid redundancies whenever possible: redundancies lower morale.
- Review how far the organisation's practices reflect its values: employees tend to have low trust in the organisation if the values are not put into practice.
- Train line managers in people-management skills: employees are more likely to trust their line manager than 'the organisation'.
- Ensure middle managers commit to key messages: mixed messages will have a negative influence on employee attitudes.
- Inform and consult employees: they are more likely to see the outcome as fair.
- Take care to fulfil commitments you make to employees: managers say employees show more commitment to their employer than vice versa.
- Consider if you need to renegotiate what employees are entitled to expect: they may feel let down when circumstances change.
- Put more effort into managing change: employees believe change is badly managed.
- Give employees more responsibility: autonomy increases satisfaction.
- Use employee attitude surveys to get a clear idea of what is happening in the organisation: employees often do not share senior managers' views of reality.
- Don't rely on tight management and close supervision: this will reduce employee satisfaction.

- Use recruitment and appraisal processes to clarify the 'deal': employee expectations are influenced by a number of factors.
- If you can't keep a promise, explain why: failure to do so is often punished by loss of trust.
- Trust employees to do a good job: most are highly motivated to do so and will respond to the trust you show in them.
- Don't rely on performance management systems to motivate employees: you need to engage hearts and minds.

Case study

6.28 The merger of Safeway and Morrisons illustrates some of the principles of managing the psychological contract at a time of change (People Management December, 2003).

6.29 Morrisons, the supermarket chain, made a bid for retailer Safeway in January 2003. Fierce competition in the retail sector prompted other supermarket chains to get involved, resulting in a referral to the Competition Commission. The long, drawn-out process of review subjected Safeway to months of uncertainty and presented them with the challenge of maintaining a 'business as usual' approach in difficult circumstances. The senior managers and the Human Resources team realised they needed a strategy to maintain employee motivation and morale.

6.30 Initially, employees went through the traditional change responses of feeling shock, denial and blame. Safeway's Human Resources Director recognised that the motivation and commitment of Safeway's people would be the key to its survival during this period.

6.31 The Human Resources team developed an overall strategy and action plan with two broad objectives: first, to retain as many good people as possible, and second, to improve morale and motivation of colleagues.

6.32 Financial incentives were introduced to encourage people to stay, but the Human Resources team also recognised that many employees at Safeway had a relational psychological contract, in that they were long-serving and not motivated purely by money. So the Human Resources team knew they had to appeal to them in different ways.

6.33 The retention strategy focused on giving enhanced redundancy entitlements to more than 2,000 employees, at all levels of the company, who would be most vulnerable to redundancy after a takeover. In the motivation strategy there were four main streams of activity: a leadership programme, communication, reward and recognition, and learning and development.

6.34   Rather than turning off learning and development because of uncertainty about the future, Safeway invested in it more and ran more courses and programmes than before. They placed emphasis on helping people to prepare for the future, cope with the uncertainty and review their strengths and development areas. Also, they implemented a leadership programme for more than 250 senior managers to update their skills on leading and coaching their teams in times of uncertainty. The outcomes of this programme, which were changed leadership behaviours, were linked with the senior-level bonus incentives.

6.35   They also created a new model of leadership behaviour to help leaders become more visible and approachable and introduced a development programme covering the new behaviours needed by leaders, with greater focus on leading in times of ambiguity and resilience during change.

6.36   Clear communication was also fundamental. Safeway set up an area on the intranet called 'Our Future', to keep people informed of new developments. There was a 'Meeting for everyone', at least every four weeks at the Hayes head office where board members discussed the situation and opened the floor to questions. This was video-linked to distribution depots and regional offices, so people could gain access nationwide. Five 'colleague councils' were also set up where employee representatives met senior people for briefings, the results of which were then cascaded throughout the organisation, and social events were arranged, to create a sense of team camaraderie.

6.37   The company also made motivational payments to 25,000 staff, as part of their efforts to maintain business performance, put in place outplacement services and offered financial advice. Safeway also maintained a credible business performance, with no significant change in labour turnover, which amazed city speculators who believed that the company would haemorrhage staff.

6.38   From January to December 2003, the customer-service monitoring programme showed that Safeway consistently improved performance every month.

Failure to communicate effectively

6.39   One of the more common risks associated with major change is the failure to communicate effectively about the change, both in advance of the 'kick off' and during the implementation phase. There are many reasons for this. For example:

- In the period following a merger or introduction of a major change, workloads increase significantly. Managers are often working frenetically to organise and structure their parts of the new organisation, select people for new positions, introduce new work processes and meet their work targets. While all this is going on, they are expected to make time to draft plans and prepare for regular communications sessions with their employees.

- Middle managers are often largely in the dark about plans and progress and do not know what is happening when change is going on. Not surprisingly, they do not feel confident about standing in front of their employees to act as a spokesperson for the organisation.

- Managers may not have the skills needed for managing major change. Often they have never had to do anything like this in the past and feel less than confident about how to go about it.

- The managers may be concerned about their own position in the new organisation and be wrestling with their own fears and uncertainties about the future:
    - Will I have a job in the new organisation? What will happen to my pension/school fees/mortgage if I am made redundant?
    - If I do get a job in the new organisation, what will my new boss be like to work with?
    - Do I want to commit to taking apart the department or group I have built up lovingly over the years and rebuilding it?
    - How will I handle the stress of telling some of the people I have worked with over the years that they are going to lose their jobs?
    - What is the strategy for this change anyway, and would I agree with it if I knew what it was?

6.40   For all of these reasons, it is important to have a well-thought-through strategy and plan for regular communication throughout the organisation. The Human Resources professional and the communication specialist can work together to play an important part in addressing the risks associated with poor communications. The first task is to get commitment from the senior team, not just to giving nodding assent to the importance of communication, but to a sustained programme of communication. They need to be seen to 'walk the talk' and model the behaviours to their middle managers – and to budget for the costs of communications. Then Human Resources professionals and the communication specialist need to prepare an innovative communications strategy that makes the best use of the many communications vehicles available. For example, intranet, newsletters, emails, merger magazines, communications cascades for face-to-face briefings, the use of video and telephone-conferencing when groups are geographically remote, question and answer sessions, meet the management 'town hall' sessions. Human Resources professionals can encourage and support their client group managers in holding regular communications meetings. This is especially important when it seems as though there is nothing to communicate, as this allows employees to ask questions, or just to be reassured that nothing significant has happened or has been planned since the last communication. Grapevines and rumour love a vacuum. If managers do not talk to their people because, 'there is nothing to communicate' you can guarantee that the grapevine will generate some juicy 'facts' for people to worry or gossip about.

6.41   The element of the strategy that is most often missed out is the need for targeted training for managers *and* employees on the change process and how to survive and thrive under change. The approach taken needs to be creative and focused on the specific needs of the people and organisation at the time.

Case study

6.42   Two companies were in discussion about the possibility of merging. As soon as the merger talks were announced, the Human Resources function designed a series of one-hour workshops or briefing sessions on change for employees and managers that addressed the relational aspects of the psychological contract. These were delivered successively over several months, addressing the change process, the psychology and emotions that arise during mergers, effective communications and the factors that make for success or failure in mergers. These workshops were designed and delivered separately for managers and employees. Once the merger was underway, this set of programmes was followed by another series of briefing sessions on the policy and processes that would be used for people issues, such as selection, job grading, promotion and redundancy – the transactional aspect of the psychological contract. This modelled the need for continuous two-way communication and provided the opportunity for questions and discussion during the period of uncertainty. It also provided information for both employees and managers and gave them confidence that they were involved in generating policy and practice for the new organisation. It enabled managers to communicate with a sense of authority when they met with their employees.

IMPORTANCE OF RELATIONSHIPS

The effect of change on relationships and trust

6.43   Our definition of organisations is that they are networks of relationships between people who come together with a common purpose. Most people would agree that the quality of relationships among people in an organisation is important to business performance. Yet not many people or organisations devote sustained effort to building and improving the quality of relationships at work. One way in which this is approached is through team-building or team-development activities, although these activities often have only limited benefit in terms of the whole organisation. The proliferation in the UK since the 1970s of reward policies and philosophies that reward individual performance has not helped to build organisational cultures that value relationships and relationship-building activities.

6.44 It is only possible to make things happen at work by working with and through other people. Few people have such an individualist role that they can work completely independently from other people in the organisation.

6.45 At times of change there is an increased risk that relationships may become strained or weakened, with a consequent negative effect on business performance. This is a serious risk for the organisation. What can Human Resources professionals do to assess, maintain and improve the quality of relationships at times of organisational stress? What criteria would they use to decide on the quality of relationships and how would they measure them? At a gut level they might decide that the quality of a relationship – whether it is good or bad – could be judged by how the partners feel about each other and their relationship; how well their interactions serve a given purpose; and also by how they treat each other. It is not easy to measure aspects of personal relationships such as intimacy, mutual feelings, level of trust, responsibility, accountability and obligation.

Five dimensions of relationships

6.46 There are well-established psychometric approaches for looking at interpersonal or team relationships, but there are not many well-established methodologies for assessing the quality of organisational relationships. The Relationships Foundation, led by Michael Schluter, has done some ground-breaking work in this area in recent years (Schluter and Lee, 1993; Baker, 1996). Schluter and Lee have developed the concept of 'relational proximity', which they describe as a description, not of the personalities or geographical positions of two individuals, but of the interaction between them. They argue that a sense of mutual responsibility, duty and obligation will only develop generally when there is relational proximity. They define this according to five dimensions, which they label:

1   **Commonality – valuing similarity and difference** – This is the extent to which people share a common purpose, vision or experience. It is the motivation that drives the development and growth of a relationship. It describes the conditions that enable mutual understanding and trust to

exist between people and includes valuing similarities and differences. The importance of sharing common values and a clear vision of the future reflects commonality.

2   **Parity – the use and abuse of power** – This reflects sharing of mutual respect and involvement in a relationship and the balance of power between the parties. It recognises that there is not necessarily equality in a relationship in terms of role or status, but that there is equality in terms of mutual recognition of personal worth. It recognises that there will be, to some extent, a sharing of power, for example, in terms of participating fully in decision-making. The importance of parity is reflected in the relative smoothness in introducing change when employees are involved in the change process, rather than imposing the change on them unilaterally.

3   **Multiplexity – breadth of knowledge of the parties about each other** – Multiplexity looks at the breadth and scope of the relationship – the extent to which people have contact in more than one role or relationship. If people have contact in a wide range of situations, they are more likely to understand each other's experiences, abilities and feelings and less likely to misinterpret each other's motives, behaviours or words. In business transformations, such as mergers and acquisitions, the lack of multiplexity can lead to misunderstandings.

4   **Continuity – shared time over time** – Continuity reflects the length and stability of the relationship – the frequency and regularity of the contact and the period over which contact is maintained. The length and stability of the relationship creates the opportunity for individual rapport and improved mutual understanding to develop. Loss of continuity in relationships in times of change can lead to some of the problems experienced in implementing change.

5   **Directness – the quality of the communication process** – Directness is the amount of direct, face-to-face contact in the relationship, as distinct from indirect communication by mail, telephone or Email. It reflects the quality and effectiveness of communication in the relationship. Direct contact, in itself, will not build the relationship, unless the communication is open and honest.

6.47   It is perhaps unfortunate that Schluter and Lee have developed this jargon, but on the other hand it is understandable that this is necessary in order to define something as nebulous as the quality of relationships. The five dimensions are seen as preconditions for close relationships to exist. They are regarded as necessary, but not sufficient, conditions for effective relationships. In other words, relational proximity does not guarantee a sense of co-operation and mutual obligation, but they will not exist without it.

Relational Health Audit

6.48 The Relationships Foundation has developed the Relational Health Audit, based on the five dimensions of relational proximity, as a diagnostic tool to enable organisations to develop and pro-actively manage their key internal and external relationships. It has been tested in a wide variety of organisations and contexts leading to improved relationships and performance. It offers Human Resources professionals an effective mechanism for surfacing key issues and enabling a structured discussion between individuals and groups on how to improve their working relationships.

Specific examples of risk from changes that impact relationships

6.49 Some of the relational risks that can occur as a result of organisational change have been discussed under the section on the psychological contract. Others that can arise are discussed in this section.

Leadership style

6.50 When organisations undergo major change, the styles of leadership that were effective in the 'old' organisation may no longer be fully effective in the new scheme of things. For example, the removal of levels of control to reduce bureaucracy and increase speed and decision-making, with the consequent increase in the traditional span of managerial responsibility, requires different approaches to leadership and management.

6.51 Leadership, in an organisation that embraces the value of growing and developing its people, is not something that derives primarily from role or status. It is a relationship of influence. It is a relationship between two people or between a person and a group where one person seeks to influence the vision, values, attitudes or behaviours of others. If this definition is accepted, it follows that everyone in an organisation may exercise leadership, regardless of role or status. The days of command and control organisations and styles of leadership are largely over. Leadership, particularly in organisations employing highly skilled people and knowledge workers, or in organisations that require their people to work with a high level of autonomy or accountability, is not solely or primarily about power or control, although these may be necessary attributes for leaders to display. Organisationally, effective leadership is a relationship of influence with a purpose – namely maintaining the community and achieving the desired mission.

6.52 When organisations are undergoing change, the dynamics of the relationships are also in flux. If this is not recognised and leaders are not paying attention to the evolution in the relational dimensions of the psychological contract, there is a real risk to the effective implementation of the change. The Human Resources professional needs to be in touch with this aspect of the change and to coach the senior managers and others in how they need to develop their attitudes, skills and behaviours in order to lead effectively.

Increasing size and globalism

6.53   During the 1980s and 1990s, consolidation of companies was a recurring theme in business and commerce. This resulted in the emergence of ever-larger companies, often at a global level. The effect on relationships has been considerable. People who used to walk down the corridor for a business discussion or meet over lunch are now based in different locations, often in different countries – or even in different companies if there has been outsourcing of some of the services. Day-to-day communication is, at best, by telephone and, more likely, by email. Face-to-face communication is diminished and relationships can only be developed slowly, if at all, through time-consuming travel. The time demands of increasing travel mean that people are more pressured and do not have (or resent the opportunity cost of) the time to develop close working relationships with colleagues with whom they are interdependent. Some companies have relocated people to larger sites from several smaller sites, which, while improving the ease of communication at work, has had a negative effect on family, community and social relationships. Because of the amount of travel, people schedule a series of meetings at the destination to make the most effective use of their time. When the CEO or other senior managers change top-level meeting dates to suit their changing agenda, this has a horrific impact on the work programmes and planning of people throughout the organisation as the rescheduling of meetings of the people affected by the top-level change cascades down to their direct reports and onward throughout the organisation.

6.54   The results of consolidation affect the culture of the organisation. Either a new culture will emerge by default – in which case it may not necessarily be supportive of the organisation's objectives – or Human Resources professionals will identify the stresses and strains in the organisation and implement initiatives to develop organisational behaviours and practices that will be functional. There are no universal panaceas. Some areas that can be considered to include the following.

MEETING STRATEGY AND TRAVEL POLICY

6.55   Is there discipline to ensure that meetings are only cancelled or rescheduled if this is absolutely essential? Are management meetings scheduled for the year in advance to ensure that people can schedule their diaries and plan their annual schedule in advance to make the best use of travel time? What discipline is there to keep the amount of travel to a minimum? Is travel time and cost monitored?

WORKPLACE DESIGN

6.56   The increasing size of organisations makes the free-flowing, informal contact between people whose work is interdependent more of a challenge to achieve. More attention needs to be given to workplace design to support and facilitate these interactions. Human Resources professionals, in consultation with the Facilities Director, can contribute to the design of new facilities or redesign the floor plate of existing facilities to facilitate good communications and interactions between interdependent working groups.

Case study

6.57   Following a relocation of people from several sites to a single site, the Human Resources Director for the area worked together with the senior managers to investigate the possibility of locating all the members of multidisciplinary project teams in a common floor area in buildings. This was a major shift in past practice as people had always been located in departments according to their disciplines. It required detailed consultation to review the pros and cons of the proposal until eventually an implementation plan was agreed to. The resultant improvement in work interactions and quality of relationships was remarkable and led to a significant improvement in job satisfaction and reduction of stress as well as increase in productivity.

Busy-ness

6.58   Reduction in headcount, removal of layers of management and increasing focus on delivery of results has led to increasing pressure on people. The days when there was time for a conversation at the coffee machine are long since past. People are often quoted in the media as saying that much of the fun has gone out of work, as colleagues do not have time to chat or to tell a joke. A 'hurry culture' has developed in many organisations. This hurry culture is to be distinguished from the pressure of work that will exist in any high-performance organisation. It is more of a mindset where people feel over-pressurised all the time and do not make time to plan and organise their priorities effectively. Hurry is not usually the result of a disordered schedule; it is the result of a disordered mind. Ultimately it is one of the causes of stress-related illness that are on the increase in the western world. Carl Jung is quoted as saying: 'Hurry is not of the devil, it *is* the devil.' It can lead to superficiality, mediocrity and lower standards in our approach to work. A concomitant area of damage is to the quality of relationships. The danger is that people become too busy to help each other; too busy to listen properly; too busy to take time to establish rapport and understand the unspoken as well as the spoken communication; too busy to coach and develop their employees.

6.59   There are no simple answers. The challenges for Human Resources professionals is to ensure that they are keeping their finger on the pulse of the organisation and are aware of the existence of the hurry culture and its effect on organisational effectiveness. They need to engage different levels of managers and employees in discussion on causes of, and solutions for, the 'hurry culture' when it arises. Ultimately, the organisation (that is, the people in it) needs to decide what it values most; whether driving for the utmost profit in the short term at the expense of its most important asset is more important than investing in the long-term development of that asset. We believe that, ironically, investing in people and paying attention to the relational aspects of work will lead to greater profitability as well as a better quality of life.

IMPLICATIONS FOR HUMAN RESOURCES

6.60   There are many risks in planning and implementing change to achieve business transformation. In our opinion, the most significant risk to success is the potential to fail to manage the relational aspects of the change. Consideration of the foregoing raises some important issues and questions for Human Resources professionals. It indicates a number of areas where they can take the lead in helping organisations to respond more effectively to influences driving organisational transformation. It sheds light on some priorities they need to develop to enable organisations to be more agile and responsive to internal and external influences in order to renew themselves and to maintain competitive advantage in times of rapid change. Some suggested priorities will now be discussed.

Relational Health Audit

6.61   The Relational Health Audit can be used to identify areas of strength and weakness in working relationships in organisations. The outcomes of the audit can form the basis of discussions within the working groups to understand the issues and to agree steps to improve them.

Relational Impact Statement

6.62 Another value-adding risk assessment step that the Human Resources professional can contribute to the organisation in times of change is to consider the potential effect on working relationships of proposed changes – in other words, to draw up a Relational Impact Statement (Clark, 1996) using the dimensions of relational proximity as a framework. This will provide a basis for senior managers to consider objectively the implications of their proposed changes that stretch beyond the immediate business and organisational objectives.

A new core competency for Human Resources professionals?

6.63 The ability to assess the relational impact of change programmes on organisations should become a core competency for Human Resources professionals. In the efforts of organisations to become employers of choice, this could provide a source of competitive advantage. People are looking for organisations to become more flexible in their approach to work, enabling them to achieve a better integration or harmonisation of the various domains in their life – sometimes called 'work–life balance'. When Human Resources professionals become more proficient at understanding and communicating the potential impact on working relationships of changes, this will enable dialogue to take place with employees around their needs and expectations in the light of changes.

Relational leadership – a new model?

6.64 Models of leadership that are relational, driven by vision and shaped by the values of the leader are not new. Books and publications have hit the bookshelves from a steady stream of authors, such as Peter Drucker, Peter Block, Warren Bennis, Max DePree, Tom Peters, Steven Covey, Charles Handy and Peter Senge. One of the greatest challenges to leaders, as organisations continue to surf the white water of continuous change in technology, market economics, consolidation in sectors and globalisation, is to provide leadership that enables people to respond with resilience and energy to change and to thrive on it. This requires leadership that values the individual in deed, not just in word; that encourages people to take intelligent risks; that forgives honest mistakes if people are prepared to face up to them and learn from them; that invests in people's development and personal growth. This type of leadership has a focus on the long-term success of the organisation. It requires strong character and courage from senior leaders in the face of an investment community whose horizons are often no longer than the next quarter's results and who are impatient if the steady growth in the share price stumbles even for one quarter. The ever-increasing rate of change in the population of the FTSE 100 and the S&P 500 indicates that few companies are surviving unchanged, which perhaps encourages short-term thinking for survival or an 'eat or be eaten' philosophy.

6.65   In this environment, leadership that nurtures a vision and values and a relational leadership style that will attract and retain top talent in an increasingly competitive recruitment market is more likely to develop the resilience, agility and flexibility required for success in today's markets and to be the employer of choice for the new generation of employees. Nurturing the appropriate leadership style for the organisation remains a continuing challenge for Human Resources professionals. The risks of failing to do this are high.

REFERENCES

Baker, N, (ed) *Building a Relational Society*. Aldershot: Ashgate Publishing, 1996

CIPD, *The People Management Implications of Mergers and Acquisitions*. London: CIPD, 2000

CIPD, *Reorganising for Success*. London: CIPD, 2003

CIPD, *Managing the Psychological Contract*. London: CIPD, May 2003

Clark, M, Relational Impact Statements, in Baker, N (ed), *Building a Relational Society*. Aldershot: Ashgate Publishing, 1996

IDS, *The International Human Resources Due Diligence Checklist*, London 2000, ISBN 0 905525 79 5

The Journal News.com, 25 June, 2004

A. Arking, 'Perfect Fit' People Management, 25 September, 34–35, 2003

V. Garrow 'Pact to the Future' People Management, 18 December, 26–30, 2003

Relationships Foundation, see www.relationshipsfoundation.org

Roffey Park, *Managing on the Edge: Psychological Contracts in Transition*, Research Report, 2003

Schluter, M, and Lee, D, *The R Factor*. London: Hodder and Stoughton, 1993

Watson Wyatt Worldwide, Mergers and Acquisitions Survey 1998/1999, 1999

CHAPTER 7

Building partnerships – the way forward

INTRODUCTION

7.1   This chapter describes the model of Human Resources involvement as business partners with senior managers, other managers and with employees. It also discusses the importance of partnership between line managers in different functions, between managers and employees and between employees.

7.2   It reviews the importance, for risk management, of trust levels within organisations. It discusses factors that build or destroy trust and proposes how Human Resources professionals can influence these. It addresses the relevance of limiting beliefs for risk management and discusses how these limiting beliefs can be surfaced and changed. Finally, it reviews situations where trust is not appropriate.

MANAGING PEOPLE RISK BY BUILDING STRATEGIC PARTNERSHIPS WITHIN THE ORGANISATION

7.3   People risks pervade the whole organisation. Although the primary accountability for identifying people risks lies with Human Resources professionals, they are not able to solve all the underlying issues, in order to mitigate the risks, by themselves. They need to work together with other people and departments to deal with issues. This includes both line and other staff functions. In many organisations this interdepartmental and interpersonal co-operation works well, at least between the Human Resources function and some other support departments. But, in our experience, such co-operation is not universal. So what are some of the strategic partnerships that Human Resources professionals need to build within the organisation?

7.4   We suggest that there are three primary areas where Human Resources Professionals need to build partnerships:

- With the senior management of the organisation.
- With other line and support functions.
- With employees.

Managing people risk by building strategic partnerships with senior management

7.5   In **Chapter 2**, we discussed the challenge for Human Resources professionals to become strategic partners with senior management in the organisation by establishing their credibility in contributing to the development and delivery of the business strategy and plan and thereby gaining a place at the table with the senior management team.

Benefits

7.6   Many benefits arise from the establishment of these partnerships. These include:

- Ensuring that people risks and opportunities are incorporated into the organisation's strategy and business plan.
- Ensuring that the managers are tuned in to people issues and risks, and take these into account in their day-to-day work and planning.
- Ensuring that the Human Resources professionals are involved in the business activities of their client groups and they are able to diagnose people issues and partner with the management team to address them.
- Enabling Human Resources professionals to influence the way things are done in the organisation to develop a culture that supports the mitigation of people risks and encourages innovation and intelligent risk-taking. For example:
  - By addressing the 'blame and excuses' culture that exists in many organisations and ensuring that mistakes and perceived failures are used as an opportunity for individual and group learning.
  - By identifying people who take intelligent risks and recognising and celebrating their efforts.
  - By developing reward and recognition policies and practices that encourage the desired behaviours.
- Modelling a win–win philosophy and behaviours of openness, directness and accountability that encourage people to contract openly about their expectations and requirements from each other in their working relationships. It provides a vehicle for confronting, openly and productively, failure to deliver what was contracted.
- Facilitating the development of a learning strategy that supports the business strategy and has the full commitment of senior management.

Risks

7.7   Although many benefits result from this partnership between Human Resources professionals and the senior management of the organisation, there are also risks that need to be recognised and minimised. The primary risk that we have encountered is the risk of loss by the Human Resources professionals of an independent view and of the ability to be the 'therapeutic thorn in the flesh' for managers.

7.8 As a result of their close identification with the organisational strategy and business plan, many Human Resources professionals have, or are perceived by employees to have, lost their ability to seriously challenge, or offer an independent perspective on, the policies and practices of the organisation. They are seen as agents of the organisation. They are not seen as being able to understand and influence the many changes in the psychological contract that have been made unilaterally by managers, as we discussed in **Chapter 6**.

7.9 Employees (including many managers) feel that their job security and promotion prospects, which they thought were part of their deal with the organisation, have been lost in the sustained activity of cost-cutting, downsizing and delayering. This unilateral breach of the psychological contract has soured relationships and engendered feelings of betrayal and a breakdown, to some extent, of trust between individuals and the organisation.

7.10 At the same time, employees perceive the senior management in the organisation to be getting a much better bargain in terms of pay increases, even when they do not hit their performance targets. Even if they lose their jobs, whether it is due to mergers or reorganisations or even due to their failure to deliver the organisational performance that was expected, senior managers appear to other employees to be well protected with large severance deals.

7.11 A further, perhaps more subtle, factor that has contributed to feelings of betrayal and loss of trust is the perceived failure by senior management to balance the requirements for cost-cutting with those for innovation, investment in human capital and improvements in quality of service. Many employees and managers feel that they have been let down in their desire to provide high quality in the products and services they deliver. They feel that some of the cost-cutting has been ill-considered and short-term, and that they are unable to work to the high standards that they wish. The evidence reported in the PricewaterhouseCoopers (2002) survey we discussed in **Chapter 2** provides some support for these views. Human Resources professionals need to address the potential risk to the organisation of this decline in levels of trust.

Managing people risk by building partnership with other line and support functions

7.12 Some of our comments about building partnerships with senior managers apply also to partnerships with other line managers. This partnership between the Head of Human Resources and the top-level managers needs to be replicated by the other levels of Human Resources professionals with other staff functions and with their client group managers and their management teams.

Benefits

7.13 People are a source of risk in organisations. They are also important for managing risk. Well-trained and aware employees can understand, anticipate and respond effectively to risks. People risks pervade the whole organisation. Effective management of risk, therefore, requires an organisation-wide approach and an avoidance of a 'silo' approach where each department addresses (or fails to address) the risk independently of others. Human Resources professionals need to take a lead in establishing a co-ordinated organisation-wide approach to the management of risk, building partnerships with line and other support functions.

BENEFITS OF PARTNERSHIPS WITH OTHER SUPPORT FUNCTIONS

7.14 By enabling individuals and groups to work synergistically to bring their individual experience and skills to the management of the organisation-wide risks, Human Resources professionals can take a lead in building partnerships with other support functions that benefit the organisation. Often, the Finance Department takes the lead in cost-cutting exercises, as they have access to all the financial data. They sometimes, however, appear not to understand, or choose to ignore, the people consequences and costs of some of the actions they recommend. If Human Resources professionals have built up a partnership with their Finance counterparts, they can work powerfully together to draw up a more comprehensive plan, which minimises the people risks.

CASE STUDY

7.15 On one occasion the head of a global business unit had made the decision in principle to close a site in a European country, as it appeared to him that this would result in a significant cost saving. He asked the Finance Director to produce a paper to demonstrate the cost savings to the company. As this was at a very early stage, the exercise was highly confidential and the executive committee had not been involved in discussion about the plan. The Head of Human Resources had established a very strong partnership with the Finance Director. The latter recognised that there could be hidden people risks that he was not aware of and asked the Human Resources Director to work with him on producing the plan. When they considered all the direct and indirect costs, they discovered:

- Employment law in the country where site closure was to take place required the creation of a social plan and its negotiation with the Works Council. This plan outlined in detail the support that would be provided to employees at the time of the site closure. The costs of the social plan, legally required to close a site in that country, were much greater than in the UK or the USA, and would significantly add to the pay-back time.
- There were many people at the site with skills in rare supply, and that the company would not want to lose. If the site were to close, the company would need to consider options for retaining those skills.
- There were significant employee relations implications, due to the militant trade union activity at the site under threat. There was a manufacturing site (part of another business unit in the company) near the site under threat and the Head of Human Resources was aware that there was a high risk of a strike at the manufacturing site if closure of the other site were to be proposed.
- The Head of Human Resources was also aware that the local Member of Parliament was a government minister who had expressed public concern about the activities of multinationals in shutting down operations in the country. He would be likely to get personally involved if the proposal were to proceed.
- The Head of Human Resources knew that there had been rumours amongst the country management team about closure of the site and that the country management of the other business unit were opposed to this.

7.16   As a result of the partnership between Finance and Human Resources, they were able to put a much more thorough report to the Head of the Business Unit outlining the true costs and cost savings, the political risks of the proposal and making recommendations about how to proceed. They saved the Head of the Business Unit a great deal of embarrassment within the company and enabled him to consider all the options and to come up with a plan that took into consideration all the risks and opportunities.

Case study

7.17   In one company, the Human Resources function were beginning to build partnerships with other support functions, and were vaguely aware that there was a risk management group that looked after insurance risks for the company. One day the insurance function was contacted and asked a question about insurance cover for the company car fleet. During the discussion, it was discovered – to the surprise of

Human Resources – that the organisation also insured against many of the people risks, such as tribunal claims, litigations against the company for alleged transgressions of employment law, medical insurance and sickness insurance. Perhaps Human Resources should not have been surprised? When the matter was explored further, it was discovered that the insurance function was largely unaware about Human Resources policy and practices in these and other areas. As a result, Human Resources were able to set up discussions to explore how the two departments could work more closely together and, as a result, were able to save the company large amounts of money.

BENEFITS OF PARTNERSHIPS WITH LINE DEPARTMENTS

7.18   Many people risks are common across departments in the organisation. To address them effectively, Human Resources professionals need to gain the confidence of line managers that they will not encumber them with numerous restrictions and bureaucracy and make their life difficult. They need to be able to demonstrate that they will, in fact, help them to improve the effectiveness of their departments.

7.19   Managing people is managing risk. If managers fail consistently to manage performance effectively, introducing remedial or disciplinary action when appropriate, the performance of the organisation is negatively affected. Similarly, as we discuss elsewhere in the book, there are risks if managers are not able to have open and honest discussions with their people about performance improvement and career development. Human Resources professionals need to establish credibility with line managers and to partner with them on managing their people risks.

Risks

7.20

- Fear of interference – even though managers have the best will in the world to co-operate, there is an inherent tendency for many to want to protect their area of work from interference by 'outsiders'. Unfortunately, they sometimes see Human Resources professionals as outsiders. Life is too short and managers are under too much pressure to deliver their results to want to take the risk of letting someone they perceive as a bureaucrat ferret round in their departments finding problems and issues that will require them to use some of their valuable time to solve.
- Turf issues – protection of 'turf', or territory, is perhaps one of the greatest risks in gaining co-operation between line managers. It is just

as great a risk for co-operation between staff functions. Would Human Resources professionals ever admit to being guilty of not wanting the Finance manager to get too involved in, or knowledgeable about, their budgeting activities and where they hide the fat in their budgets against emergencies? Or what about the legal department or the tax department? Have Human Resources professionals ever kept them at arm's length, because of the perception that they might be advised that they cannot do what they want to do?

- Competition – another risk is the desire to be seen to be the primary contributor to solving problems and issues so that the 'hero' gets the recognition and reward. Of course, in most organisations the players are too sophisticated to do this openly. More often the lack of co-operation, or even competition, is subtle and under the surface. Some manager's work to a win–lose script. They do not seem to be aware, or to want to accept that, if there is sufficient trust and co-operation, everyone can win in many situations. Unfortunately, many reward systems, at least as they are applied, do not always encourage co-operation between managers.

7.21   The core issue here is one of trust. Do the parties involved trust each other to have their best interests at heart? We will return to a discussion of trust and its importance for managing risk later in this chapter.

Benefits of managing people risk by building partnership with employees

Benefits

7.22   Earlier, we discussed the impact of changes in, and perceived betrayals of, the psychological contract on employees' motivation, morale and levels of trust. The following research supports this perspective:

- In an opinion poll commissioned by the *Financial Times* (Worcester 2003), 80% of the people polled said that Directors of large UK companies cannot be relied on to tell the truth.
- Jones (2001) reported that, in a Wirthlin Worldwide study of employees, 67% said that they were committed to their employers. Only 38% felt their employers were committed to them.
- Maitland (2003) suggested that distance breeds mistrust. Employees invariably hold their immediate supervisors in higher regard than their senior managers.
- Kourdi and Bibb (2004) reported that, although 96% of people rated

trust as either 'important' or 'essential' in the workplace, on average respondents trusted only 57% of their colleagues.

7.23   The indicators are that there is room for improvement in the levels of trust in the workplace – trust between colleagues and trust between employees and senior management.

7.24   Human Resources professionals have an important part to play in acting as honest brokers in the organisation, in encouraging openness and communication about impending changes and their effect on the psychological contract and in maintaining a positive environment where mistakes are recognised as part of doing business and do not lead to blame and sanctions. They can be key agents in coaching managers in order to facilitate an environment where trust can flourish. Even more importantly, in their interactions with managers and employees, Human Resources professionals can model behaviours that build trust.

Risks

7.25

- There is a danger that Human Resources professionals can be perceived by managers as the 'shop stewards' of employees.
- Managers might perceive them as not sufficiently business focused.
- This could reinforce the perception of Human Resources as primarily welfare orientated.
- Confidences must be kept absolutely by Human Resources professionals. Betrayal of confidential discussions with an employee to a manager could destroy trust in the Human Resources function.

TRUST AND RISK MANAGEMENT

7.26   Building successful working relationships and partnerships is of fundamental importance in managing risk in organisations. Trust is fundamental to creating these relationships. In the current climate of pressure for growth and profits, corporate greed, cost-cutting and changes in the psychological contract, that all have the potential to destroy trust, Human Resources professionals have a key role to play in acting as the agents for co-ordination of the tensions and conflicting interests in organisations. They are uniquely placed to encourage leaders and employees to invest sustained, focused attention on building and maintaining trust within the organisation.

7.27   Failure to build levels of trust in organisations carries the risk that it could result in:

- Turf issues and less than effective working across organisational inter-
  faces.
- Employee commitment and discretionary effort being suboptimal.
- Disconnection between the interests of the organisation and those of the
  employee.
- Loss of innovation, risk taking and creative energy.
- Reduced organisational performance and increased operating costs.

7.28   Although these are significant people risks that Human Resources
professionals need to manage, there does not appear to be much evidence that
Human Resources professionals recognise that building and maintaining trust
needs to be a specific objective.

7.29   In the following sections we explore the meaning of trust in the
context of the workplace, factors that build or destroy trust, the value of trust
to the organisation, and the role of Human Resources professionals in
developing trust in the organisation.

What is trust?

7.30   The concept of trust is, in some respects, complex. There have been
many high-profile issues in recent months that have caused much debate
about trust:

- The failure of governance and integrity that led to corporate scandals
  such as Enron, WorldCom, Parmalat.
- The shortcomings by the UK financial services community such as the
  misselling of endowment mortgages and pensions.
- The so-called 'fat cat' syndrome, whereby top management in some
  companies seem to feather their own nests while employees lower in the
  organisation do not see their prosperity increasing at even a fraction of
  that pace.

7.31   Newspaper columnists debate whether, as a society, levels of trust are
increasing or decreasing. Our view is that discussions on generic levels of
trust can be confusing and are probably meaningless. Although it can
sometimes be helpful in the debate to consider a hypothetical deposit in a
bank of trust, this is not a universally useful concept. Usually we think of trust
much more specifically. We trust a specific person to do something they have
promised. We trust them to tell the truth and not to deceive us. If they
consistently fail to deliver what they have promised or to tell the truth, then
we will probably become suspicious about them and think we do not trust that
person at all.

Definition

7.32   There have been many definitions of trust, some of which ascend into the realms of moral philosophy. In the context of trust at work, we consider three types of trust:

1   'I trust you to do what you say you will do' – This relates to contracting between parties and the (old-fashioned?) concept in business and finance that 'my word is my bond'. If I say I will do something, then I will do it. Or if there is some reason why I am not able to deliver what I promised, I will come back to you, explain what has changed and seek to renegotiate the contract.

2   'I trust you to have the competency or the capacity to be able to do what you promise to do' – If a manager promises that he will guarantee his people that there will be no redundancies under any circumstances, their experience of the market conditions might lead them to judge that he is incapable of delivering that promise, even if they think that he believes what he says. For example, the company might be taken over by a competitor.

3   'I trust you to have my best interests at heart' – This touches on the area of mutual support and co-operation. I trust you not to deceive me or manipulate me for your personal benefit. I trust you to share information that I need to enable me to do my job. If things go wrong, I expect you to look after my interests as well as your own. In a manager/employee relationship, it would include the expectation that the manager will support the employee if things go wrong, rather than putting all the blame on the employee. It includes the values of openness and honesty.

Developing trust takes time

7.33   Trust is built up over time. If we have found that you are trustworthy over several deals, then we are likely to be more open and trusting in the way that we work with you. We will trust commitments that you make, rather than looking for penalty clauses or checks and balances and controls to be built into the deal. Also, if our experience of people over the years is that they are trustworthy, we will be more likely to be ready to enter into a trusting relationship with new people.

WHY TRUST IS IMPORTANT

Trust and co-operation

7.34   Is trust essential? We have all worked reasonably well with people we did not trust. We knew that they were motivated primarily by self-interest and that we could expect them to look for opportunities to advance themselves at our expense. In a convoluted sense, we could trust them to be untrustworthy. Yes, of course we could work with them. But we did not enjoy the working relationship as much as we did with those we could trust. Also, there were occasions when we did not share information with the other people, because we knew they would use it to their advantage and our disadvantage. They probably acted the same towards us. The working relationship was not as effective as it could have been if we had trusted each other and co-operated together. To achieve co-operation and optimum working relationships, a degree of trust is an essential ingredient. Before we decide to co-operate, we ask ourselves whether we trust the other party. The same applies to co-operation between departments as well as individuals, or between the organisation and the employee. There is an element of reciprocity in co-operation and trust. In relationships that involve frequent interactions we are more likely to trust people if they demonstrate trust in us. Conversely, if I co-operate because I trust you to reciprocate, but then you don't, I will be less likely to co-operate when we next interact.

'Trust lubricates cooperation. The greater the level of trust, the greater the likelihood of cooperation. And cooperation itself breeds trust' (Putnam, 1993).

7.35 Or, as Warren Bennis (1985) said,

'Trust is the lubrication that makes organisations work.'

Trust and innovation

7.36 Trust is important for co-operation. It is also important for the release and exercise of creativity and innovation. Trust and risk are inextricably intertwined. People feel able to take intelligent risks when there is trust. The more trust that exists in a relationship, the more people feel free to take intelligent risks. As trust and risk grow, so does creativity. Conversely, fear or insecurity tends to reduce trust, creativity and restrict intelligent risk taking. When people move into new areas of thinking or try to develop new ways of doing things they often, consciously or unconsciously, feel vulnerable. Because of their vulnerability, people often need a supportive relationship to encourage them to press on when the inevitable difficulties arise. There are, of course, always the exceptions of people who are so confident or so inspired by their quest that they will press forward into new areas regardless of, or in spite of, lack of support or opposition. But, in organisations in general, innovation and intelligent risk taking thrives in a supportive environment.

DEVELOPING AN ENVIRONMENT THAT BUILDS AND MAINTAINS TRUST

7.37   Leaders cannot legislate for trust or demand it. They must model trustworthy behaviour and demonstrate trust in others in order to grow trust in the organisation. If people prove they are not trustworthy, leaders need to confront the negative behaviour. The role of the leader is to promote an environment where trust can flourish and where deviousness and intrigue is exposed. The easiest way to destroy trust is to let untrustworthy behaviour go unchecked.

7.38   There are a number of factors that build and maintain trust, and these will now be discussed.

Factors that build trust

Commitment

7.39   'I believe that the person is sufficiently interested in me to invest time and effort in our relationship.' Leaders need to invest in the personal and professional growth and development of their people.

Communication

7.40

'I believe the person is open and honest and will tell me the whole truth. He will not hold back information from me. He will listen to me and understand my viewpoint, rather than forcing his views on me.'

7.41

- There needs to be good two-way communication between different levels of management and employees. Managers need to tell the truth even when it is difficult.
- Employees need to be involved appropriately in decision-making and consulted about changes, in an appropriate way (remembering that consultation covers all points in the spectrum between the two extremes of 'We have decided to do this and are telling you about it in advance so that you can comment on it' to 'We need to introduce a change and we want to involve you in considering alternatives and making recommendations on how we should proceed').

- Employees need to be able to take proposals and concerns to their manager and know that their viewpoint will be listened to and considered fully.
- There needs to be high levels of integrity in the organisation. If people agree to do something, then they need to deliver it.
- Managers need to be prepared to hear hard truths and celebrate people who point up tough issues to them. They need to avoid shooting the messenger at all costs.

Competence

7.42

'This person understands the implications of what he has promised and has the skills and abilities to deliver what we have agreed will be done.'

People need to be trained so that they are able to perform to a high standard of competence. Inability by a person or a team to deliver results effectively and on time destroys trust. Departmental managers need to introduce performance measures for what their department delivers to their internal (and external) customers and review the results with them regularly. They should survey their client groups to gather information on how the performance of their department is perceived.

Fairness

7.43

'She will treat me fairly and will look after my best interests as well as her own.'

In the work context, this means that remuneration and recognition policies and practices demonstrate that the rewards are shared fairly. People need to feel that they are treated with respect and fairness when it comes to performance appraisal or career development discussions. They need to feel that their boss will support them when things go wrong and not try to put the blame on them.

Integrity

7.44

'This person is reliable. She will do what she says she will do.'

People need to know that their peers and manager will not behave one way on one occasion and in a different way on another occasion; that they will behave honourably and not say one thing to their face and a different thing behind their back. Managers and employees need to 'walk the talk'.

7.45   Miles Protter (2004) uses the illustration:

'Integrity builds trust

Trust builds relationships

Relationships build business (profits)'

7.46   Leaders can build trust by practising zero tolerance on any behaviour that lacks integrity or respect or shows signs of intrigue.

Purpose

7.47

'We share a common purpose and values.'

People need to know what the values of the organisation are and to feel confident that these will act as a touchstone for everyone's behaviour. Although there will be differences of viewpoint between managers and their people, the manager needs to provide an environment where these differences can be talked about and managed openly and positively.

Contracting skills and accountability

7.48

'I know what is expected of me and I am held accountable. Equally, others hold themselves accountable to deliver on agreements.'

Human Resources professionals need to facilitate the development of good contracting skills within the organisation so that people are very clear about their mutual expectations of what will be delivered, in what manner, by whom and by what date. On too many occasions, situations arise where conflict arises due to failed expectations, because people have made assumptions about what they have agreed with each other, rather than specifying precisely what has and has not been agreed.

7.49   Once the 'contract' has been agreed, it is important that both parties accept their individual accountability for fulfilling it. In our experience accountability is more talked about in organisations than it is practised. Often it takes a degree of courage to confront failure to deliver on an agreement, particularly if it is a more senior person who is failing to deliver to a more junior person. The danger is that the event is glossed over and that the subsequent feelings of betrayal eat away at trust and respect. Equally, however, some managers seem reluctant to confront, in a calm and open way, failure to deliver by their employees. We have heard managers say that it would alienate the employee if the manager were direct in confronting failure. Usually the opposite turns out to be the case when the manager is persuaded to confront the issue.

7.50   Equally, if an employee has promised to complete a task by a certain date, then, if there is slippage, they should go to their manager and explain what is happening and negotiate over what needs to be done to achieve the date, or renegotiate the date and agree what can be done to minimise the consequences of the slippage. Failure to do this diminishes the manager's trust in the employee.

7.51   It is also important that people accept mutual accountability for the delivering of an agreement. It is not good enough for one party to say, 'Well he promised to do it, so it is entirely his responsibility.'

7.52   In the preceding example, if it becomes clear to the manager that the employee is not delivering a result by the time that was agreed, the manager has two options. Either they can feel disappointed or angry and can wait until the delivery date has passed and then discipline the employee (assuming they do not gloss over the failure). This may occasionally be appropriate if this is a recurring pattern of behaviour for the employee. Or they may recognise that the employee is, for example, feeling embarrassed or fearful about admitting failure, in which case they can remind them of what was agreed and explore the reasons for the slippage, using the failure as a learning event. In other words, the manager can hold the employee accountable for what was promised. By modelling openness and directness, she can coach the employee on how to act with accountability.

7.53   Similarly, hard issues need to be confronted in a timely manner. If an employee has excessive absences or wastes time at work, it is important to confront the behaviour. Other employees will watch what the manager does. Confronting inappropriate behaviour will build trust and reduce risk.

Recruitment practice

7.54

'We hire managers who support the values of the organisation and live according to them.'

Personal qualities are as important as technical or professional capabilities in managers. To enable trust to grow, Human Resources professionals need to ensure that the organisation hires leaders who are capable of forming positive, trusting interpersonal relationships with people who report to them and to their peers and higher management.

Role of Human Resources

7.55 Human Resources professionals play a special role in promoting trust. They coach managers and supervisors about all the appropriate factors that build trust we have described above. They also influence the way power and control is used in the organisation by initiating debate with senior managers and developing and implementing suitable policies and practices. They are influential in growing and developing the appropriate social norms among people. Above all, they model the appropriate behaviours to build trust.

7.56 As Mahatma Gandhi said,

'First we must become the change we want to see.'

Factors that destroy trust

7.57 Trust is built up over a period of time. But it can be destroyed in an instant when someone betrays our trust. In **Chapter 2** we discussed how betrayal of the psychological contract destroys trust. Insecurity and fear for the future can also destroy trust and openness, as can over-harsh punishment of failure.

7.58 People at the top of organisations are often driven, ambitious people who have been ruthless in achieving their ambitions. Top managers are surrounded by ambitious people who are impatient to move into their positions. The way senior managers behave sets the tone for the rest of the organisation. If they are seen to be jockeying for power and position, then people below them will take the cue that this is the way to get on in the organisation – unless their personal values are different. Leaders can provide fertile ground that encourages intrigue and destroys trust by ignoring the factors in the preceding section.

REBUILDING TRUST

7.59 Rebuilding trust once it has been betrayed is difficult. In an earlier section, we discussed the reductions in levels of trust due to job insecurity, outsourcing, lack of investment in training, cost-cutting and inequitable distribution of reward between top managers and employees. Many organisations urgently need to address the issue of trust and commitment. Human Resources professionals are ideally placed to play a leading role in this activity.

Return to strong core values

7.60   One possible solution is to return to strong core values.

- This does not mean top management producing laminated cards to post on the walls of the workplace. A sincere initiative to debate and re-establish consensus on the core values with all the employees in the organisation can build trust, promote strong working relationships and cement mutual commitment to a common purpose. Trust needs to be one of the core values to be discussed. We have found that many managers find it difficult to engage employees in open discussion on trust and betrayal. Human Resources professionals need to coach and support them and provide them with suitable 'scripts', as appropriate, to enable them to get started.
- This is not a quick fix. It will require investment of time, money and energy. It will be important to spend time debating and understanding what the values would look like in terms of behaviours in the organisation. Then these behaviours or competencies will need to be built into the performance review and reward systems. It will be important to make clear that these values and behaviours are aspirational rather than something that can be introduced by management edict. They will act as a compass and a touchstone for everyone to hold themselves and each other accountable while the values and behaviours become part and parcel of the way things get done in the organisation.
- People will need to support and challenge each other when behaviours do not match the values. Leaders will need to walk the talk and be prepared for their team to challenge them when they fall short. Employees will need to have the courage to speak up when the behaviours of their colleagues or leaders fail to measure up to the values. The important thing is that this is done in a spirit of support and co-operation rather than as a witch-hunt.

7.61   This provides a great opportunity for Human Resources professionals to take a leadership role in gaining leadership commitment and engaging the organisation.

Explore limiting beliefs

7.62   When trust is damaged in an organisation, the 'shadow side' of the organisation often becomes important. The shadow side represents the beliefs about what really happens in this organisation and what behaviour really gets rewarded, regardless of the official view. It may seem cynical when uncovered, but it represents people's perceptions about what life is really like in this organisation. We call it the shadow side because it is hidden. People do not like to talk openly in front of managers about these perspectives, because trust levels are low and these beliefs are often diametrically opposite to the espoused values and beliefs in the organisation. They are represented by the comments that people make in the corridors after meetings or the work topics that get talked about in the pub after work.

7.63   Examples of comments representing the shadow side would be:

> 'We say that we value people, but did you see how the boss shouted at John in the meeting because he did not like him saying that it was irresponsible to promise the customer a delivery date we could not meet?'

Or,

> 'We say that integrity is a core value, yet the pay award for staff was 3%, whereas the top managers got an increase of 18% this year. Call that fair!'

7.64   The risk is that managers may expect employees to accept, and to behave in line with, the stated values even if leaders do not model these values. Employees observe how people behave in contradiction to the stated values and how this is rewarded. They learn to behave in the way that achieves reward and advancement.

Case study

7.65   An organisation stated that customer care and the health and safety of its employees were core values. In an efficiency drive to increase profits, field service engineers were given increases in their targets from an average of eight calls per day to ten. The outcome was that measures of customer satisfaction decreased sharply. When they investigated, managers found that this was because the service engineers were spending less time with customers and were not listening to their issues carefully. They had also cut corners in the way they did the servicing in order to meet their tougher targets. In addition, the number of vehicle accidents increased because of the time pressures in getting between customers on the tighter schedule.

7.66   The limiting beliefs in an organisation need to be identified and then brought out into the open, discussed and acted upon. These limiting beliefs exist in every organisation. They grow when trust is low or has been damaged. They are rarely explicit. They are demonstrated by the difference between what people say and what they do. Their importance is that they demonstrate where the beliefs and behaviours in the organisation are misaligned with the espoused core values and the statements about how things should be done.

7.67   Examples of limiting beliefs might be:

- In this organisation you need to keep your head down if you disagree with the boss otherwise you will get it shot off.
- It is not worth complaining in communications meetings because nothing ever gets done.
- You need to cover your back when you deal with other departments because you can't trust them to do what they say.
- Innovation is supposed to be a value, but if you try something new and it doesn't work you'll get roasted.
- Development reviews are a waste of time, because nothing ever gets followed up.

7.68   Human Resources professionals have an important role to play in getting the senior managers' support to identify and address these limiting beliefs and in coaching them to understand what they demonstrate. The danger is that managers could react impatiently, because the limiting beliefs challenge the espoused values and expose behaviours that are perceived negatively by employees. Human Resources professionals can model openness and trust in the way that they gather the information and facilitate managers' responses to it.

7.69   Engaging in open, honest dialogue and not denigrating people who have the courage to speak out and tell it how it really is, are essential behaviours that are needed to bring limiting beliefs to the surface. Of course, the problem is that these are precisely the behaviours that are lacking in organisations with a strong shadow side. Initial actions to move to open dialogue will probably be met initially with cynicism and mistrust. It is important to persist through this initial stage and demonstrate commitment to changing the way things are. Encouraging a climate of openness by talking with employees and listening will assist in identifying the limiting beliefs. Ensuring that action is taken to realign behaviours with the core values and related behaviours will contribute to restoring trust. One way to realign behaviours is to identify, through discussion and participation, a new set of beliefs to replace the limiting beliefs.

7.70   It is important to remember that trust is not a matter of technique but of character. General Eisenhower illustrated this, as recorded by his biographer, Stephen Ambrose (1983):

> 'I know only one method of operation,' Eisenhower wrote in his diary; 'To be as honest with others as I am with myself.'

> 'When President Roosevelt pressured him to get tough with the local French, Eisenhower refused, saying, 'My whole strength in dealing with the French has been based on my refusal to quibble or to stoop to any kind of subterfuge or double dealing.'

'The French responded. One official told him, 'As long as *you* say that I believe it.' Another said, 'I have found that you will not lie or evade in any dealings with us, even when it appears you could easily do so.'

'Indeed, whenever associates described Eisenhower, there was one word that almost all of them, superiors or subordinates, used. It was 'trust.' People trusted him for the most obvious reason – he was trustworthy.'

7.71   General Norman Schwarzkopf '(Stormin' Norman' of 1991 Gulf War fame) said,

'Almost every leadership failure in the last 50 years has been a failure in character and not a failure in competence.'

7.72   Human Resources professionals need to be able to demonstrate strong character within the organisation and to model this for other leaders.

THE VALUE OF TRUST

7.73   The existence of high levels of trust in an organisation is a source of competitive advantage. Mari Sako (2000), who investigated the impact of trust on business performance, argues that trust is a value because:

- It reduces transaction costs. It reduces the cost of doing business.
- It allows investment to increase future returns, for example with a supplier or an employee.
- It results in continuous improvement and learning. It supports and encourages innovation.

The value of trust is illustrated in the following paragraphs.

Distrust costs money

7.74

- People who do not trust each other will only co-operate if there are sufficient rules, regulations, checks and balances built into the relationship. The breakdown of trust between small investors and financial advisers due to misselling of endowments and pensions and over-hyping of the e-business boom has resulted in a web of regulations that slows down and adds cost to the work of the financial advisors and investment funds. If people had acted with integrity and maintained the trust of their investors, these costs could have been avoided.
- The oil multinational, Shell, had a good reputation overall in the

business world. When it was caught deliberately misleading its share-holders and the public by overstating its oil and gas reserves, its share price plummeted and it had the expense and discontinuity of replacing key members of its senior management team.

- We discussed in earlier chapters the breakdown of trust by employees in their employers. This is also reciprocated. Many employers no longer trust their employees to stay with them. They face the risk of key employees leaving them for a better offer from competitors and there-fore try to put in place non-compete agreements. These can lead to expensive litigation. Some employers do not trust their employees in how they work or how they use their time. CCTV is used covertly to film their employees and monitor their actions. Emails and telephone usage are monitored – all an increased cost. For example, the negotia-tions caused by a lack of trust between British Airways and its employees over their use of time off for sickness (17 days a year, on average, compared with an industrial average of seven days) almost led to a stoppage of work over the 2004 late summer holiday. The cost to the airline in terms of lost sales and future customer confidence is incalculable.

Implementation of change

7.75 We discussed the importance of good working relationships in imple-menting change in **Chapter 6**. Kim and Mauborgne (2003) have argued that introducing fair process, engaging employees in change implementation and setting clear expectations will engender trust and commitment, which will maximise co-operation and business performance, ie reinforcing the rela-tional aspects of the psychological contract. On the other hand, introducing control of resources, economic incentives and target setting will tend to produce feelings of coercion and inducement and a lower level of perform-ance, ie reinforcing the transactional aspects of the psychological contract. This is borne out by experiences of many organisations, not least the UK National Health Service. Introduction of targets that are seen by the work-force to be less than fully relevant to the core objectives and deliverables produces a response such as: 'Well if that's what you want and that's how we are going to be rewarded, then, OK, that's what we will deliver!' Intelligent employees soon learn how to deliver the targets, especially if there are rewards attached to this, even if this does not produce the most effective outputs.

Trust increases profits

7.76 Earlier in this chapter we described one type of trust as 'I trust you to do what you say you will do.' Maintaining behavioural integrity, or the perceived pattern of alignment between managers' words and deeds is essential for the building and maintenance of trust. It also reduces risk and builds profits.

7.77   A survey of employees at 76 hotels (Simons, 2000) found that employees' perceptions of managers' behavioural integrity – both keeping promises and demonstrating espoused values – had a huge impact on hotel profitability. Simons demonstrated an impact both on the revenue and on the cost side of the profit equation. His analysis also demonstrated that, on a five-point scale, a one-eighth of a point improvement in employee ratings should improve hotel profitability by an average of $250,000 per year. This increase was traceable in part through impacts on employee retention and guest satisfaction.

7.78   Changing everyday practice is never easy. Simons' findings, however, suggest that companies that focus employee surveys, manager training and performance reviews on the issue of integrity can build effective working relationships, optimise profits and build powerful competitive advantage.

Trust encourages organisational learning and innovation

7.79   There is a direct and strong relationship between organisational trust and both innovation and creative problem solving. A survey by Pricewater-houseCoopers (1999) of 300 large companies reported:

> 'At the heart of the issues impacting how people work together is trust. Of the quantitative data in the survey, trust between people, which enabled them to share ideas freely, was the single most significant factor in differentiating successful innovators.'

7.80   Trust, not only between management and employees, but also between colleagues, has a part to play. Trust between colleagues supports the sharing of ideas and experience and hence leads to innovation. Trust between management and employees is essential to build self-confidence and to encourage employees to take the inevitable risks that accompany experimenting, or trying out new ideas. If employees feel that managers are waiting for them to make a mistake so that they can put a black mark beside their name, why should they risk trying something new? If managers are continually critical of new ideas and can usually find something wrong with a proposal, the new ideas will soon dry up. Employees will learn that it is safer to be a critic. It is more fun and less risk to make critical comments at meetings and to write memos pointing out the shortcomings in what other people have done. And you will never get anything wrong yourself, which will enhance your salary assessment. If this is the employees' perception why would they take intelligent risks that may not always achieve the desired results?

7.81 One of the obstacles to team and organisational learning is lack of openness. As mistakes are made, pilot exercises are run and experiments are carried out, learning can occur. Unless the results of the pilots and the learning are openly shared, everyone is reduced to learning from their own experience and, perhaps, repeating the mistakes of others. Human Resources professionals need to encourage the celebration of 'glorious failures' so that the maximum learning can be extracted and shared. They need to ensure that the reward systems recognise people who take intelligent risks that sometimes do not work out as planned.

Case study

7.82 One pharmaceutical company was very successful in using trust to encourage innovation. The development stage of producing a medicine for market is a lengthy and very expensive process. It is important that scientists and managers recognise at an early stage the signs that the potential product may not make it through the development process – and make the decision to end the project. The costs of development increase exponentially the longer a development project continues. Also, while potential products remain in development they are using up finite resources and preventing other, perhaps more promising, candidates from getting into the development pipeline.

7.83 But there are subtle forces that work against this. The scientists are highly motivated to get 'their baby' through development successfully. There is always the temptation to do another experiment just to prove that the early signs of problems were false. Also, there is great kudos and reward for getting a product to the market. These and other forces operate against early decisions to pull the plug on a development compound. Although 'failure' is, by definition, built into the development process, as only a small proportion of potential products get through the development process to market, still there was a limiting belief in the organisation that to be associated with a failed development project was somehow damaging to your career.

7.84 The executive committee of the Research and Development organisation decided that they needed to take decisive action to change the beliefs and attitudes of the scientists. One of the steps they took was to celebrate each time a potential product failed to get through the development process. They held an open review of the project and recognised the efforts of the scientists by getting them to share the learning from the project and to write up a learning report for other projects to learn from. Over a period the culture changed and the process of 'failing' compounds became more open and occurred at an earlier stage in development.

WHEN TRUST IS NOT APPROPRIATE

7.85   Power and the dynamics of influence are inherent in organisations. The existence of ego goes with the role of the senior executive. The higher people rise, the more they feel that they can influence the direction of the organisation. It is probably essential for senior executives to identify their own destiny with that of the organisation. But the danger is that the executive's personal goals could have little to do with the good of the organisation and all to do with personal advancement or enrichment. Often over-ambition can drive an executive to compete with colleagues or people higher in the organisation rather than with the external competition. The senior executive with a trusting leadership style is vulnerable in this situation. They could be open to manipulation or intrigue.

7.86   Holding the value of trust strongly does not mean that you must trust everyone. It means that you will promote and develop an atmosphere and working relationships that will enable trust to grow. It means that you will be prepared to demonstrate trust in people unless they betray it, at which time you will confront the dysfunctional behaviours vigorously and rapidly.

7.87   Healthy organisations depend for survival on mistrust as well as trust. This is the case, for example, with scientific investigation and research. The advancement of science depends on critical peer review of the scientist's findings, with the aim of finding shortcomings in the experimentation or faults in the reasoning of the scientist. It would be inappropriate for the scientists to trust that, because someone is a respected scientist, it should be assumed that the findings are justified.

7.88   It is worth noting that trust is not always appropriate at every stage of the innovation process. An environment of trust encourages people to think up new ideas and to start to put together proposals for new ways of doing things. At this early stage, people need to be encouraged to work up the germ of an idea into a proposal for action. But when it gets to the proposal stage, the manager's role is not to trust that the proposal will work. The manager's role at that stage is to work with the proposer to test the recommendation to destruction – and only after it passes that test, does it get through to implementation.

7.89   It would be inappropriate for auditors to trust the management of the companies they audit to have the competence always to recognise errors in their organisation. The collapse of Enron at the end of 2001 was not helped by the inappropriate degree of trust from auditors Arthur Andersen towards the client. It cost both organisations their existence.

7.90   Trust has to be earned. It is naive to trust totally someone whom we do not know.

'Our ambition is not to place trust blindly, as small children do, but with good judgement. In judging whether to place our trust in other's words or undertakings, or to refuse that trust, we need information and the means to judge that information ... Reasonably placed trust requires not only information about the proposals or undertakings that others put forward, but also information about those who put them forward' (O'Neill 2002).

REFERENCES

Ambrose, S E, *Eisenhower* (2 Vols). New York: Simon & Schuster, 1983, 1984

Bennis, W and Nanus B, page 43 (1985) Leaders: The Strategy for Taking Charge, New York: Harper and Row

Jones, D, Gannett News Service, 2001

Kim, W C, and Mauborgne, R, Fair Process – Managing in the Knowledge Economy, *Harvard Business Review*, July/August 1997

Kourdi, J, and Bibb, S, Trust Matters: For Organisational and Personal Success. London: Palgrave Macmillan, 2004, ISBN 1403932530

Maitland, R, A Question of Trust. *People Management*, 6 November, 2003, 51

O'Neill, R, *A Question of Trust – The BBC Reith Lectures, 2002*. Cambridge: Cambridge University Press, 2002

PricewaterhouseCoopers, *Innovation Survey*, 1999

PricewaterhouseCoopers, *Strange Days Survey*, 2002

Protter, M, *The Values Partnership*, informal communication, 2004. www.the-valuespartnership.com

Putnam, R, *Making Democracy Work – Civic Traditions in Modern Italy*. Princeton University Press, 1993

Sako, M, Does Trust Improve Business Performance? in Lane, C, and Bachmann, R (eds), *Trust Within and Between Organisations*. Oxford: Oxford University Press, 2000

Simons, T, The High Cost of Lost Trust. *Harvard Business Review*, September 2002, 18–19

Worcester, R, Trust in Business, 28 June 2003, www.mori.com/pubinfo/review/trust-in-business.shtml

CHAPTER 8

Getting started – increasing your contribution

INTRODUCTION

8.1 This chapter discusses how Human Resources professionals can develop a strategy for increasing their contribution to the management of risk within their organisation, which will increase their influence, and contribute significantly towards the performance of the organisation.

8.2 The development of the strategy will be tackled in two parts:

1   The identification of Human Resources risks, and how to classify/ prioritise them to build an action plan.
2   The development of a strategy and the use of organisation-wide processes to increase influence.

8.3 In **Chapter 2** we outlined some approaches to the identification and assessment of risks. We explained that one method is to place risks into three categories – compliance, productivity and growth – whilst another method is to view risks based on the level of intervention required – remedial, preventive and systemic. We also explained that the assessment of risks should take account of two dimensions – the possible impact or consequence of the risk remaining untreated, and the likelihood of the risk occurring. These two dimensions can be used to plot risks on a four-quadrant matrix to assist in the assessment/prioritisation of risks and decisions on risk treatment and control.

8.4 In this chapter we will not specify which method of risk assessment or categorisation is used, but do commend these approaches, as it is important to use a formal process to ensure consistency of approach. The organisation may already use a formal system – as part of its organisation-wide risk management system that can be adopted, so Human Resources professionals can demonstrate that they are using the same process as other risk management processes. If the organisation does not have an organisation-wide process, then Human Resources professionals should approach relevant functions within the organisation that are already identified with some aspect of risk management, e g insurance, capital, business continuity, health and safety, to gain insights and obtain advice about a process that would be appropriate for the Human Resources function to use.

8.5 The focus of this chapter will be the detailed identification of risks, methods of classification/prioritisation, and showing how Human Resources professionals can build an effective Human Resources risk management strategy that can make a significant contribution to the organisation's management of risks and the achievement of its objectives.

8.6   A key theme is that Human Resources professionals should base their contribution to risk management on the principle that the organisation within which they operate is one large 'system' of interconnecting pieces that, together will achieve the organisation's objectives. Our definition, first spelled out in **Chapter 1,** is that:

> 'An organisation is a network of relationships between people who come together for a common purpose.'

8.7   Using the key words from the above definition, we can see that the Human Resources function can support an organisation and its senior management in the following ways:

- Help to identify and maintain its common purpose, strategy and objectives.
- Help to manage the relationships.
- Help to maximise opportunities and minimise risks to people in the network and the organisation as a whole.
- Help to ensure that the people in the organisation have the competencies, knowledge and skills to build effective relationships and successful networks.

8.8   In earlier chapters we have prompted Human Resources professionals:

- To create initiatives to increase their influence at higher levels of management decision-making.
- To increase their added value, all within a new business- and risk-management-focused approach.
- To put aside the organisation's and manager's perception of its contribution and professional image.
- To create a strategy to enhance their professional and personal development.
- To adopt a risk-based approach.

8.9   We also mentioned in earlier chapters that, if Human Resources professionals are to get on 'the risk and business agenda', and start to increase their influence and contribution, then they need to identify the 'hooks' that will generate a favourable response from the rest of the organisation. Reducing risk and the exposure to unplanned direct and indirect costs that have financial and other implications for the business will assist the achievement of the organisation's objectives, and increase the contribution and influence of Human Resources professionals.

8.10 It is important to use a structured process for creating a strategy aimed at increasing influence, and in our experience this should be tackled in two stages:

1 Identify the current status, the supporting evidence and the implementation challenges.
2 Create a strategy for increasing influence, and identify processes to assist with the implementation of the strategy.

IDENTIFICATION OF HUMAN RESOURCES RISKS

8.11 In general terms there is a need to identify in total where the organisation, the Human Resources function and Human Resources professionals (both professionally and personally) are 'at risk', arising from the management of the organisation's people risks, and all related aspects.

8.12 As discussed in earlier chapters, Human Resources professionals have the opportunity to influence the organisation at the strategic, tactical and operational levels. However, the credibility of Human Resources is often affected by the internal view of their ability to manage operational-level functions. If Human Resources are unable to get the 'basics right', then any attempt to get involved at the tactical and strategic levels will be resisted. It is unfortunate that the following statement can still be levelled at some Human Resources functions:

'Come back when you have put your payroll, records systems, recruitment and selection process, etc, in order. Then we might be interested in other ideas. In the meantime leave us to get on with running the business.'

Identification factors

8.13 In **Chapter 2** it was explained that the process of identification, assessment, prioritisation and treatment of people risks should not be different to that used for managing other risks.

8.14 We believe that it is important for Human Resources professionals to be able to demonstrate to the organisation that a systematic and consistent approach has been used. Additionally, where appropriate, we have included the identification of potential risk treatments, as this information will be useful when building a strategy.

8.15 In our experience the successful management of Human Resources risks will be affected by four main factors:

- **Factor 1:** Organisational context within which the organisation is operating, eg the organisation's activities, where they are based, the ownership status, organizational factors.
- **Factor 2:** Policies and systems for general risk management.
- **Factor 3:** People risks, and Human Resources operational, professional and personal risks.
- **Factor 4:** Risks generated by the organisation's business and operational processes, which either have a direct or indirect effect on the management of people risks.

8.16   This section will use these four factors to show how risks can be identified. Additionally, at the end of this section, we describe a review tool that focuses on these factors. It can be used by Human Resources professionals to get a 'handle' on the organisation's Human Resources risk profile, and therefore provide valuable input to the development of a strategy for improving the management of these factors. It can also be used to contribute to thinking within the organisation about the content of its Operating and Financial Review (OFR) where this is required.

Recording the outputs – Risk Register

8.17   It is vital that output from the identification process is recorded. For this purpose we have created the concept of a 'Human Resources Risk Register'.

8.18   The Risk Register should be used to record all the Human Resources risks that are identified. Any measurement and performance data that is available, eg turnover rates or absence rates, should also be included to assist with the assessment of the risk in later steps.

8.19   The content of the Risk Register will enable identification of how the Human Resources function is performing and how certain elements of its contribution might be improved.

8.20   One example of a Human Resources Risk Register is included towards the end of this section, with some risk examples and example risk treatments. The list is not intended to be definitive or exhaustive and the content should be tailored to suit the organisation's needs and circumstances.

Factor 1: Identify risks – organisational context

8.21   The best place to start is by undertaking an exercise to identify organisational factors and the organisational context within which the organisation and the Human Resources function have to operate. A list of organisational factors, taken from **Chapter 1**, and used as the structure for this factor, is set out below:

- Vision statement.
- Senior management commitment.
- Core values.
- Leadership style.
- Organisational culture.
- Hidden belief systems.
- Psychological contract.
- Responsibility framework.
- Occupational stress.
- Job/role design.
- Business strategy and goal-setting process.
- Performance management system.
- Compensation and rewards policies.
- Communication.
- Learning and development.

8.22   We have provided some explanation of each organisational factor and its relevance to risk identification, and under each factor we have listed a series of questions. We recommend that the whole Human Resources function be involved in creating a consensus about the answers, and only when a consensus is agreed should the risk be entered into a risk register. As a starting point, if the answer to any of the questions is 'no', then you have created an item for your Risk Register.

- **Vision statement** – a statement of the organisation's vision for its future (sometimes called a 'mission statement') that underpins everything it says and does. Many organisations create vision statements, but develop the words as if the exercise was part of their public relations or general marketing/sales campaign. In the absence of a clear and demonstrable vision, the organisation lacks a clear statement around which many other things need to revolve. For example, if an organisation says that its vision is: 'To deliver outstanding customer value, provide exceptional customer service, create excellent returns for its shareholders, and make itself the employer of choice', then all of its value statements, strategy, goals and objectives must flow from that vision. However, many organisations will publish such a vision, and not engage people in establishing the values and behaviours that will ensure that the vision can be achieved. Or they will publish a vision statement, and the associated values, but not link them to the organisation's strategy, goals, objectives and leadership competencies.
  Questions:
  1   Does your organisation have a vision (mission) statement?
  2   Is it clear, demonstrable and well-communicated?
  3   Does it underpin everything that the organisation says and does?
  4   Is it linked to the organisation's strategy, goals and objectives?

     5   Are there clear, demonstrable and well-communicated value statements that are derived from the visions statement?

- **Senior management commitment** – the extent to which management are committed to the management of risk and the management of an organisation's people risks.
  Questions:
  1. Do senior management actively and publicly support the management of risks, including people risks?
  2. Do senior management take part in risk management project teams?
  3. Do senior management discuss risk management and internal-control processes at main management meetings?
  4. Do senior management involve themselves in reviews to establish the current status and past performance of the organisation's risk management and internal-control processes?
  5. Do senior management performance measurements include those related to the management of risk and internal control?

- **Core values** – as we have discussed above, core values need to derive from the organisation's vision statement. Core values describe what particular aspects the organisation focuses on and what core values it sets for the organisation and its employees.
  Questions:
  1. Does your organisation have core values?
  2. Are they clear, demonstrable and well-communicated?
  3. Do people accept the core values?
  4. Do they create the attitudes/behaviours that the organisation requires?
  5. Are definitions of leadership behaviours that demonstrate these values included in the personal development planning process?
  6. Does the organisation's strategy, goals and objectives fit with the core values?

- **Leadership style** – the energy and inspirational qualities of an organisation's leaders are a major factor in creating an effective organisation.
  Questions:
  1. Do they create and live by the organisation's vision and core values?
  2. Do they run the organisation on strong values and principles, especially related to employees, customers and suppliers?
  3. Do they genuinely care for their people?
  4. Do they involve their people and give them freedom?
  5. Do they show appreciation and ensure that work is fun?
  6. Do they show real trust?
  7. Do they listen and act on what they hear?

- **Organisational culture** – what value does the organisation place on the effective management of risk and, in particular, people risks?

Questions:

1 Does your organisation see the management of risk as a valuable process that can protect all stakeholders?

2 Does the organisation accept that considered risk-taking is part of creating a vibrant and dynamic organisation?

3 Is the taking of risks seen as a core value of the organisation?

4 Will people who take considered risks be 'rewarded' rather than blamed, when planned outcomes are not achieved?

5 Does your organisation give a clear lead on the management of its people risks?

6 Are Human Resources professionals able to proactively influence the organisation's strategy, goals and objectives?

7 Are Human Resources professionals part of the organisation's business and commercial processes, including the management of risk?

• **Hidden belief systems** – what hidden belief systems are actually in place, and what influences attitudes and behaviour when no formal 'rules' are available?

Questions:

1 Does your organisation have hidden belief systems that are different to its vision and core values?

2 Do the organisation's vision and values take precedence in influencing attitudes/behaviours?

3 Do your senior management recognise that the organisation has a hidden belief system?

4 Could your senior management describe, in writing, the content of the organisation's hidden belief system?

5 If the current hidden beliefs are contrary to the organisation's vision and values, would your senior management accept the need to create a new set of beliefs that could support the organisations vision and values?

6 What information do you have on levels of trust in the organisation?

• **Psychological contract** – the psychological contract is an unwritten set of expectations between everyone in an organisation and, unlike the written contract, is continually changing. In this context we need to ask ourselves to what extent are the 'original' psychological contract 'terms' (in the view of each employee) still in existence? Has, for example, the removal of final salary pension schemes started to erode the contract and the trust between employers and employed?

Questions:

1 Does the organisation recognise the existence of a psychological contract?

2 Would management be able to describe, in writing, their interpretation of the contract and its value to the organisation?

3   What information do you have/need on the quality of relationships and trust in the organisation?

4   Is there a 'single' contract that all employees would consider as applying to them?

5   Has the status of the contract remained static in recent times?

6   Have the changes been for 'the better', ie have they improved confidence and trust between employees and management?

- **Responsibility framework** – to what extent are responsibility, authority and the allocation of resources delegated to the correct level at which action is most effective?

  Questions:

  1   Is responsibility and authority clearly defined and communicated?

  2   Are decisions taken at the most effective level?

  3   Are managers effective at delegating responsibility and authority?

  4   Does budgetary authority match general management authority?

- **Occupational stress** – occupational stress has many negative consequences for organisations, and therefore it is a strategic risk that can be identified, quantified and managed. Numerous studies have shown that workplace stress adversely affects work performance, morale and commitment to the organisation.

  Questions:

  1   Has the organisation used absence, health monitoring and other data to identify the existence of occupational stress?

  2   Does the data show how and why occupational stress is affecting the organisation?

  3   Has the organisation undertaken any audits and/or employee surveys to identify the existence of occupational stressors?

  4   Have the results of any audit/surveys been built into an effective action plan?

  5   Is there a current system for identifying, at an individual employee level, the presence of occupational stress?

  6   Have managers been trained to recognise and manage occupational stress?

- **Job/role design** – the ability of an organisation to create a structure, management style and work environment that encourages the best aspects of team working is a vital component in successfully managing any activity within the business, especially risk management.

  Questions:

  1   Has the organisation set clear guidance for the design of jobs/roles and team working?

  2   Is the management structure aligned to the jobs and roles that the organisation has created?

  3   Does the management structure enable people to fulfil roles that will enhance the achievement of organisational objectives?

4   Are active communications outside of formal management structures and team-working naturally encouraged?

5   Are active communications and effective team working rewarded over individual performance?

- **Business strategy and goal-setting process** – to what extent are these elements integrated and are goals and objectives formally set, cascaded, monitored and amended to take account of changing circumstances?
Questions:

  1   Are the organisation's vision, values, strategy, goals and objectives all interlinked?

  2   Is there an effective formal process for communicating and cascading the organisation's strategy, goals and objectives so plans can be developed at the most effective level?

  3   Are managers allowed latitude in developing plans that meet their goals and objectives, rather than being imposed from higher levels?

  4   Are the plans used to create performance indicators that are used during performance reviews, and related to reward and recognition processes?

- **Performance management system** – to what extent are performance goals agreed, measured and managed to ensure active action-oriented activity?
Questions:

  1   Does the organisation require that regular performance review and development discussions occur for each employee?

  2   Do managers regularly discuss performance and development with their people?

  3   Have participants received training in the system?

  4   Are managers rewarded for being good people-developers? Are penalties imposed on managers if they do not undertake regular performance reviews?

  5   Is the process used a genuine two-way dialogue rather than an imposed result determined by the manager?

  6   Is anyone other than the employee's manager required to 'sign-off' the results?

  7   Is the employee given an opportunity to 'appeal' against the results of performance assessment?

  8   Are performance measures determined and agreed with the employee?

- **Compensation and rewards policies** – to what extent are compensation and rewards policies aligned to the business, linked to business goals and objectives, including risk management; and do they reward those behaviours that are consistent with the organisation's core values, cultural framework and hidden belief systems?
Questions:

1   Are your compensation and rewards policies linked to the organisation's vision, values, strategy, goals and objectives?
2   Are they designed to produce specific attitudes/behaviours that reward the employee for the actions required?
3   Have those attitudes/behaviours been created?
4   Have they achieved the desired result?
5   Do the policies provide an equitable distribution of the benefits generated by the policy?
6   Are individual performance measures related to reward and recognition processes?

- **Communication** – ensuring that communication systems are effective is a challenge in most organisations, but the issue becomes ever more relevant when related to the management of risk. Effective communication is the foundation on which risk management systems are based.
  Questions:
  1   Is there a formal communications strategy?
  2   Are there different methods used to only distribute essential information to those who need to act upon it?
  3   Are any 'mass' communication systems focused on 'face-to-face' and active involvement?
  4   Are communications methods 'two-way', and are there effective feedback arrangements?
  5   Are the matters raised during communication actively recorded, and is timely feedback provided?
  6   Are regular employee surveys used to gain understanding of employees' issues and concerns and alignment with the organisation's vision, values and strategy?
  7   Is the information gained from these used to engage employees at work-group level in discussions on how to improve areas of weakness?

- **Learning and development** – to what extent are the organisational and individual needs for learning and development considered as part of the means by which the organisation will achieve its objectives, and a key method used to enhance the contribution and productivity of the individual employee and teams?
  Questions:
  1   Are there formal systems to identify organisational core learning needs?
  2   Do individual performance reviews identify personal development needs?
  3   Do managers and employees accept mutual accountability for delivering the development plan?
  4   Are these compared with and amalgamated with the organisational core requirements to produce a complete organisational perspective and priorities?

5   Based on those priorities, is an annual learning and development plan created and adequate resources allocated?

6   Are the results of learning and development expenditures formally evaluated to assess their contribution to the organisation and individual?

8.23   Additional organisational factors that may be considered are:

- Organisational activity.
- Locations of sites/people.
- History/background to organisation.
- Ownership.
- Particular political and external influences.
- Exit plans (where appropriate).
- Organisational structure/style.
- Strategies/goals/objectives.
- Commercial status.
- Internal control systems.
- Management control systems.

8.24   These factors will themselves vary considerably between and within organisations, depending on a whole variety of factors. Consequently the impact of the organisational context on the management of its people risks will also vary. Human Resources professionals need to identify the factors that are relevant to their organisation, evaluate the impact, and record any additional risks in the Risk Register. As mentioned earlier, at the end of this section we will give details of a tool that can be used to focus in on the organisational context and factors that are particularly relevant to the management of people risks within an organisation.

Factor 2: Identify risks – risk management processes

8.25   The policy, strategy and processes that already exist within an organisation for general risk management, internal control and corporate governance will have a greater or lesser impact on the management of Human Resources risks, depending on the extent, coverage and sophistication of existing systems. There is a clear need for Human Resources professionals to adopt a structured and systematic process that takes account of existing systems, especially a risk management vocabulary, methods of risk assessment, classification of risks and project management. The three main areas that Human Resources professionals should consider are any existing arrangements for:

- Risk management strategy and organisational framework.
- Internal controls and processes.

● Project management methods.

8.26 Human Resources professionals need to discuss with existing 'risk management' functions, e g insurance, business continuity, health and safety, to identify existing arrangements and create and dovetail an approach that is consistent and does not produce conflict, misunderstanding or confusion.

8.27 The two risk management standards described in **Chapter 1** provide some excellent guidance towards creating an organisational process framework for managing risk.

Factor 3: Identify risks – Human Resources risks

8.28 The next step is to use a systematic process to identify and record people risks and Human Resources operational risks that are:

● Created by an organisation's management of its human capital.
● Created by the activities of the Human Resources function.
● Potentially reduced/improved by the input of the Human Resources function.

8.29 We see these risks falling into three main categories:

1   General people risks.
2   Human Resources operational risks at three levels – strategic, tactical and operational.
3   Human Resources professional and personal risks.

General people risks

8.30 In earlier chapters, we emphasised the need to take a fresh risk-based approach when thinking about the organisation's people policies/procedures and administrative systems. In addition, the issues raised in other chapters should be used to identify people risks. Human Resources professionals need to build a list of all potential people risks using information from earlier chapters and the example Risk Register detailed later in this chapter. The list of potential risks, and options for risk treatment for an organisation will contain many of the examples in the Risk Register, along with others that will be specific to the organisation.

8.31 We recommend that you use the concept of a Risk Register and enter each applicable people risk area into your Risk Register and identify potential risk treatments. If measurements or other data are available, then also enter these into the appropriate risk area as this will assist with the subsequent risk-assessment process.

Human Resources operational risks

8.32   These risks are dealt with in detail in **Chapters 4 and 5**. The first step to identify operational risks is to look at any previous audit reports that have been undertaken on the Human Resources function, policies, procedures and record systems.

Audit

8.33   If the Human Resources function has not been audited, then serious consideration should be given to undertaking an audit using an external auditor, either external to the function or external to the organisation. Normally an auditor, external to the Human Resources function, but from within the organisation, eg a quality specialist, is preferred in the first instance. An audit will provide a very useful insight into the current perform-ance level, but need not study every activity or process in detail. In our experience, the most effective audits are those that combine a 'horizontal' and 'vertical' processes. By 'horizontal' we mean a study horizontally across the whole function, at a certain level of activity, eg operational, tactical or strategic. By 'vertical' we mean a study of a particular activity, eg recruitment and selection, from 'top to bottom' or 'beginning to end'. We recommend that you use a 'horizontal' approach at the strategic and tactical levels, and a 'vertical' approach for a study of the main operational activities. Remember during the audit, especially the 'vertical' elements, that you actually look for any evidence rather than assuming it 'will be here somewhere'! In addition, ensure that every opportunity is taken to identify and capture any performance data that can be used to assist with the risk-assessment process. The audit results and data can be used to create entries for the Human Resources Risk Register.

8.34   If an audit has been undertaken, the Human Resources professional needs to consider:

- What were the results, and have all actions been implemented?
- If not, then enter those items in the Risk Register.
- What is the overall level of absence within the organisation and is it in excess of the norm for the sector or area?
- Are absence levels particularly high in some areas?
- What is the overall employee turnover percentage?
- Are employee turnover levels particularly high in some areas?
- What is the cost of your employee injury and employment tribunal claims?
- Are costs showing an upward or downward trend?
- What involvement has Human Resources had in the management of absence, turnover and other costs?

8.35 The answers to these questions will potentially create entries for the Risk Register. In addition, any performance data or analysis that can be used for the risk-assessment step should be added into the Risk Register.

Other methods

8.36 There are two other methods that could be used to identify Human Resources operational risks:

1   Input-activity-output approach.
2   'Process' approach.

Input-activity-output approach

8.37 In addition to thinking about the risks that can be created by a particular activity; it is equally vital to identify the risks that are initially caused by factors that affect a particular activity – called 'input risks'. There is also a need to consider the 'knock-on' effect of the Human Resources activity or organisational aspect – called 'output risks'. In addition, when thinking about the organisation as a complete system it is clear that 'input risks' to a particular activity or aspect are generally 'output risks' from another part of the overall organisational system.

8.38 The following diagram demonstrates the relationship between input risks, activity risks and output risks.

8.39 Too often, the area for risk identification is drawn far too tightly, and misses the realities of the risks being created by a business activity. In our experience, the identification process is frequently restricted to the 'activity' risks, and the risks created by the inputs and those transferred to the outputs are not usually even considered. In addition, the 'activity' itself is often assessed at a superficial level, based on the assumptions of what is taking place and the inherent risks, rather than on a detailed observation of what actually happens.

8.40 The reality is often very different. We will explain these points by using a simple case study. This shows how the input of incorrect information can cause a Human Resources activity – handling a new starter – to be at risk, which then causes output risks for the employing department and the organisation.

Case study

8.41   Nothing in this case study is meant to an indication of 'good' or 'best' practice. The content is designed to demonstrate that, when identifying risks, an 'input-activity-output' approach should be used.

INPUTS

8.42   An organisation has service employees working throughout the country. A vacancy was created 300 miles away from the headquarters where the Human Resources function was based. As there was an urgent need to get the job filled, the regional manager undertook the recruitment and selection process. No Human Resources input was provided due to a combination of the pressure of work within Human Resources, the location of the vacancy and the urgent need to fill the position. The regional manager was aware that a previous applicant was available and still interested, so he telephoned the person and held a quick interview. No specific requirements were mentioned as both the regional manager and applicant based their discussions on the previous job details. No mention was made about qualifications or a driving licence during the discussions – even though it was generally under-stood within the organisation that new employees are required to hold a particular current type/level of servicing certification (ie not just proof that training of that type/level had previously been undertaken) and a full, clean driving licence. (The company's insurers had recently changed the insurance policy by removing cover from any person who drove for the company if they have been previously convicted of a drink-driving offence. The policy change was listed in the insurance documents, and accompanying letter, but was not specifically discussed with the company's insurance manager). No formal application form was used. The manager verbally advised the applicant that they had been selected. The manager asked the applicant whether they have been trained on the particular type/level of servicing and whether they had a driving licence. The candidate answered 'Yes' to both questions. The specific requirements were not mentioned and no proof was asked for at any stage.

HUMAN RESOURCES ACTIVITY

8.43   The regional manager telephoned Human Resources, to provide them with details about the successful candidate. Human Resources sent a formal written offer of employment to the candidate. The letter did not include the requirement to produce a copy of the required qualification certificate and a copy of their driving licence. It was assumed by Human Resources that the regional manager had resolved these matters at the interview; otherwise the manager would not have made a verbal offer. No structured offer letter system was in use, to ensure that specific requirements of a particular function or job were discussed during the compilation of the offer.

8.44   The successful candidate accepted the job. During the induction process, carried out by Human Resources, it was discovered that the new employee had not provided a copy of their training certificate and driving licence. They were advised to provide a copy of both documents to their manager, for copying to Human Resources. No mention was made of any specific requirements. Human Resources did not advise the manager that the new employee had been asked to provide those copies. The manager assumed that Human Resources had obtained copies. No diary note was made by the Human Resources function to follow-up the request to the manager.

OUTPUTS

8.45   The new employee started work and was provided with three months of formal training. After about 18 months, the employee was involved in a vehicle accident, and was arrested on suspicion of drink-driving. It was then discovered that the new employee had a previous disqualification from driving due to a drink-driving offence. This information prompted the Human Resources manager to ask for a copy of the specific qualification certificate which, it transpired, had expired prior to employment commencing. The employee was immediately suspended on full pay until the police action had been completed and the disciplinary hearing had been completed – in total, a period of three months. The employee was subsequently found not guilty of a drink-driving offence, but the company decided to dismiss the employee because of the situation with the documentation. The employee was awarded compensation at an employment tribunal for unfair dismissal because the need for the certain type/level of qualification and the requirement for a full, clean driving licence had not been mentioned at any time. The insurance company refused to pay the cost of the accident because of the previous drink-driving disqualification, drawing the company's attention to the change in policy terms introduced two years ago.

Case study risks

8.46 The risks under each category can be summarised as follows.

8.47 Input risks:

- Urgent need to fill vacancy.
- No formal recruitment and selection process.
- No training of line managers in recruitment and selection techniques or basis processes.
- No Human Resources involvement prior to their 'formal activity'.
- No clear description or complete awareness of the job requirements.
- No checking that the process indicated the need for a current qualification or full, clean driving licence.
- No formal application form, that could have asked the relevant questions.
- No prior notification to applicants to bring required documentation to the interview or induction.
- No awareness of the change in insurance cover or effective management of the insurance process.

8.48 Activity risks:

- No structured offer letter process.
- Formal offer based on incomplete and incorrect information.
- No formal application form to refer to.
- No mention in the formal offer about the need for a current certificate or clean driving licence.
- No mention in the formal offer about the need to provide the documents before the offer was formally confirmed and before they resigned their existing job.
- Induction process was not structured and did not ask for copies of the required documents to be produced at the induction.
- No follow-up process for matters raised during the induction process.

8.49 Output risks:

- Unqualified employee undertaking servicing.
- Employee with unknown previous drink-driving disqualification.
- Insurance company condition had made the insurance invalid.
- Financial costs and time resources needed to deal with employment tribunal case.
- Potential reputation risks arising from the employment tribunal case and associated publicity.
- Full costs of accident – company and third-party not covered by insurance.

- Cost of overtime to cover the absence of new employee during the extended suspension, and until vacancy is eventually filled.
- Cost of employee pay, etc, during suspension.
- Cost of recruitment and selection to replace employee.

8.50   We recommend that this case study be used to prompt the creation of a list of 'input-activity-output' exposures that are related to the Human Resources function. Each potential 'input-activity-output' exposure should then be analysed to identify the risks. The risks should be added to the Risk Register, together with any data for the risk-assessment process, and details of potential risk treatments.

Process approach

8.51   In **Chapter 2** we referred to the need for Human Resources professionals to think about their function as a series of 'processes' that come together to provide an integrated and co-ordinated service to the organisation. When identifying risks, Human Resources professionals not only need to think about the concept of 'input-activity-output' risks within their own 'processes', but also those generated by 'processes' that are not so clearly identified as parts of a broader process within a Human Resources function or a much larger complete organisational process. The above case study shows the risks that can be created within a simple 'recruitment, selection and appointment' system (you are reminded that the case study is not intended to show good/best practice). However, this is not the complete picture as that 'process' is itself part of a broader resourcing 'process' to ensure that the correct people with the right skills, competencies, etc, are available when and where the organisation needs them and are managed to provide maximum benefit for the organisation and the individual.

RESOURCING PROCESS

8.52   To illustrate the point we have created a simple model of a resourcing process:

1   Resourcing and recruitment.
2   Modifying and improving.
3   Monitoring and feedback.

8.53   Set out below is a diagram that helps to explain this model.

8.54   We will discuss each in turn.

1   **Resourcing and recruitment** – this process starts with the organisational resourcing plan based on the organisation's strategy, goals and

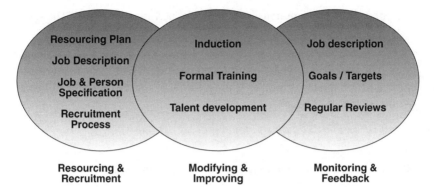

| Resourcing & Recruitment | Modifying & Improving | Monitoring & Feedback |

objectives. The plan will be used to determine the detailed requirements for each area of the organisation and the specific requirements for an individual job (see job/role design in **Chapter 3**). Each job should have a job description that should be an accurate description of the job functions and objectives, plus the levels of authority and responsibility. The job description should be the base on which everything else is built. As we have seen from the earlier case study, there is a need to ensure that the process of recruitment and selection is based on accurate and relevant detail, coupled with a clear understanding of the process and the respective responsibilities under the process. The person that is appointed as a result of this process must be as close a fit for the organisational needs as it is possible to achieve – at that point. The risks that are created by not selecting the most suitable person for the position are huge and very often long-term.

2   **Modifying and improving** – following appointment, the employee needs to be brought within the organisation and initially provided with all the relevant information that will enable them to work effectively and efficiently. The first stage is induction, where the vision, values, strategy, goals and objectives of the organisation, and the particular area where they are to be initially employed, must be clearly outlined. Next, necessary formal training must be provided before a task is undertaken, to ensure that the skills that are required by the individual and organisation are of the right type and at the required level. The next step is talent development, where the capabilities and talents of the individual employee are identified and nurtured, so that their contribution in their existing role is maximised and their potential contribution in future roles can be evaluated and developed.

3   **Monitoring and feedback** – this process is linked to job requirements and the context within which the job operates, eg organisational, departmental strategy, goals and objectives. It relies heavily on the job description, to ensure that the monitoring and feedback processes are linked to the base document, which was key during the 'resourcing and recruitment' process. Personal goals/targets should be linked to job and

organisational requirements, and regular performance reviews should be undertaken for each employee so there is effective feedback.

8.55   Use this example to prompt the creation of a list of broader Human Resources 'processes'. Then identify additional risks within those processes, and 'knock-on effects' for other Human Resources processes; and add those risks to your Risk Register.

HUMAN RESOURCES PROFESSIONAL AND PERSONAL RISKS

8.56   In earlier chapters we have discussed the way that Human Resources professionals can help an organisation to achieve its objectives. In this section we have listed some professional and personal risks that are important in understanding how the contribution of the Human Resources function is restricted, and what potential risk treatments are available. The list is not intended to be exhaustive, and should be used by Human Resources professionals to prompt the generation of a list that is relevant to a particular organisational context.

HUMAN RESOURCES PROFESSIONAL RISKS

8.57   Professional factors that can create risks for Human Resources include:

- What is the organisation's opinion of the contribution made by Human Resources to the achievement of the organisation's objectives?
- What is the organisation's opinion of the Human Resources function, and what areas does the organisation think Human Resources does well or could be improved?
- What is the organisation's perception of the ability of the Human Resources function to increase its influence, and in what areas?
- Being too closely aligned to the management process, therefore not able to provide impartial advice or take a balanced view.
- Being seen by the organisation and 'general' management as an administrative function, thereby not recognising or asking for a more effective contribution.
- Focusing on operational-level functions, thereby restricting their ability to make a more effective contribution.
- Being seen as a 'blocker' to progress and a guardian of a risk-averse legal compliance activity.
- Seeing themselves in the role of legal-compliance enforcer.
- Not 'speaking' a business language, and not making a contribution to business and commercial strategy, goals and objectives.

- Focusing on the cost of intervention and not considering the cost of inaction.
- Focusing only on the minimisation of risks/costs and not including a focus on the maximisation of opportunities.
- Not using available data, eg absence and turnover data, to identify risks and to influence methods of cost control.
- Not maintaining an active continuing professional development (CPD) process for those working in the Human Resources function, which covers both professional and personal development.

8.58 Add any identified risks to the Risk Register, along with any 'evidence' or data, plus consider potential risk treatments.

8.59 In addition, the Human Resources function should create a professional development plan that covers the whole function and is linked to the current roles that members of the team undertake. Each team member should identify where professional development opportunities exist and where their relationship with, and support for, parts of the organisation or the management of particular support activities can be enhanced. In particular input should be sought from the Human Resources professional's client group. The obstacles that are currently preventing such developments being implemented should also be identified. These individual development opportunities and obstacles should be amalgamated to create a schedule for the whole function that can then be used to identify priorities and key actions.

HUMAN RESOURCES PERSONAL RISKS

8.60 Human Resources professionals are no different to any other job-holder, in that their contribution to an organisation can be restricted by the 'constraints' of their current role or the historical perception of the abilities of previous job-holders. However, to ensure that the job or the historical perception does not constrain a particular job-holder, the application of a different blend of personal competencies, skills and experience must be brought to bear so the individual can 'rise above' the expected contribution. The personal risks that can affect an organisation and the Human Resources function can be tackled by understanding what competencies, skills and experience are required and what development opportunities are available.

8.61 In very general terms, the types of people who are attracted to the role of Human Resources professional, take a broader, longer-term, more organisationally relevant view that is not restricted to the constraints placed on them, or the perception of the Human Resources function. This is often the reason why some Human Resources professionals ignore the operational-level activities in favour of the tactical and strategic-level activities. Again another sweeping generalisation, but entrepreneurs or very business and commercially focused people often take a more function, results oriented and short-term view that can sometimes be to the detriment of the organisation. To be successful, an organisation needs to harness the competencies, skills and experience of both types of individual, and combine them to create an effective management process.

8.62 Human Resources professionals need to develop the key skills of facilitation and relationship-building to ensure that the organisation maintains an open culture and challenging corporate 'mind' and is prepared to operate as a matrix of opportunity 'teams', rather than each activity within the organisation protecting its own responsibility areas and not thinking about or contributing to the overall strategic objectives. In addition, they need to develop and bring to bear the key skills of generic influencing, facilitation, blue-sky thinking and non-silo-constrained skills to provide a focal point for those aspects within the organisation. However, the Human Resources professional will often need allies within the organisation to start the process of getting on the risk and business agenda.

8.63 As mentioned in **Chapter 1**, the UK Chartered Institute for Personnel and Development (CIPD) has recently published draft core Human Resources management standards. These standards include ten core competencies and state: 'The business competence of human resources professionals is an important issue.' The draft standards also recognise the need for Human Resources professionals to become 'thinking performers' and make a contribution, directly and indirectly, to organisational profitability.

8.64 The CIPD vision for the professional standards and competencies is to ensure that all CIPD members are effective and possess a mixture of the following ten competencies.

1 **Personal drive and effectiveness:** the existence of a positive, 'can-do' mentality, anxious to find ways round obstacles and willing to exploit all of the available resources in order to accomplish objectives.

2 **People management and leadership:** the motivation of others (whether subordinates, colleagues, seniors or project team members) towards the achievement of shared goals not only through the application of formal authority but also by personal role-modelling a collaborative approach, the establishment of professional credibility and the creation of reciprocal trust.

3 **Business understanding:** adoption of a corporate (not merely functional) perspective, including awareness of financial issues and accountabilities of business processes and operations, of 'customer' priorities, and of the necessity for cost-benefit calculations when contemplating continuous improvement or transformational change.

4 **Professional and ethical behaviour:** possession of the professional skills and technical capabilities, specialist subject (especially legal)

knowledge, and the integrity in decision-making and operational activity that are required for effective achievement in the personnel and development arena.

5 **Added-value result achievement:** a desire not to concentrate solely on tasks, but rather to select meaningful accountabilities – to achieve goals that deliver added-value outcomes for the organisation, but simultaneously to comply with relevant legal and ethical obligations.

6 **Continuing learning:** commitment to continuing improvement and change by the application of self-managed learning techniques, supplemented where appropriate by deliberate, planned exposure to external learning sources (mentoring, coaching, etc).

7 **Analytical and intuitive/creative thinking:** application of a systematic approach to situational analysis, development of convincing, business-focused action plans, and (where appropriate) the deployment of intuitive/creative thinking in order to generate innovative solutions and proactively seize opportunities.

8 **'Customer' focus:** concern for the perceptions of personnel and development's customers, including (principally) the central directorate of the organisation; a willingness to solicit and act upon 'customer' feedback as one of the foundations for performance improvement.

9 **Strategic thinking:** the capacity to create an achievable vision for the future, to foresee longer-term developments, to envisage options (and their probable consequences), to select sound courses of action, to rise above the day-to-day detail, to challenge the status quo.

10 **Communication, persuasion and interpersonal skills:** the ability to transmit information to others, especially in written (report) form, both persuasively and cogently, display listening, comprehension and understanding skills, plus sensitivity to the emotional, attitudinal and political aspects of corporate life.

8.65 Each member of the Human Resources team should use the above list to develop a personal risk assessment. That should be fed into a personal development plan and CPD objectives, and listed in the Risk Register. In that way the organisation will see that the Human Resources function is considering all factors to increase its contribution, including personal development. A programme of CPD can also include professional courses and skills courses that have relevance for the individual and the professional development needs of the Human Resources function. Of particular relevance would be sessions on risk management that have a Human Resources implication, eg human capital risk management, operating and financial review reports, corporate governance.

Factor 4: Identify risks – other related risks

8.66 This area of risk identification needs to consider all the organisation's business and operational risk areas that have a direct or indirect impact on the management of people risks and the service that the Human Resources function provides to the rest of the organisation. If this factor is not included, then a significant number of risks could remain undetected (until something goes wrong!). In addition managers in those areas can take the view that the Human Resources function is only really interested in those aspects that are organisationally relevant (strategic) and those that relate to the core function of Human Resources – people risks – and not those that relate to the general operations of the organisation.

8.67   Many of the risks should have been identified during earlier reviews, especially when using the 'input-activity-output' and the 'process' approaches. However, to ensure that no risk has been missed, we recommend that you list all the organisation's business and operational risk areas and activities and identify the links to the management of people risks, and the activities of the Human Resources function. Having created the list, you will then be able to use the 'input-activity-output' and the 'process' approaches in new areas of investigation to identify additional risks.

8.68   The table lists examples of business and operational risk areas:

Business strategy and Planning	Sales and service	Facility and plant management
Reputation and legal	Distribution and transport	Health and safety, quality and environment
Capital and insurance	Procurement and supply chain	IT, fraud and security
Marketing and development	Operations and production	Business continuity

8.69   Add any identified risks to the Risk Register, along with any 'evidence' or data, plus consider potential risk treatments.

Risk Register

8.70   This example of a Risk Register is designed to prompt the identification of Human Resources risks. It is not an exhaustive list and should only be used as a base from which to start the identification process.

Risk area	Potential risk exposures and assessment data	Potential risk treatments

Vision and values and organisational 'culture'	No core vision and values. Core vision and values are not linked to organisational strategy, goals and objectives. Organisation culture is based on hidden belief systems that are not officially recognised or accepted. Hidden belief systems largely condition individual attitudes/behaviours, rather than formal systems or reward/recognition processes. Individuals operate without reference to authority and responsibility rules.	Clarify and embed a set of core vision and values that align the organisation to its employees. Ensure the vision and values are based on a clear and open review of existing 'hidden belief systems' and proactive decisions to create a new set of 'belief systems'. Use this process to develop an organisational culture that encourages, recognises and rewards employees for intelligent risk-taking, changing their mindsets and adopting a new set of beliefs. Communicate the visions and values in a committed way from the top.
Corporate Governance	No identification of current status and existing non-compliance. Inadequate policies and procedures are in place. Managers/employees acting in an inappropriate manner and/or not following the procedures.	Identify current status and existing non-compliance. Ensure adequate policies and procedures. Ensure that organisational values, policies and approach are well-communicated to all, via initial induction/training and ongoing processes.

Strategic planning process, strategic thinking capability and training	Reactive management decision-making. No process for reviewing medium-/long-term organisational strategy, goals and objectives. No competitor analysis or market information. No marketing strategy and no service/product development plan. No proactive link to organisational design, resource plan, etc. No structured strategic process and training.	Implement formal process for strategic thinking, including allocation of authority and responsibility for process. Identify skills and competencies required and available, with link to core skills register and resource plan. Provide training and/or recruit internally or externally.
Organisation design and development	Design is out-dated and does not fit the current requirements, either in functional terms or organisational 'culture', management style, etc. Authority and responsibility allocation is not clear. Poor design prevents effective management of key activities, leading to stress, reduction in productivity, de-motivated employees.	Regularly review design to make sure it fits needs of organisation. Link design to organisational strategy, goals and objectives. Establish clear lines and areas of authority and responsibility. Communicate design, authority and responsibility allocation to all likely to be affected.

Organisation memory, core skills and talent	During major reorganisations, mergers, takeovers or downsizing, key performers are not specifically 'managed', increasing the likelihood of unwanted resignations. Either no system or an inadequate system is available for performance assessment and succession planning. Performance assessments and succession planning output, especially for key performers, is not considered. No core skills register or individual development plans are available or considered.	Plan and manage merger processes to focus on the human capital impact as well as financial and other impact. Ensure an effective system for performance assessment and succession planning. Ensure an effective system for a core skills register. Use the output to manage key performers.
Employee satisfaction and commitment Communication processes	Management do not see the need or value in communicating with employees. Management's often-favourable view of the situation is not based on 'hard-facts'. Employees' views are not considered. Employees are potentially de-motivated, with a reduction in productivity and an increase in absence and turnover.	Implement a two-way communication process that enables employee's views to be proactively obtained and that ensures people understand and are committed to the organisation's vision, values, strategy, goals and objectives. Ensure output is communicated to all concerned and acted upon. Ensure timely and relevant information is provided.

| Building trust, effective working relationships and team working | There is an absence of trust between management and employees, and between employees with each other. This prevents effective team working, reduces productivity, de-motivates employees and increases turnover and absence. The organisation's vision, values, strategy, goals and objectives are not clear and employees have no faith in the ability of the management to manage. Individual employees are unsure of their authority and responsibility limits, which stifle creative thinking and decision-making. | Clarify and embed a core vision and a set of values that align the organisation to its employees. Instil in senior management a culture where they 'walk the talk'. Ensure the vision and values are based on a clear and open review of existing 'hidden belief systems' and proactive decisions to create a new set of 'belief systems'. Use this process to develop an organisational culture that encourages, recognises and rewards employees for intelligent risk-taking, changing their mindsets and adopting a new set of beliefs. Ensure that the allocation of authority and responsibility is clear and unambiguous and is well-communicated to all concerned. |

| Diversity | No identification of the current status of employees and no evaluation of the lost opportunities or risks. Failure to utilise full potential of the people available. Inappropriate policies and procedures are in place. Managers/employees acting in an inappropriate manner and/or not following the procedures. Employment tribunal cases/costs. | Identify current status and evaluate lost opportunities and risks. Ensure adequate policies and procedures. Ensure that organisational values, policies and approach are well communicated to all, via initial induction/training and ongoing processes. Ensure systems for recruitment, selection, performance management, training, etc, take full account of diversity aspects. Ensure managers are trained in the possible risk areas and practical application of policies to protect the needs of the organisation. |

Performance assessment	No system of performance assessment. System of performance assessment is inappropriate for the organisation. System is not linked to organisational goals, objectives and personal development plans. System is implemented piecemeal and the output is not acted upon. De-motivated employees. Reduction in productivity. Increase in absence and turnover.	Ensure that organisational strategy, goals and objectives are formally determined and communicated. Ensure that system is proportionate for organisation and agreed with participants. Ensure adequate training for all participants, both managers and those being appraised. Ensure output is acted upon.
Succession planning	No system and no use of output from performance assessment process. Overlooking individual potential. De-motivated employees. Reduction in productivity. Increase in absence and turnover.	Ensure that output is communicated and discussed with employees and linked to organisational strategy, goals and objectives, plus individual performance assessments. Ensure adequate training for managers.
Leadership development	No formal process. Reactive recruitment decisions. No link to organisational strategy, goals and objectives. No link to succession planning, core skills process and resource plan.	Use outputs from succession planning process, core skills process and individual development plans to create list of leadership candidates. Implement enhanced individual development plans, including training.

Attracting and retaining talent	No medium-/long-term resourcing strategy that identifies the skills and competencies required for the organisation's strategy, goals and objectives. Specific shortage of required skills and competencies leading to reduced productivity, missed or delayed implementation of plans including R&D.	Create a resource plan by consolidating the output from the organisation's strategy, goals and objectives process and individual performance assessments; succession planning and core skills register.
Recruitment strategy	No strategy and reactive recruitment processes. No effective linkage to other elements, e g strategy, goals, objectives, core skills register, succession planning.	Identify potential skill shortages in the recruitment market and feed into resource plan. Identify recruitment sources for particular skills in advance of need. Create service-level agreements with recruitment specialists and gain commitment to them.

Reward and recognition	Either no system or an inconsistent system is available to link reward and recognition to individual performance, goals and objectives. Reward and recognition systems are not linked to organisational strategy, goals or objectives. System does not recognise and reinforce behaviours and attitudes required to develop the desired organisational culture. Participants use the system for personal gain only.	Ensure that any system is consistent, fair, well-communicated and linked to personal goals, objectives and performance and organisational strategy, goals and objectives. Ensure that the system is designed to produce the attitudes/behaviours that are linked to organisation goals and objectives.
Core skills training	No identification of core skills requirements. No linking between training requirements and organisational strategy, goals and objectives. No register of internal core skill capabilities.	Ensure employee record system captures core skills and other training. Ensure training/recruitment plan is linked to strategy, goals and objectives.

Discrimination (all forms)	No policies or inappropriate policies and procedures are in place. Managers/employees acting in an inappropriate manner and/or not following the procedures. Employment tribunal cases/costs.	Ensure adequate policies and procedures are in place. Ensure that organisational values, policies and approach are well-communicated to all, via initial induction/training and ongoing processes. Ensure that managers are trained in best practice for operation of procedures to protect the organisation.
Harassment, bullying or violence in the workplace	No policies or inappropriate policies and procedures are in place. Managers/employees acting in an inappropriate manner. Employment tribunal cases/costs.	Ensure adequate policies and procedures are in place. Ensure that organisational values, policies and approach are well-communicated to all, via initial induction/training and ongoing processes. Ensure that managers are trained in best practice for operation of procedures to protect the organisation.

Stress	Employee health and performance is adversely affected, with a reduction in 'productivity', and increase in turnover, absence, etc. No management awareness or system to identify and resolve causes of stress. Inappropriate policies and procedures are in place. Managers/employees acting in an inappropriate manner and/or not following the procedures. Employment tribunal cases/costs.	Create management systems to identify individual and organisational stressors, to facilitate action planning and case handling. Ensure adequate policies and procedures, are in place. Ensure that organisational values, policies and approach are well-communicated to all, via initial induction/training and ongoing processes. Ensure awareness training and guidance in case handling is provided to managers.
Absence management	No records system. System has inadequate data capture and retrieval capabilities. No analysis of data or proactive data and advice to managers. Link to accident reporting to identify accidents that have caused work related injuries or ill-health. No action, or inconsistent action by managers. No return to work interviews.	Ensure adequate system for data capture and retrieval. Link to accident management system. Analyse data and provide proactive advice to managers. Ensure adequate policies, procedures and training for managers. Ensure that organisational values, policies and approach are well-communicated to all, via initial induction/training and ongoing processes.

Employment law	Failure to identify legal changes. Organisation unaware of the need for, or not prepared to implement, compliant policies and procedures. HR failure to advocate adequate policies and procedures. HR/organisation's failure to communicate and train those responsible for implementation and compliance.	Use an external notification system to identify changes. Use all 'arguments' to demonstrate the need to implement and ensure compliance. Ensure full understanding of the requirements via a process of CPD. Only use proportionate communications methods to 'target' required audience, ie only send them what they need to know, not sending everything to everyone.
HR policies and procedures	No or inadequate policies and procedures. Out-of-date or non-existent employment contracts or terms and conditions. Managers/employees acting without formal guidance and in an unlawful or inappropriate manner. Employment tribunal cases/costs.	Undertake a systematic survey to identify current status and what is required. Create policies and procedures that will support the organisation to achieve its strategy, goals and objectives. Ensure all legally required documentation is created, implemented and updated.

Human resources operations	Incomplete documentation and inadequate training create inconsistent and inaccurate advice. Issues of interpretation and application are resolved 'locally' and not passed to the 'centre' for review of decisions. Lack of control creates inaccurate record systems and incomplete data from which decisions can be made.	Ensure that all internal policies and procedures are fully documented and up-to-date. Create and implement training and development programmes so all HR employees fully understand the content and application of HR policies and procedures. Ensure a record of issues identified, so that amendments can be considered and acted upon.
Payroll and benefits management	Incomplete or inaccurate records. Late, missed or inaccurate payments and deductions. Inland Revenue investigation. Formal penalties.	Establish formal, robust, compliant, confidential and consistent process for payroll and benefits management.

Employee records	No, incomplete or inaccurate records. Restricted access to records is not maintained. Records and data are not kept in line with legislation. Employees are not given access to records to check the accuracy and content. Incorrect decisions and calculations are made, e g redundancy, sickness pay, and maternity leave. Lack of confidence/trust in the HR function. Employment tribunal cases/costs. Poor security can lead to inappropriate access to employee records.	Establish formal, robust, legally compliant, confidential and consistent process for recording, storing, accessing employee records and data. Implement a process for a formal employee review of their record. On an annual basis, proactively provide each employee with an extract of the data held on the HR system, and require them to sign that it is accurate. Implement adequate security and controlled access arrangements for employee records.
Disciplinary and grievance procedures	Inappropriate policies and procedures are in place. Managers/employees acting in an inappropriate manner and/or not following the procedures. Employment tribunal cases/costs.	Ensure adequate policies and procedures are in place. Ensure that organisational values, policies and approach are well-communicated to all, via initial induction/training and ongoing processes.
Health and safety	Managers/employees acting in an unsafe manner. Reduction in productivity. Reduction in morale due to accidents and inadequate organisational focus.	Ensure that organisational values, policies and approach are well-communicated to all, via initial induction/training and ongoing processes.

Occupational health	New employees may have pre-existing conditions that can be exacerbated by their employment. Existing employees can be adversely affected by work activities.	Use pre-employment medicals, ongoing health monitoring and absence data to identify exposures.
Accidents	Accidents at work and 'work-related' driving accidents that cause personal injury are reported as sickness absence, and not linked to actual 'accident'. Prosecution cases and costs.	Ensure managers know the distinction between the various types of absence and how each has to be handled and reported.

Risk-profiling tool

8.71   We have included details of a unique risk-profiling tool that we have developed specially for Human Resources professionals, to assist them in identifying Human Resources risks. The tool is called 'Human Resources Risk Management' and is the copyright of RiskFrisk®.

8.72   This unique tool is used to undertake a top-level risk-profiling review. It focuses on the way in which an organisation's risks and the interrelationship between them can have an impact on the management of its people risks and the Human Resources function. It reviews four major factors:

- **Factor 1:** Human Resources risks.
- **Factor 2:** organisational context.
- **Factor 3:** general risk management policies, strategies and processes.
- **Factor 4:** business and operational process risks.

8.73   The methodology adopts a holistic approach and includes the 'input-activity-output' and 'process' approaches, as outlined in earlier sections.

8.74   Benefits to Human Resources professionals are:

- Knowing the keys areas where their organisation is at risk.
- Being able to use the outputs to support informed decision-making about priorities for improving the management of people risks.
- Understanding the options for managing people-risk exposures and costs.

- Understanding Human Resources operational, professional and personal risks.
- Understanding how risks in other areas of the organisation relate to and influence the management of people risks.
- Understanding how Human Resources can influence the management of related risks.

8.75 It also provides Human Resources professionals with:

- Valuable insights into key organisational processes.
- A view of the organisation as a complete system.
- An opportunity to feed the results into the organisation's strategy and plans.
- An awareness of current silo thinking.
- Information to prompt a review of insurance and other costs.
- An ability to reassure shareholders.
- Knowledge to help support organisational development.

8.76 The business-focused and commercially relevant outputs are specifically designed to enable Human Resources professionals to demonstrate where improvements to Human Resources risk management can be made. Additionally, the output can be used by Human Resources professionals to demonstrate an understanding of the interrelationships between risk areas, and an understanding of the organisation of a complete system. This gives Human Resources professionals an excellent opportunity to increase their influence and professional standing within the organisation by demonstrating that they are aware of the broader implications and can more easily provide advice about the opportunities and risks facing the organisation.

8.77 Human Resources professionals can use the tool to:

- Review their organisation as a total system.
- Demonstrate business and commercial understanding and relevance.
- Demonstrate an integrated approach, and not just a focus on compliance.
- Identify the impact of existing organisational and people risk factors.
- Identify Human Resources operational, professional and personal risks.
- Identify management system status and required improvements.
- Become aware of (a) actual activity risks, (b) input risks (risks that affect the actual process), and (c) output risks (risks that are created by the actual process and become an input risk for another process).
- Improve the awareness of the specific risk area and its interrelationships, and how changes in one process need to consider the implications for other processes.
- Obtain vital information to enable them to propose business-relevant solutions that are focused on the cost-benefit analysis of an improvement rather than just concentrating on the intervention costs.

- Set the scene and then establish a baseline position statement and profile.

ONGOING USAGE

8.78   The use of the tool is not a single event. Human Resources professionals can apply the process to future changes that are being considered by their organisation, that require a fresh look at risk management and internal control systems and especially the implications for Human Resources risks. In this way Human Resources professionals can contribute to the 'risk and business agenda' on an ongoing basis. This inevitably results in Human Resources professionals demonstrating their business and risk credentials, and their added value to the organisation.

STRATEGY FOR INCREASING THE HUMAN RESOURCES CONTRIBUTION

8.79   In this section we will:

- Consider the development of a Human Resources strategy, mainly referring back to **Chapter 2**.
- Look at some additional considerations to assist in explaining how an enhanced Human Resources strategy can benefit the organisation.
- Explain some organisational processes that can be used by Human Resources professionals to increase their involvement and influence throughout the organisation.

8.80   What are the key objectives of a strategy? We suggest they are:

- To influence the inclusion of 'risk management' on the broader business agenda, particularly at board level, and influence corporate governance and internal control processes.
- To assist management in developing the organisation to ensure that it effectively balances the management of its opportunities, whilst minimising its risks, thereby supporting the achievement of its strategic objectives.
- To develop the role of Human Resources professionals, and the acceptance of the role change, to one of managing risk within the total range of Human Resources activities, and to increase the added value of the Human Resources function across its range of activities.
- To increase the influence on the business by changing the Human Resources role from 'admin' to 'business partnership'.

8.81   In **Chapter 2** we outlined the steps for the development of a strategy for developing the effectiveness of the Human Resources function. The main steps are repeated here for ease of reference:

- Client survey.
- Establish targets.
- Process mapping.
- Business partnership.
- Employee sensing survey.
- Strategic human resources.

8.82   We will not discuss each step again, but have set out below some additional considerations that are intended to help format and explain a particular strategic approach.

Risk assessment and classification

8.83   Where to start? This phrase springs to mind – 'Get a quick win', eg, tackle a situation:

- Where the risk is self-evident.
- Where the assessment can be undertaken using existing evidence, and the priority is likely to be high.
- Where risk treatments are available to the Human Resources function.
- Where risk controls can be implemented.
- Where the resolution of the issue can have a quick and effective impact, especially if a reduction in costs is a real possibility.

8.84   However, whilst we appreciate that it is very tempting to 'rush off' to tackle a particular risk, we strongly recommend that a longer-term perspective is taken and that the risk-assessment process is tackled in a systematic manner. In that way those who Human Resources professionals seek to influence, and those who will need persuading that Human Resources is part of risk management, will see that there is some substance to the approach.

8.85   Tackling some risks is going to take time, and the creation of a carefully structured strategy and plan. There are no 'quick-fixes' that are going to resolve certain risks overnight, especially those that relate to organisational factors and Human Resources risks.

8.86   As mentioned before, we recommend that a structured risk assessment process is used. In addition to considering the 'probability' and 'impact' variables, we recommend that consideration is also given to the cost-reduction opportunities for each risk, and the cost of the intervention. This will create a 'cost-benefit' analysis approach that will show that there is a business and commercial focus to the analysis, which will appeal to many within the organisation. An additional 'selling point' that we have found very successful is to translate the cost of inaction into the cost of providing a service or the profit on a particular product. We find that this concentrates the mind of business managers very well, if they understand that the cost of inaction is actually higher than the cost of the intervention, especially if the cost, eg the cost of additional recruitment, is to be charged to their cost centre.

Classification process

8.87 When the risk-assessment process is completed, and Human Resources are aware of the level of risks, they will then need to prioritise the risks for implementation and building into the strategy. Whilst all risk-assessment processes do provide a 'ranking order', often the risks to be tackled first are decided by other broader considerations, including the availability of resources – financial, people, time – to implement the risk treatment(s) and risk control methods identified. Consequently, we recommend that a simple process be used to consider each item listed in the Risk Register and to establish an overall classification. This process should be undertaken as quickly as possible, by asking these questions:

1   Is it within the Human Resources professional's authority and responsibility to implement the risk treatments option(s) listed?
2   Does the Human Resources professional have the current resources – money, people and skills – to implement the option(s)?

8.88 If the answers are 'yes', then consider those as *priority 'A' actions*. The implementation of these items, and the communication of the action and the benefits in managing the risks, will start the process of the rest of the organisation realising that Human Resources are also in the business of 'risk management' and are as equally business and commercially focused as other parts of the organisation.

8.89 If the answer is 'no' to either of the above questions, then there is a need to ask some further questions:

1   Could the risk treatment option(s) listed be implemented by agreeing the option(s) with the Human Resources professionals' immediate superior – either line or functional – or 'local' management team?
2   Can the immediate superior – either line or functional – or 'local' management team agree to provide the resources – money, people and skills – to enable the option(s) to be implemented?

8.90 If the answers are 'yes', then consider those as your *priority 'B' actions*.

8.91 If the answer is 'no' to either of the above questions, then you need to ask some further questions:

1   Could the risk treatments option(s) listed be implemented by agreeing the option(s) with the ultimate authority within the organisation, ie chairman, chief executive, board of directors?

2   Will the ultimate authority within your organisation, ie chairman, chief executive, board of directors, agree to provide the resources – money, people and skills – to enable the option(s) to be implemented?

8.92   If the answers are 'yes', then consider those as your *priority 'C' actions*.

8.93   If the answer is 'no' to either of the above questions, then those actions are your *priority 'D' actions*, but do not delete them from your Risk Register. Remember there may be an opportunity to input your ideas at a later date, especially if you have successfully implemented your 'A', 'B' and 'C' actions.

8.94   However, this simple approach should not restrict consideration of any of the risk treatments as a higher priority. Senior management may decide that certain risks should be tackled first, even if they are more of a challenge than, say, Priority 'A' risks, and more resource intensive, simply because they are more strategic and can deliver a better added value to the achievement of organisational objectives.

Additional considerations

8.95   Referring again to the classification system described above, there will exist a classification for each risk detailed in the Risk Register and a justification for each change – or, as a minimum, the priority 'A' items.

8.96   In **Chapter 2** we suggest that the way to create a strategy is to agree with the organisation – using client surveys and employee sensing surveys – to determine what the two groups require. This should, in theory, enable those changes to be implemented with limited resistance, but may restrict changes to those that the organisation is prepared to accept. However, it is a start.

8.97   So what is your strategy for moving forward from this point? We suggest that, in general terms, you have three options:

1   Proceed with the changes on a piecemeal basis – priority 'A', then priority 'B' and so on.

2   Identify the changes that will be required to implement priority 'C' items and develop a plan to change the thinking within the organisation to implement those changes.

3   Combine the two options; start on priority 'A' items but, at the same time, start a process of discussion with other members of the team about the priority 'C' items.

8.98   Clearly your decision on an option will be conditioned by organisational, professional and personal factors that we have discussed previously. In general terms, organisational factors are more likely to be priority 'C' items, and professional and personal factors priority 'A' items. In addition, it is generally easier to determine and explain your strategy if it is structured in a systematic manner, and/or is explained as a model. We have set out some ideas below.

8.99   One way to look at your strategic contribution is to view it as a model, with the organisation being shown as a system for producing a product or service to create a profit for shareholders.

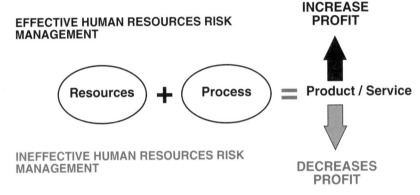

8.100   The model shows that if the organisation ignores the contribution that can be made by the management of Human Resources risks, then directly or indirectly the combination of resources + process can affect the output of products and services that create the profit for the organisation.

8.101   Another way to look at it is to consider each major function of the organisation as a system. However, as we have discussed earlier, if the organisation and each separate activity does not adopt an integrated process approach, then each activity will operate within its own silo. What do we mean by 'silo'? The term means that each area will only view its contribution to the organisation within its own boundaries, which are generally seen as a vertical process. Consequentially, each function tends to operate in isolation from any other and will not appreciate or concern itself with the concept of 'input' and 'output' risks. Typically such organisations are very bureaucratic and operate along rigid vertical reporting lines. The tendency is for contact to be made between the functions via the vertical 'chain of command' rather than a more flexible arrangement, where people are encouraged to work with anyone within the organisation who can support their objectives – sometimes called a 'matrix approach'.

8.102   Viewed another way this can produce an organisation that looks like this:

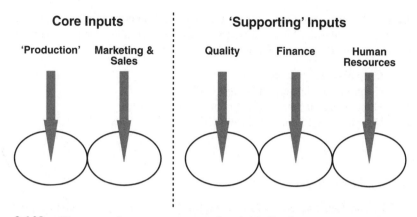

8.103   However, the consequences of a rigid silo-focused organisation are significant. Each function concentrates on its own activities and does not consider the benefits of a more co-operative organisational system approach. We do not have the space in this book to debate the benefits and consequences of each type of organisation structure, but in our experience the following approach is significantly more beneficial for all stakeholders. This creates an organisation where each activity overlaps or is co-ordinated with each other. In this example, 'input' and 'output' risks are identified both within each area but also between areas.

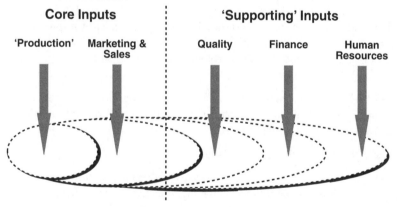

Other strategic development opportunities

8.104   We have identified several organisation-wide internal control systems that provide an excellent opportunity for Human Resources professionals to increase their involvement, contribution and influence. By deciding to involve themselves in these systems, Human Resources professionals can build these activities into the Human Resources strategy and demonstrate that the strategy has considered all the factors we discussed earlier in this chapter.

8.105   We have provided outline details of each and explain how they can become part of the Human Resources strategy for increasing the Human Resources functions contribution to the management of risk:

- Corporate governance (CG)
- Corporate social responsibility (CSR)
- Human capital management review (HCM)
- Operating and financial review (OFR)

Corporate governance (CG)

8.106   We first discussed CG in **Chapter 1**. In summary, CG relates to the senior-level internal control processes of an organisation, and in particular the arrangements for managing risks. In the case of the private sector, this includes:

- Guidance for the appointment of the Chairman, directors and non-executive directors, their roles and responsibilities.
- The creation of a system for internal control.
- The auditing of the board's performance.
- The principal duties of the remuneration and nominations committees.

8.107   The Combined Code on Corporate Governance, issued in July 2003, includes matters taken from the Turnbull Report mentioned in **Chapter 1**. The Guidance in the Turnbull Reports makes reference to the need for a sound system of internal control in the particular circumstances of the organisation (company).

8.108   Human Resources professionals have an opportunity to conduct their activities in accordance with the principles of internal control and to make an effective contribution to the organisation's overall internal control systems.

8.109   In addition, the Guidance states:

'All employees have some responsibility for internal control as part of their accountability for achieving objectives. They, collectively, should have the necessary knowledge, skills, information and authority to establish, operate and monitor the system of internal control.'

8.110   Human Resources professionals can make a major contribution to CG in three ways:

1   By advising on, and supporting, the remuneration and nominations committees in managing the process of the selection, appointment and remuneration of directors and non-executive directors. Human Resources professionals are well-placed to provide the necessary skills or can advise on the attainment of the specialist skills of selection,

appointment and remuneration. These skills are vital to ensure an effective process of selection and appointment, and to achieve the correct level and balance of remuneration. Following that input, the Human Resources professional should be actively involved in the construction and execution of an induction process for directors and non-executive directors. In addition, the Chairman will need advice on the training and development of the directors, which Human Resources professionals are ideally placed to provide or facilitate.

2   By seeking to influence the organisation's strategy through contact and discussion with the directors and non-executive directors. The information that Human Resources professionals have included in the Risk Register, and the output from the other processes, will be of particular interest to those internal control systems that are a major concern of the organisation. In addition, the list of priority 'C' actions (these, if you recall, are the organisational level items) can help the organisation to understand and focus on the organisational-level risk areas that are likely to be having a significant impact on the ability of the organisation to achieve its strategy, goals and objectives.

3   By identifying those areas where Human Resources can make an enhanced contribution to the management or risk within the organisation. Some activities are as follows:

- Establishing clear recruitment criteria – skills, competencies, experience.
- Ensuring effective internal communication systems.
- Determining a sound organisational structure, plus responsibility and authority frameworks.
- Creating systems for setting and measuring goals and objectives.
- Implementing a system of talent management and succession planning.

8.111   The Human Resources strategy should include an analysis of the opportunities for increasing influence in corporate governance systems, either directly or indirectly, and use this analysis to produce an action plan.

Corporate social responsibility (CSR)

8.112   CSR is essentially about how an organisation takes account of its economic, social and environmental impacts in the way it operates, maximising the benefits and minimising the downsides.

8.113   In May 2003, the UK Department of Trade and Industry and the Forum for the Future hosted a workshop for business, non-government organisations, academics and government to debate the links between competitiveness, productivity and the increasingly important role of intangible assets, as well as sustainability and CSR. The broad conclusion, with some qualification, was that sustainability makes a positive contribution to business success. The key is to look at CSR as an investment in a strategic asset or distinctive capability, rather than an expense. The debate highlighted the importance of taking a balanced approach to assessing performance, rather than concentrating solely on one aspect, for example shareholder value.

8.114   The Forum for the Future has described on its website what a sustainable society should look like using 'The Twelve Features of Sustainable Society', which are grouped under five 'capitals' – Natural Capital; Human Capital; Social Capital; Manufactured Capital; and Financial Capital. They go on to say that 'IF we invest appropriately in all capital stocks, AND achieve the flow of benefits' the statements under each Capital would be true. That means that the statements 'represent the OUTCOME of a successful capital investment strategy for sustainable development – that is, a sustainable society.'

8.115   Work is continuing on identifying the links between CSR and organisational effectiveness and success, and there are some examples, eg British Telecommunications, of companies that have carried out a lot of work in this area, with particular reference to reputational risks.

8.116   There are clear links to the management of people risks, the activities of Human Resources and the development of a strategy to increase the influence of Human Resources. For example, how would the organisational agenda for CSR be communicated throughout the organisation so that the CSR policies are an integral part of the way that the organisation is managed? How would individual practices and behaviours be brought together to ensure that the CSR policy is consistently maintained? How could performance-management systems discuss and recognise employee CSR initiatives and success? How can incentives be used to focus managers and employees on the CSR initiatives?

8.117   Human Resources professionals should therefore seek to influence the CSR debate within an organisation and identify ways of supporting the implementation of CSR policies. The Human Resources strategy should include an analysis of the opportunities for increasing influence in CSR policies and initiatives, either directly or indirectly, and then use this analysis to produce an action plan.

Human capital management

8.118   Human capital management (HCM) is an approach to Human Resources management that treats it as a high-level strategic issue and seeks systematically to analyse, measure and evaluate how people policies and practices create value. HCM is winning recognition as a way of creating long-term sustainable performance in an increasingly competitive world.

8.119 HCM treats human capital as a positive – and active – asset to be developed, not a passive cost.

8.120 The 2003 'Accounting for People' Taskforce, sponsored by the UK Department of Trade and Industry (DTI), states:

'We believe that greater transparency on how value is created through effective people policies and practices will benefit organisations and their stakeholders. Managers, investors, workers, consumers and clients all have an interest in knowing that an organisation is striving to adopt those features of HCM that are associated with high performance. We also see clear strategic value for organisations themselves. The process of identifying those aspects of HCM that drive performance and enhance value should itself lead to better management.'

8.121 But what elements are to be reported, and what process should be used to undertake the assessments? The report discusses options of a regulated framework and a complete free hand, and states:

'We take as our starting point the need to communicate clearly, fairly and unambiguously the directors' understanding of the links between the organisation's approach to HCM, its business strategy and its performance, and identify some areas that are likely to be relevant in the overwhelming majority of cases.'

8.122 So what should be included and how do Human Resources professionals start the process and include the results within their strategy for increasing their influence?

8.123 Some organisations already use HCM processes and, although some guidance can be obtained from reviewing their processes, the best processes are those that undertake HCM based on the needs and context of the organisation.

8.124 However, some general guidance can be given:

- Size and composition of workforce – is the workforce expanding or shrinking; does the workforce profile fit the business strategy; how reliant is the organisation on external workforces?
- Retention and motivation – is turnover running at the best level for the business; are there differences between different parts of the workforce; is everyone working to the same goals?
- Remuneration and fair employment – does remuneration practice support business strategy; how to reward non-financial performance; what assurances can be given about no unfair discrimination?
- Skills, competences and training – what is the fit between skills and business needs; is the fit set to improve; what is the contribution from formal training?

- Leadership and succession planning – what profile of leadership skills is needed; do existing managers fit the bill; how reliant is the organisation on externally recruited leaders; can more leaders be developed internally; how effective is succession planning?
- Diversity – has the organisation committed itself to a broad diversity strategy; are all elements of the organisation's workforce treated equally and have the same level of opportunities; does the organisation's workforce reflect the diversity of the local population; does the organisation ensure that the products/services it provides are accessible to all sections of the population?

8.125   The above list is very general and is only designed to prompt thinking about what could be included with an HCM process. We recommend that Human Resources professionals review the list and undertake an initial analysis of each item, to produce a clearer description that helps to link it with the context of the organisation. The review will identify which of the above points are of particular relevance, those to be discarded and any additional items to be included. The next step is for Human Resources professionals to discuss the concept of HCM, and the initial list/descriptions with their various business partnerships – described in **Chapter 7** – to get feedback on the aspects of HCM that others within the organisation believe should be included. When the list is complete, the Human Resources function should create a detailed description of each item and the measurement criteria to be used.

8.126   These details can be built into a report to senior management to seek agreement to start the process of HCM. Experience shows that, in general, organisations appreciate the contribution that can be made by HCM. Human Resources professionals can use HCM to show that they are interested in a business and commercial focus and are willing to put themselves and the Human Resources function into the limelight of the mainstream of the organisation. Human Resources professionals can use HCM as a key element of their strategy to increase their contribution.

8.127   The outcome of HCM systems can be used as an input to the next strategic development opportunity and the relatively recent operating and financial review (OFR), discussed in the next section.

Operating and financial review (OFR)

8.128   The 2003 'Accounting for People' Taskforce, sponsored by the UK Department of Trade and Industry (DTI), recommended that companies should clearly communicate the links between their HCM policies and practices and their business strategies and performance, and the information should be reported in operating and financial reviews.

8.129   In May 2004, the government published a consultation document on 'Draft Regulations on the Operating and Financial Review and Directors Report'. This was in response to the work of the Task Force and other inputs, including the recommendations of the independent Company Law Review and the Accounts Modernisation Directive from the European Union.

8.130   Paragraph 2.5 in part states:

'Directors deciding in good faith what would be most likely to promote the success of the company, taking account of a wide range of factors, within and outside the company, which are relevant to achieving its objectives and to an assessment of the business. These factors may well include the company's impact on the environment and on the wider community, and its relationships with employees, customers and suppliers.'

8.131   A clear implication is that the management of people risks is a key component of this review and report, and Human Resources professionals should ask that the management of people risks are considered and comment included in the review and report.

8.132   When finalised, the requirements will apply to financial years starting on or after 1 January 2005, recently changed to 1st April 2005, for large- and medium-sized companies. Companies should be actively studying the consultation document to determine what actions they need to take.

8.133   Many organisations are currently reviewing their response to the OFR, and in general see the OFR as a progressive move, but it is unclear at this stage whether it will actually create a willingness and appetite to take the management of people risks more seriously. It will largely depend on whether the Director who signs off the OFR actually thinks that people issues are a real risk to the business and shareholder value. Human Resources professionals are anticipating such willingness, but time will tell. Human Resource professionals can assist and contribute by asking the questions set out below. Human Resources policies and processes need to be incorporated efficiently and effectively into the organisation's risk management process in order to answer many of the questions being raised.

8.134   Human Resources professionals can assist and contribute to the thinking and the preparation of the review and the report's contents by posing the following questions.

- Does the organisation currently undertake such a review and publish such a report?
- Does it include aspects related to the management of people risks?
- Are people risks a significant aspect of your organisation?
- Has the organisation started to review its current practice to take account of the likely changes?

- Have Human Resources professionals considered the matters relating to the management of people risks that could be appropriate for inclusion in the review and report?
- Have Human Resources professionals been involved in the broader discussions?
- Have Human Resources professionals sought out and created new internal 'partnerships' to ensure that their contribution is timely and effective?

8.135   The answers to these questions are particularly important, as the consultation document does not indicate that the recommendations of the Accounting for People taskforce will be made mandatory. Paragraph 3.37 of the consultative document states:

> 'The Accounting for People taskforce reported in November 2003, having looked at ways in which organisations can measure the quality and effectiveness of their Human Capital Management (HCM). The taskforce has provided very useful guidelines on the issues companies should consider when reporting on HCM. The government hopes that companies will use the guidance in the Accounting for People report when preparing their OFR.'

8.136   However, in paragraph 3.35, the draft regulations state:

> 'Similarly, the way a company manages and utilises its workforce can have a significant impact on the performance of the company. Companies need to be able to recruit and retain the staff they need to achieve their business objectives, so a reputation as a good employer will often be an essential factor in business success. For companies with particular skills needs, training may be a crucial factor in the company's future development and performance, and therefore need to be described in the OFR. Companies with large numbers of employees in contact with customers will need to pay particular attention to motivation and morale.'

8.137   Paragraph 3.36 goes on to say:

> 'All companies preparing an OFR will need to consider their employment policies and practices, and the Government expects that most if not all will consider that some aspects of employment are relevant to an understanding of the company. But it is for the directors of each company to review and identify the relevant factors in their particular case.'

8.138   Consequently Human Resources professionals will have to use the outputs from their risk identification process, and the information from the other strategic development opportunities outlined above, to seek opportunities to discuss and influence the content of the OFR with directors and senior managers.

IMPLEMENTATION CHALLENGES

8.139 At this point a great deal of information will be available:

- Human Resources Risk Register.
- Risk assessments.
- Classifications.
- Selected risk treatments and risk controls.

8.140 The information should be discussed and agreed with the Human Resources team. The risk treatment and controls should be appropriate and proportionate. However, before any decisions are made about 'risk treatment' options, or decisions made about 'risk control' measures, you will need to identify the obstacles to implementation.

8.141 As discussed in **Chapter 7**, Human Resources professionals should seek out and create business partnerships with those parts of the business that have influence through other mechanisms, eg financial control, legal and company secretariat. In that way it will increase its influence via direct and indirect routes. In our experience, if Human Resources professionals can establish a partnership with the finance function, then there is very little that anyone in the organisation can do without needing to speak to one or other of the partnership! If they create an effective working partnership, then there is an excellent chance that the risk agenda will be welcomed and more readily accepted.

8.142 By using the classification system described above, the implementation challenges will have been anticipated. What is now needed is to develop a formal justification for the implementation of each risk treatment and risk control option. We suggest that this is even undertaken for the priority 'A' items, even though it has been decided that the change can be implemented without reference to others or the need for additional resources. This is for several reasons:

1 It will provide practice in thinking in 'risk' terms and thinking of the improvement in managing people and Human Resources risks.
2 It will provide practice in determining the benefits to business and commercial processes, and what contribution it will make to improving the management of the organisation's risks.
3 It will provide readily-available answers, should they be required, to enable a start to be made in the process of increasing influence.
4 It will justify the change should the organisation decide that resources need to be reduced, costs to be cut, etc.

8.143 Creating a Human Resources Risk Register, using a classification system to determine priorities, and developing a rationale for each risk treatment and control option will not necessarily result in unqualified success on every occasion. There are some implementation challenges that will need to be considered and these can be the most significant challenges to over-come. This is especially relevant if the decision to embark on a Human Resources risk management programme is the first major excursion by the organisation into the world of risk management, other than the traditional insurance function.

8.144 In our experience, the 'first' major excursion into a new area of internal management control, be it quality, IT, environment, health and safety or customer service, Human Resources is the most challenging because a control mentality is often not part of the organisation's management style. Most organisations that have not faced a new potentially all-embracing management control process will find it difficult to accept the actual change and the need to implement controls which at first seem to be bureaucratic. The 'second' management control process that is introduced will proceed much easier because an element of the 'control mentality' from the first process has become ingrained in the organisation, thereby reducing the level of resistance to change that happened on the first occasion.

8.145 We recommend that the following aspects be considered during the implementation of any new risk management process, and especially during any move to increase the influence and involvement of the Human Resources function:

1   What is the extent of the change and what impacts will the change have outside of the Human Resources function?

2   Is an effective internal communication process available that can be utilised to communicate the change and the supporting information?

3   While senior and middle management may support the concept of risk management, it requires discipline, time and effort to implement a regular, systematic process. Managers need to truly feel that risk management work is of value and understand that it is not an add-on, but a better way of doing business.

4   The start-up phase of a risk management process can require some time and effort to overcome the inertia of current practices. However, as risk management becomes integrated with management systems and business processes in general, people will realise that additional resources may not be required.

5   Senior management should be required to report progress on the implementation of risk management processes, so that the momentum is maintained and managers are held to account for their agreed actions.

6   The implementation of risk management processes will impact on both priority setting and longer-term plans to achieve organisational objectives.

FINAL STAGE

8.146 None of the approaches or tools outlined above provides all the information needed to create and implement a strategy for Human Resources professionals to increase their contribution to the management of risk within the organisation, and especially Human Resources risks. However, each can provide valuable assistance at a different level and at a different stage in the process of building the strategy. Therefore, Human Resources professionals should use a combination of the approaches or tools that are a best fit for the organisation, closely reflect the current status of the Human Resources function and provide the insights and outputs that are desired.

8.147 At this stage the following information is potentially available:

- A Human Resources Risk Register.
- The output from one or more of these approaches or tools:
    - RiskFrisk® – Human Resources Risk Management.
    - Corporate governance.
    - Corporate social responsibility.
    - Human capital management review.
    - Operating and financial review.
- An outline action plan with priorities.

8.148 A combination of the outputs from the above approaches and tools will provide Human Resources professionals with sufficient information and supporting evidence to create a draft strategy.

8.149 The draft strategy should then be discussed with the Human Resources team, the 'business partner(s)' or line/functional manager to agree an actual action plan, with priorities, timescales and measurement criteria. The plan should include adequate monitoring processes and regular reviews of the progress of implementation.

REFERENCES

Chartered Institute of Personnel and Development. Core Management standards (http://www.cipd.co.uk/mandq/standards/prac/cms/)

Code of Professional Conduct, Chartered Institute of Personnel and Development (CIPD) (http://www.cipd.co.uk)

Combined Code on Corporate Governance – UK Financial Services Authority, 2003. The Financial Reporting Councils' Combined Code – Listing Rules for UK Stock-Exchange listed companies (http://www.frc.org.uk)

Draft Regulations on the Operating and Financial Review and Directors' Report – a consultation document – UK Department of Trade and Industry, May 2004 (http://www.dti.gov.uk/cld/condocs.htm)

Forum for the Future (http://www.forumforthefuture.org.uk)

Turnbull Report, *Internal Control: Guidance for Directors on The Combined Code*, The Institute of Chartered Accountants in England and Wales, September 1999 (http://www.icaew.co.uk/internalcontrol/)

UK Department of Trade and Industry and the Forum for the Future, workshop for business, non-government organisations, May 2003 (http://www.societyandbusiness.gov.uk

CHAPTER 9

Pulling it together

9.1 This chapter will pull together the key points from earlier chapters and summarise the way forward for Human Resources professionals to identify and assess Human Resources risks.

9.2 The theme of this book has been that, where Human Resources professionals operate at a strategic level, they are ideally placed to make a significant and effective contribution to organisation-wide risk management. Risk management succeeds or fails depending on altering employees' perceptions, attitudes, behaviour and performance with regard to risk. Success will depend on effective training, performance management, reward and sanction systems and developing work practices and procedures that limit human error, increase job satisfaction and reduce stress. The above mechanisms are cross-functional and interrelated, hence the need for involvement, at the strategic level, of a Human Resources professional with a cross-functional remit.

9.3 In **Chapter 2** we have seen that risk management should be seen as a core competency and a key responsibility of Human Resources functions. However, Human Resources professionals do not always perceive this as a positive obligation and emphasis is placed in this chapter on the need to change mindsets.

9.4 One way to think about people risk or human capital risk is to view it as being made up of three aspects – compliance, productivity and growth – which can incorporate a variety of areas. The challenge for the Human Resources professional is to decide which of the many potential human capital risk areas to address. One useful approach is to assess the risks across two dimensions:
1   The possible impact of the risk in terms of costs, or impact on business effectiveness.
2   The likelihood of the event occurring.

9.5 In the area of corporate governance, along with the areas of corporate strategy and organisational change Human Resources professionals are often invited in at a late stage in the process when the plans have been made, rather than being involved in the strategic thinking and planning stages. Failure to deliver full and effective people-related strategies in these areas is an unacceptable risk to the organisation.

9.6 The role of the Human Resources function is developing to become more of a strategic partner with line managers. However, in many companies they are still expected to, and in many cases apparently content to, operate at an administrative or policy-policing level, providing pay and employee benefits. The Human Resources professional must show determination, vision, business acumen and high-level professional capability to change the mindset, both within their function and the business as a whole. This will be particularly important where the expectation of the organisation is that the role of the Human Resources function is merely as an implementer of decisions made elsewhere.

9.7 Where a Human Resources function is determined to operate at a strategic level it must have a strategy for developing the capabilities and competencies of the Human Resources professionals within it. In order to influence the thinking of the senior managers about people risks, they need to be able to operate in strategic partnership and to contribute to the strategic thinking of the organisation. Unless they are able to do this, the function will be ineffective in enabling the organisation to manage people risks and opportunities.

9.8 Often Human Resources professionals will feel that they have too much 'routine' work to do to be able to move up to the more strategic levels in the organisation. However, the first step in establishing a strategic Human Resources function is to focus on achieving operational excellence. One aspect of this process should be talking to internal clients to find out which aspects of the Human Resources activity they value and which they would like done differently, better or not at all. A similar line of questioning should also be used within the Human Resources function to gain a full perspective on where operational and administrative processes and procedures can be improved. The benefits of this to the organisation and to the Human Resources function include improvements in effectiveness and efficiency, better client relationships, stronger customer focus and improvements in the reputation of the Human Resources function.

9.9 Human Resource professionals will undoubtedly find the prospect of such a change in approach daunting, particularly when their clients look on them as operational specialists. A considerable amount of work will need to be undertaken by Human Resources professionals to become involved in some of the longer-term issues that their client groups are tackling as well as their own day-to-day operational issues. Human Resources professionals should not be put off by this challenge since the benefits of such an approach can be seen in the improved professionalism of the Human Resources function. In turn this affords huge benefits to the organisation as a whole, in the management of people related risks.

9.10 Human Resources professionals will need to develop additional skills and capability in a variety of areas, including consulting, facilitation, strategic thinking, influencing, marketing, change leadership and process management.

The function as a whole will need to develop a robust, long-term development strategy that will gradually build on the skills and capabilities needed.

9.11 In **Chapter 3** we saw how organisational psychology provides a valuable perspective in managing organisational risks. We also saw how this approach to risk management has evolved to provide Human Resources professionals with a key perspective in understanding the causes and motivations associated with risk-related behaviour in the workplace.

9.12 We considered two perspectives, which are brought together to demonstrate an integrated approach to risk management. First, organisational factors – the structures and processes that determine the culture of an organisation, and include factors such as responsibility frameworks, communication frameworks and job/role design. Second, human factors – the perception of risk, the nature of human error and what motivates individuals in the workplace to take risks.

9.13 Human Resources professionals operating at a strategic level are best placed to manage the risks associated with organisational and human factors. They alone take a cross-functional view of organisations. The focus of Human Resources professionals on people management through such activities as training, performance management and reward mechanisms provides, Human Resources professionals with the opportunity to become an integral and vital part of the risk management process.

9.14 The input of Human Resources professionals to the risk management process is about implementing the procedures and practices that lead to changes in behaviour, attitudes and values. A systematic focus on limiting human error at every stage and process within an organisation acts as a mechanism for organisational development as the potential for human error is largely synonymous with inefficient organisational systems.

9.15 Learning and development are key components in establishing a positive risk culture. Ineffective learning (or training) is a fundamental cause of loss and accidents in the workplace. Human Resources professionals must seek to implement a risk management system. As with any organisational change, this will require training to provide management and employees with the necessary skills, knowledge and attitudes to achieve the organisation's new strategic goals.

9.16 It is difficult, if not impossible, to eradicate human error from organisations. However, Human Resources professionals can do a significant amount to reduce the risk of human error, by designing organisational systems that seek to limit risk-related behaviour.

9.17 In **Chapter 4** we saw that organisations need to have a top-level strategy for managing internal risks. It is the responsibility of the board or senior management team not only to protect the interests of the shareholders but also to ensure a safe and effective working environment for employees. It is here that Human Resources can have a major impact. Implementing effective policies/procedures is key to managing Human Resources risks. Where Human Resources are effective in managing Human Resources risks, the board or senior management will be able to fulfil an important part of their obligations to stakeholders.

9.18   The approach that Human Resources take to drafting policies/ procedures will determine whether this key business obligation is achieved. Policies will be more likely to be adopted at a senior level where a robust process is followed and where Human Resources professionals ensure that the final policies achieved are appropriate to the style and culture of the organisation. The most effective way to do this is to take a risk-based approach to the exercise. This will mean identification of potential risks in respect of the policy issue, evaluation of the risk of introduction of the new policy or of taking no action, and then drafting the policies in light of this information. The use of such an approach will minimise the people risks and maximise organisational opportunity. When the Human Resources professional comes to communicate the revised policy to management and employees, there is more chance of acceptance, because the need for the policy has been researched and can be demonstrated.

9.19   We have seen, though, that this approach may require a radical change in style by some Human Resources professionals since some of the reasons for developing new policies are neither risk nor organisation driven.

9.20   In order for Human Resources professionals to effectively cover the full range of operational Human Resources activity, they must not only ensure the consistent application of such policies, but also ensure that they are effectively and accurately administered. This will provide the best value to the organisation and, when coupled with effective communication to employees, will minimise the organisation's people risks. It is therefore clear that Human Resources policies, procedures and administration are closely linked.

9.21   We further explored this in **Chapter 5**, where we showed that it is essential for Human Resources functions to carry out administrative tasks accurately, effectively and efficiently. Control measures, quality standards and review mechanisms must be put in place to maintain the accuracy and robustness of administrative systems.

9.22   The systems themselves must be aligned with the policies/procedures that are in place and must also be consistent with the style and culture of the organisation.

9.23   In addition, Human Resources professionals must have a detailed knowledge of the legislative and Inland Revenue areas that can be impacted by poor or inefficient administrative systems to ensure that there is no risk of non-compliance or of incorrect interpretation.

9.24 Systems must be regularly reviewed to ensure compliance and that they are adapting to organisational and cultural changes. It is then vitally important to effectively communicate any changes made to all involved. There is also a need for effective training and re-training for all who will be directly impacted by the change.

9.25 Human Resources professionals who achieve a detailed focus on administrative practices will ensure that the organisation has confidence in the Human Resources function and thus the organisation as a whole. They will also ensure the organisation is protected from risks of non-compliance with the legislation. More importantly, however, as we have mentioned above, it will be the key to helping Human Resources professionals to move out of the administrative 'trap' in the organisation and up to a level where they can provide significant value to the organisation.

9.26 In **Chapter 6** we saw that some people in organisations, including the Human Resources professionals, do not identify and evaluate risks appropriately. In order to balance this and to provide the best approach for the organisation, Human Resources professionals must improve their capability for risk assessment and risk management in planning for major organisational change. Ensuring that management focus on the people issues related to change initiatives as well as the organisational issues is a major challenge for Human Resources professionals.

9.27 There are many risks associated with organisational change; however, the Human Resources professional can be instrumental in working with the senior management team to minimise risks in many areas including assessing the need for, and planning, the change as well as its implementation.

9.28 As we have seen in respect of administrative changes, the key to the success of major organisational changes is in planning and then effectively communicating the change. This communication will need to incorporate the business justifications for such a change. Human Resources professionals must focus on identifying the people risks associated with major changes.

9.29 The challenge, having identified the risks, is to gain the commitment of senior management to address the problems. Human Resources professionals need to manage expectations of the senior team and also emphasise the importance of involving employees in the change process, as this will often help to influence the course of events when the unexpected occurs.

9.30 It is important to have a well-thought-through strategy and plan for regular communication throughout the process of the change. The Human Resources professional can play an important part in addressing the risks associated with poor communications and will need to take into account possible break-down in the psychological contract and trust amongst employees within the organisation. Human Resources professionals must become more proficient at understanding and communicating the potential impact on working relationships of major organisational change. This will enable dialogue to take place with employees around their needs and expectations in the light of proposed changes. This, in turn, will allow the Human Resources professionals to identify and manage the related risks.

9.31 In **Chapter 7** we saw that, in order to help them manage Human Resources risks, Human Resources professionals need to build partnerships with others within the organisation. It is important to build partnerships not only with senior management, but also with line managers, other support functions and with employees. The important factor in developing such partnerships is trust, and such trust will take time and effort to build up. It is important for all in the organisation to work together to develop an environment that builds and maintains trust.

9.32 We saw that Human Resources professionals have a key role in promoting trust within organisations. This takes place through coaching managers and team leaders in factors and behaviours that build trust. Human Resources professionals can model the behaviours that build trust and are thus instrumental in developing the accepted norms of behaviour within the organisations.

9.33 Building successful working relationships and partnerships is of fundamental importance in managing risk in organisations. Trust is fundamental to creating these relationships. Human resources professionals are uniquely placed to encourage senior managers to invest sustained, focused attention on building and maintaining trust within the organisation.

9.34 The recurring theme throughout this book is the strong emphasis on the Human Resources professional raising their profile and increasing their contribution within the organisation. The various chapters have examined the risk of the Human Resources professional being unable to achieve an increased influence. **Chapter 8** focuses on providing guidance as to how Human Resources professionals can increase their influence, and contribute significantly towards the performance and development of the organisation. The chapter shows how to develop a strategy for increasing the Human Resources contribution to the management of risk within the organisation.

9.35 Details are included of a structured process for identifying and classifying Human Resources risks, and how the results of the process can be built into a Risk Register. The concept of the Risk Register is introduced so that all identified Human Resources risks are recorded and can then be classified, to ensure that all potential risks are dealt with in an appropriate order of priority.

9.36 Four factors are used to describe the process:
1   The organisational context – these aspects vary considerably from organisation to organisation and affect the organisational impact on people risks.

Human Resources professionals need to identify the factors that are relevant to their organisation, evaluate their impact and record the risks in the Risk Register.

2   Policies and systems for general risk management – Human Resources professionals must develop a consistent approach with existing 'risk management' functions to avoid conflict, misunderstanding or confusion.

3   People risks – a Human Resources audit may need to be carried out in order to identify such risks, plus Human Resources operational, professional and personal risk.

4   Risks generated by the organisation's business and operational processes – all the organisation's business and operational risk areas that impact on the management of people risks must also be incorporated.

9.37   Details of a unique risk-profiling tool that has been developed especially for Human Resources professionals are included. The tool is called 'RiskFrisk® – Human Resources Risk Management' and it is aligned closely with the above four factors. This unique tool focuses on the way in which an organisation's risks and the interrelationship between them impacts on the management of its Human Resources risks.

9.38   In addition, an explanation is given of a process for developing a strategy to enable Human Resources professionals to use organisational processes to increase their influence. There is strong focus on processes to identify risks so that Human Resources professionals have the opportunity to influence the organisation at all levels.

CONCLUSION

9.39   Through the use of this book, we believe that Human Resources professionals will be able to carry out a complete review of the Human Resources function and its key areas of impact on the organisation. Human Resources professionals will then be able to undertake risk identification and effectively record the risk and potential risk treatments to minimise risks and maximise opportunities using a structured approach. A structured risk-identification and risk-treatment process will provide a valuable opportunity for Human Resources professionals to demonstrate their risk credentials.

9.40   Through such an approach, the Human Resources professional will begin to understand the need to develop a Human Resources risk management strategy linked to the organisation's overall risk management strategy. Such strategic-level involvement allows the Human Resources professional to demonstrate the value of its increased contribution to the organisation. The organisation should then seek to develop further these opportunities to ensure that Human Resources functions and risks are considered consistently at the highest levels within the organisation.

Index

[*all references are to paragraph number*]